Government Foresighted Leading

T0270737

Over the past four decades of reform and opening up to the outside world, remarkable economic growth has been achieved in China, and it has drawn considerable world attention. The question of how to explain that phenomenon and the road China has taken towards its modernization have been the focus of attention from worldwide economists and experts.

This book attempts to explore China's economy from the perspective of government foresighted leading, which gives full play to government functions, particularly those of regional governments. Government foresighted leading theory is an important innovation and contribution to the theoretical configuration of economics. It not only offers an explanation of China's continuous economic growth but further classifies economics into microeconomics, macroeconomics and mezzoeconomics, which includes regional economics, industrial economics or structural economics, supplementing the traditional microeconomics and macroeconomics system.

Yunxian Chen is a PhD in economics at Peking University and the founder of Guangfa Securities. He is an expert on regional economy and has many years of experience in the management of regional government in China.

Jianwei Qiu is an investment director in a branch company of Taikang Life Insurance Co. Ltd. His key research areas include health industry and financial investment.

China Perspectives Series

The *China Perspectives* series focuses on translating and publishing works by leading Chinese scholars, writing about both global topics and China-related themes. It covers Humanities and Social Sciences, Education, Media and Psychology, as well as many interdisciplinary themes.

This is the first time any of these books have been published in English for international readers. The series aims to put forward a Chinese perspective, give insights into cutting-edge academic thinking in China and inspire researchers globally.

For more information, please visit https://www.routledge.com/series/CPH.

Internet Finance in China: Introduction and Practical Approaches
Ping Xie, Chuanwei Zou, Haier Liu

Regulating China's Shadow Banks
Qingmin Yan, Jianhua Li

Forthcoming titles:

Internationalization of the RMB: Establishment and Development of RMB Offshore Markets
International Monetary Institute, Renmin University of China

The Road Leading to the Market
Weiying Zhang

Macro-control and Economic Development in China
Jiagui Chen

Economic Development and Reform Deepening in China
Jiagui Chen

Research Frontiers on the International Marketing Strategies of Chinese Brands
Zuohao Hu, Xi Chen, Zhilin Yang

History of China's Foreign Trade, 2e
Yuqin Sun

Government Foresighted Leading

Theory and Practice of the World's Regional Economic Development

Yunxian Chen
Jianwei Qiu

LONDON AND NEW YORK

This book is published with financial support from Chinese Fund for the Humanities and Social Sciences

Translated by Heming Yong and Jing Peng

First published 2017
by Routledge

2 Park Square, Milton Park, Abingdon, Oxfordshire OX14 4RN
52 Vanderbilt Avenue, New York, NY 10017

Routledge is an imprint of the Taylor & Francis Group, an informa business

First issued in paperback 2020

British Library Cataloguing in Publication Data
A catalogue record for this book is available from the British Library

Library of Congress Cataloging in Publication Data
A catalog record for this book has been requested

ISBN: 978-1-138-68703-5 (hbk)
ISBN: 978-0-367-51903-2 (pbk)

Typeset in Times New Roman
by Apex CoVantage, LLC

Contents

Figures

Tables

Foreword

Early this summer, Dr Chen Yunxian came to visit me during his business trip to Beijing. He told me that another book of his would be published by Peking University Press and hoped that I could write a few lines for it, which I accepted with great delight.

Over the past few years I have lived basically a secluded life due to my ill health but have been kept well-informed and updated, thanks to the sophisticated modern media and the frequent visits from my students.

Time is just like a long river, flowing and flowing without stop. Great changes have taken place in today's world, and China's economy has gradually integrated itself into the world's economic system, development and competition. Likewise, China's economists must embrace, with courage and confidence, the theoretical system of the world economy and be part of its construction and innovation.

I am more than happy to find my former student Dr Chen Yunxian keeping abreast of the times and standing at the forefront of economic theorization. Over 20 years ago, when few Chinese scholars knew something about securities and capital market, Dr Chen was already among the first scholars in China's economic circles in studying capital market in the United States, the United Kingdom, Germany, Japan, etc. He proposed the laws governing the relations between securities investment risks and returns. The year 2011 saw the publication of his new book *Foresighted Leading: Theoretical Thinking and Practice of China's Regional Economic Development* by Peking University Press, which attracted immediate attention from China's economists. The viewpoints and the analyses of different cases won extensive recognition. I was also told that the English version of that book has been published by Springer, Germany, which is highly worthy of warm congratulations. It is my belief that his theory will draw the attention of economists from different parts of the world.

This new book – *Government Foresighted Leading: Theory and Practice of the World's Regional Economic Development* – is a companion to the aforementioned book. One is based on the practice and thinking of China's regional economic development and the other is based on the theory and practice of the world's regional economic development. Government foresighted leading, evolving from China's regional economic development to the world's regional economic development and from practice and thinking to explorations and theorization, has undergone theoretical sublimation deeply rooted in practice and has gone beyond the Chinese scene to the world stage.

I have discovered with great satisfaction that Dr Chen's research and his theory based on China's practice have proved to be of universal significance and application to the world economy. Dr Chen's theoretical achievements have originated from his profound theoretical foundations and, more importantly, his rich practical experience. He started his career in the microeconomic sector by setting up Guangfa Securities Co. Ltd. and leading it to the position of China's top five. He then served in China's local government – the Foshan municipal government and the Shunde District government, both of which have been recognized as China's reform pioneers, with great success. He is now working as deputy governor of Guangdong provincial government. In his transformation from scholarly research to economic practice and from microeconomics to macroeconomics, Dr Chen Yunxian, as a serious scholar, has provided effective solutions to the disconnection between theory and practice and has seamlessly welded them together.

I remember that he came to discuss with me the role of regional government during one of his visits to me while he was serving the Shunde District government. He argued that local governments' role has a dual character – a quasi-macro role of representing the state in meeting the demands of macroeconomic development and a quasi-micro role of effectively allocating local resources and promoting regional economic development, which raises one fundamental issue in economics, i.e. the micro-entity of market competition. In the eyes of most economists, businesses are the sole micro-entity of market competition. The supposition of local governments playing the quasi-micro role suggests that they are part of market competition, in addition to businesses. China's development over the past three decades or so since its reform and opening up has proved that competition between local governments has indeed been an important driving force. It is not hard to see that important economic principles await to be explored underneath competition between local or regional governments. I believe that it would be unlikely for Dr Chen Yunxian to make this discovery if he had not worked for local governments.

In fact, some Western economists, such as Adam Smith, Keynes, Samuelson, Stiglitz and Paul R. Krugman, all had experience in economic administration in the government sector. Keynes, for example, was so courageous as to shatter the old theoretical shackles and put forward his theory of government intervention, thus establishing macroeconomics, which initiated the classification of economics into microeconomics and macroeconomics. The power of theory is so immense that the practice of macroeconomic theory has brought forth such international economic organizations as the World Bank and the International Monetary Fund and has propelled the sustainable development of the entire world economy. An important explanation for Keynes' theoretical breakthroughs is his experience of serving in the British government as Chancellor of the Exchequer that enabled him to have a better position to understand economic operations on the national level.

Over the past few decades, China has covered an economic journey that would have taken one or two hundred years in the West. Western economists have achieved a series of significant theoretical innovations and breakthroughs in economics on the basis of their national experiences and economic advantages, which have benefited mankind. Today, China's development, in particular its economic accomplishments, will certainly give rise to cutting-edge global advantages in China's economic theorization. Chinese economists are bound to achieve their desired goals as long as they work in a down-to-earth manner but operate from a strategically advantageous position.

Xiao Zhuoji
June 2013

Preface

China's road of scientific development has not only brought wealth and well-being to the Chinese people but provided research opportunities for economists as well. Over the past three decades or so in particular, China's reform, opening up and development embody the wisdom and efforts on the part of numerous economists and bear abundant theoretical fruit.

The publication of *Government Foresighted Leading: Theory and Practice of the World's Regional Economic Development* is one of the major academic accomplishments Chinese economists have attained. What is noteworthy is that the authors make theoretical explorations of world regional economic development from a global perspective while basing on China's regional economic development.

Dr Chen Yunxian studied under Professor Xiao Zhuoji, a good friend of mine, for his doctoral degree. Since he got his PhD degree in economics, he has been working in financial institutions and for regional government. He proposed the theory of government foresighted leading on the basis of his research findings. In his view, government can perform foresighted leading by means of foundations, mechanisms and regulations of market economy and can employ the visible hand to make up for the margins and defects caused by the invisible hand and remedy market malfunction. On the other hand, government can reduce government malfunction and the cost of remedying malfunction to the greatest possible extent through its competitive role as a regional government in a mezzoeconomy and exercising pre-process foresighted leading.

Dr Chen Yunxian is highly original in proposing the dual-component theory of market competition. He holds that judging from the perspective of global economy, market competition consists of two components – businesses and government. From the microeconomic perspective, businesses are the sole component of market competition, but when viewed from the macroeconomic perspective, there is another key component of market competition – regional government. In terms of global economy, competition occurs between countries, and on the level of national economy, there is obvious competition between regions. Competition takes place between states and cities in the United States, and between provinces, cities and counties in China. It is his view that this dual-component competition that has been driving China's economic growth and has formed the practical basis for regional governments of provincial, municipal and county level to exercise foresighted leading.

I strongly feel that Chen Yunxian's point of view is in line with the practical situation of China's economic development over the past three decades. I mentioned on several occasions that government regulation should be anticipatory and should not be limited only to "post-process regulation" and that there should be anticipated regulation under some circumstances, which accords with Dr Chen's idea.

The relation between government and market is an important issue in economics. In the course of China's reform and development, confrontations and conflicts of different forces basically revolve around the relation between government and market. However, in any case, the visible hand of government and the invisible hand of market are most important to all self-operating economies. Some economists, under the influence of Western liberal economics, have gone so far as to believe that the invisible hand is omnipotent and disregard the fact of market malfunction, which is obviously one-sided. Some other economists, under the influence of theories of government intervention, have gone so far as to believe that the visible hand is omnipotent and that macro-level economic regulations will solve all problems in economic operations, which is also one-sided.

China's remarkable accomplishments in social and economic development over the past decades are ascribable not only to giving full play to the basic role of market regulation but also to a strong and forceful government. We cannot simply put strong market against strong government: in economic development there must be strong market effectively allocating resources and strong government creating and protecting market environment. Strong government exists not to replace strong market, and strong market needs strong government protection. Only when this "double-strong" mechanism is put into place can market malfunction be remedied and government malfunction be diminished.

Then what is meant by a strong market and a strong government? How can we give full play to the role of strong market and strong government? This book provides us with illuminating ideas, i.e. let market do what it should do and let government do what market cannot do or cannot do well. Both have their own places and roles. Government foresighted leading aims to give full play to government roles in economic guidance, regulation and warning and take the lead in promoting scientific and sustainable growth in regional economy with recourse to market rules and forces, by means of investing, pricing, taxation, legal and other measures and through innovation in organization, system and technology.

One phenomenon in China's development is noteworthy. Regional economies, which are relatively self-operating and economically independent, have been in competition with each other, which propels them to give full play to their comparative advantage and helps to arouse local enthusiasm. All this gives driving forces and vitality to the whole of China's economy. Some scholars have generalized this situation under the heading of inter-county, inter-city and inter-province competition. Dr Chen Yunxian has categorized it into mezzoeconomics in the light of economic theories and from the angle of local economic practices, which is an important innovation and is well worth serious attention of the economic circles.

Mezzoeconomics represented by regions comes in between microeconomics represented by businesses and macroeconomics represented by countries. This offers not only a factual explanation of the process and characteristics of China's economic development but also a fuller and ameliorated theoretical description of economics. Just as the theory of market economy lays the foundation for microeconomics, and Keynesian theory divides economics into microeconomics and macroeconomics, so the theory of government foresighted leading further classifies economics into macroeconomics, mezzoeconomics and microeconomics.

In fact, mezzoeconomics discussed here includes regional economics, industrial economics or structural economics, which is intimately related to regional economics. I think that this theory fills in the blank of existing economic theories, guides the direction of reform in economic systems, creates a multilevel market and strengthens the stability and vitality of national economy.

As a science of close relation to practice, economics must be related to economic development, and its focus will shift with the transfer of world economic centres. Prior to the 1930s, the world-renowned economists are mainly in Europe, and in the United States after the Second World War, which is the result of the shift of the focus of world economic development. With the rise of China's economy, China's economic growth is bound to attract more and more serious attention, and Chinese economists will usher in a new era.

Li Yining
June 2013

Introduction

Chen Yunxian

Over the past three decades of reform and opening up to the outside world, remarkable economic growth has been achieved in China and has drawn considerable world attention. The question of how to explain the phenomenon that has been taking place in China and the road China has taken towards its modernization has been the focus of attention from worldwide economists and experts from various other fields. Some economists have even come to predict that whoever can explain China's economic development is definitely entitled to the honor of the Nobel Laureate in economics.

Theory is derived from practice, and unprecedented practice is bound to generate unparalleled theories. Looking back upon the development of world economy, the emergence and evolution of economics, together with all major theoretical breakthroughs, are without exception concomitant with the shift of the world economic centres from one region to the other.

Economics, with its ultimate goal of serving the good of the general public, is intertwined with practice. Not only has China created the miracle of the past 30 years' achievements, but there is a great prospect for its future growth as well. The model China has been pursuing deserves economists' serious attention and study, which will bring about significant breakthroughs in traditional economic conceptualizations and development patterns.

The greatest blessing of life is no more than its birth at the right time. As an economist, I am most blessed for being born in the great era. I am most fortunate to have been able to witness and participate in the unprecedented transformations of China's economy. In the mid-1980s, I had the great honor of studying under professor and economist Xiao Zhuoji at Peking University, where well-known economists from home and abroad converge and work, and where active thoughts and theories appear in close succession.

Chinese economists, harboring the ambition of serving the country, started to capitalize on their knowledge, wisdom and courage to propel China's reform, opening up and transformation. This atmosphere infused into us not only a strong desire for economic expertise but a strong sense of responsibility and mission of serving the country and the people as well.

In the summer of 1991, after my doctoral degree study in Peking University, I settled in Guangzhou and started to launch the securities department of

Guangdong Development Bank. We started up from a team of six people and a meager investment of a little over two million yuan. Through painstaking efforts, the securities department, which was first affiliated to Guangdong Development Bank, was later transformed into Guangdong Guangfa Securities Company, and now Guangfa Securities Co. Ltd, which has become one of the top five large-scale national securities companies, with a well-known "doctoral corps" in China's capital market circles made up of 65 doctoral degree holders and 385 master degree holders from China and overseas.

From early 2003 to July 2011, I was consecutively appointed by Guangdong Provincial Committee of CPC as executive mayor of Foshan City, secretary of Shunde District Committee of CPC, mayor of Foshan City, secretary of Foshan Municipal Committee of CPC, and now deputy governor of Guangdong Province. Guangdong Province, the first to start reform and opening up to the outside world in China, has been leading China's economic transformation. Shunde, for several years, headed the list of China's top 100 counties, and Foshan remains among China's most developed regions. Immersed in such a vast pilot zone of economic transformation, I feel a stronger impulse of China's economic development. Standing on such an economic height, I acquire a clearer panorama of its theoretical progression.

No matter whether in the capacity of scholar, business leader or government official, what remains unchanged in me is my nature of being an economist. My theoretical thinking and reflections upon China's economic reform and development have not ceased with my completion of PhD study in Peking University. Instead my thinking and reflections started to focus more on the application of theories to practical issues. It is my strong conviction that only those who stand firmly on soil can sense the real solidarity of the ground.

0.1 From "crossing the stream by feeling the stones" to foresighted leading

Regarding China's economic progress, what weighs most heavily in my mind is the role of government in regional economic development. In the case of China's most developed areas like Guangdong, Foshan and Shunde, their development path and indications for future growth have provided economists with excellent samples for their social and economic analysis.

During my stay in Shunde as party secretary in 2004, my investigation and research concerning Shunde's industrial development gave me the confidence that China's development should have got over the stage of "crossing the stream by feeling the stones" and that government should play the foresighted leading role. In the initial stage of economic development, it is safe to adopt the approach of "crossing the stream by feeling the stones" and necessary to encourage bold moves and audacious experiments on the part of regions and even work units. However, when economic development reaches certain levels, it is paramount for government to exercise foresighted leading through scientific planning and take rigorous measures to implement the plans.

Overt the following years, I began to systematically generalize my thinking about foresighted leading and the result was *Foresighted Leading: Theoretical Thinking and Practice of China's Regional Economic Development* published by Peking University Press in 2011, which gave a full description of the economic concept – 政府超前引领 (government foresighted leading, *chaoqian* (超前) meaning "foresighted", and *yinling* (引领) "leading", hereinafter abbreviated as GFL), defined as follows: *giving full play to government functions, particularly those of regional governments, in economic guidance, regulation and warning and taking the lead in promoting scientific and sustainable growth in regional economy with recourse to market rules and forces, by means of investing, pricing, taxation, legal and other measures and through innovation in organization, system and technology.*

Its publication has received considerable attention from economic circles and government organizations due to its practical cases and innovative theorization. Its influence has gone beyond the boundaries of China since the appearance of its English version published by Springer in Germany.

Joint efforts have been made by Qiu Jianwei, who studied as a postgraduate student in Postgraduate Program Division of The People's Bank of China, Beijing, to put the proposition of GFL on a more systematic basis of better theorization, combing this theoretical generalization through its proposition, prerequisites, practical background and implementation from a global perspective. It presents a fuller analysis and a more detailed description of GFL, with the commitment that this theorization justifies and further differentiates the categorization of economics into macroeconomics, mezzoeconomics and microeconomics, hence *Government Foresighted Leading: Theoretical Thinking and Explorations of World Regional Economic Development*.

0.2 Using "the visible hand" to remedy market malfunction and government malfunction

The primary issue that confronts economists is the relationship between government and market. Various theories have been proposed by Western economists to explain economic growth in different stages of social development and to lead economic policy making and implementation accordingly.

The publication of *An Inquiry into the Nature and Causes of the Wealth of Nations* (also known as *The Wealth of Nations*) by Adam Smith (1723–1790) in 1776 enabled a better understanding of market economy and established a theoretical framework for microeconomics, and Western economics evolved itself in the subsequent 160 years or so. However, the world economic depression in the 1930s made us aware of market malfunction and economists began to doubt and refute theories of free economy.

In 1936 John Maynard Keynes (1883–1946) proposed his theory of government involvement, i.e. the visible hand, in his work – *The General Theory of Employment, Interest and Money*, hence the classification of economics into microeconomics and macroeconomics, which remained in parallel development for almost 80 years. The American stagflation in the 1970s and the outbreak of the international economic crisis near the end of 2007 enabled economists to better recognize the consequences of market malfunction and government malfunction.

According to traditional free economic theories, market malfunction is inevitable, and according to Keynesian theory, government malfunction can never be avoided. Keynesian ideas dominated the period of the world economic depression, and neo-liberalism made a comeback when the economic stagflation took place.

Whatever changes those theories have undergone, they can generally be reckoned as the derivations of either Adam Smith's free economic theory or Keynesian theory of government intervention in economy, which either focuses on the major role of businesses or individuals in a microeconomy or in-process and post-process intervention of government in a macroeconomy.

Almost no attention has been paid to pre-process government intervention or the role of regional government in mezzoeconomy. Inadequacy in researches in government foresighted leading role in pre-process of economy and in the role of regional government in mezzoeconomy is a huge blank left behind in the Western theorization of economy from the incept of microeconomics and macroeconomics. It has become a serious drawback in modern Western economic theories.

Consequently, the efficiency of market economic systems and the impacts of government intervention have been reduced to a considerable extent, for lack of guidance of those theories. No better example can be cited to illustrate this point than the world financial crisis since 2007.

Neither microeconomics, which advocates free economic activities, nor macroeconomics, which emphasizes government intervention in economy, can fully explain what really happens in economic development. China's economic growth over the past three decades sets theorists thinking about new theories and making new discoveries within the general configuration of the traditional model of macroeconomics and the classic model of microeconomics.

The proposition of GFL, on one hand, enables government to exercise foresighted leading by means of the foundations, mechanisms and regulations of market economy and employ the visible hand to overcome the defects and make up the margins caused by the invisible hand, and on the other hand to reduce government malfunction and minimize the cost of remedying defects to the greatest extent through the competitive role of regional government in mezzoeconomy and its regulatory role in pre-process leading.

0.3 Competition between businesses and between regional governments

Competition lies in the core of market economy. Judging from a global perspective, business and government are the dual participants in market competition. On microeconomic level, the business is the sole entity in market competition, but on macroeconomic level, there is an additional entity – regional government. Countries are entities of competition in world economy, and within national economy competition obviously exists between regions and regional governments. In the case of the United States, regional competition takes place between states and cities, and in China between provinces, cities, and counties, and the like.

It is this dual-entity competition that forms the major driving force for regional governments, national, provincial or municipal, to exercise foresighted leading and opens up immense space for theoretical explorations in mezzoeconomics.

It is important to note that "mezzoeconomy" and "regional government" are relative concepts, referring to "countries" if viewed from the perspective of global economy and to "cities" if viewed from the perspective of national economy. So mezzoeconomics may be equivalent to national economics, municipal economics or regional economics. Regarding "global economics", not much research has been conducted yet. This presentation will set its limits within the scope of regional economics (i.e. municipal economics), focusing on different levels of "city" in various regions of a country or "a certain region" with a high density of population. It is also important to note that the notion of "city (urban)" is relative to "countryside (rural)", and "municipal government" to "rural government". So the notion of "city" is relative, either inclusive of "the administrative division of a city" or "the geographical division of a city".

Therefore, "city", "municipal government" and "municipal economy" are employed as key economic concepts when GFL or regional economy is discussed from the angle of national government.

In terms of competition between regional governments in China, Steven Cheung defines it within county-level competition in his book *China's Economic Policy* (2009). He holds that the greater the economic power, the fiercer the regional competition and the economic power mainly resides within the county rather than within the city, the province or the central government in today's China. He reasons that the right to utilize land lies in the hand of the county, which gives it strong economic power, and the most forceful county-level competition ensues.

We, however, think that as far as regional government is concerned, competition mainly takes place between municipal governments, which therefore become the real entity that is to exercise foresighted leading.

First, the municipal government enjoys greater power in economic development and as a result competition is the most intense. In China, the central and provincial governments provide guidelines for land employment and other economic policies and retain the power to appoint government officials and reallocate fiscal revenues. Of the factors of market economy, capital is mainly controlled and regulated through monetary policy of the central government, and labor is mainly determined by market. Only the power to supply and utilize land remains within the authorities of the municipal government.

Second, the city's economic independence and government interests are closely related to economic development. The fiscal revenues of the municipal government, the economic performance of officials and the status of fiscal revenues are all contingent upon project construction, investment attraction and regional growth.

Third, within a region, cities may vary only slightly in natural resources, and there is a high degree of comparability, but within a province or a state, cities may vary greatly, as they may have different locations like in the coastal or inland areas and different natural resources, and therefore there is a relatively low degree of comparability. Comparison can be made between cities with similar natural conditions.

Finally, China enjoys a good number of cities. They are mostly of large scale and possess adequate environment and conditions for competition.

0.4 The categorization of government foresighted leading

Within an economy, system, institution, technology and notion are all important components. Accordingly, GFL is classified into four types: institutional, organizational, technological and notional.

Institutional foresighted leading means giving full play to the role of government, particularly regional government, in innovation of systems by creating new and more incentive policies and standards to increase the efficiency of resource allocation and the sustainability of socio-economic development and reform. Its core part is innovation in social, political, economic and administrative systems, in regulations of human conduct and interrelations, and in organizations and relations of its external environment.

Its direct consequence is the inspiration of human creativity and enthusiasm, the creation of new knowledge, the fair allocation of social resources and the continuous creation of social wealth, which ultimately promotes social progress. Only when there is innovative government can institutional foresighted leading be realized and innovative systems and policies be formulated.

Organizational foresighted leading means the innovation of government, particularly regional government, in organizational structure, mode and regulations with the aim of strengthening foundations for economic and industrial development and eventually facilitating innovations in policies and technology.

Technological foresighted leading means giving full play to the advantage of government in allocating social resources and enabling government to participate in and lead technological innovations directly or indirectly so as to promote scientific and technological advancement and strengthen the capabilities of cities and businesses to perform scientific and technological innovation.

There are two aspects to technological foresighted leading. On the one hand, government should create a favorable environment for businesses to enhance the capabilities to perform technological innovation, for example the construction of systems for patent application and protection and product standardization. On the other hand, government should implement effective economic measures and policies to encourage businesses to take the initiatives for technological innovation, for example granting fund to support research and development in key technologies, establishing technological funds, recruiting leading experts, and so on.

Notional foresighted leading means that in the course of exercising authority and power, government should conduct foresighted investigation, rational analysis and theoretical thinking concerning newly emerged issues and problems, foresee new social and economic phenomena and generalize work experience and push it to a theoretical elevation so as to guide innovation and advancement in economic systems and institutional structuring.

In the new phase of economic development, only by continuously transforming and upgrading government notions, such as notions of civilian community, restrained government, open government and government efficiency, can government innovate administrative systems, behavior, methodology and technology and provide right value guidance and boundless innovative incentives.

The focal points of GFL may vary with economic systems, phases of economic development and economic resources. In countries where economic transformation is in progress, economic system remains to be improved and mode of economic growth is extensive, it is of special significance for government to exercise foresighted leading in systems, institutions, technology and notions. That has been amply exemplified by China's experience in reform and opening up over the past 30 years.

0.5 Foresighted leading and government performance

For government to perform effective foresighted leading, appropriate systems and measures must be set in place, including corresponding market economic system, right status of economic entities, effective competition, transparent information disclosure mechanism, perfect legal and supervisory mechanism, and excellent administrators coupled with good selectional mechanism.

Take China for example. Since 1978, when China started to implement its policy of reform and opening up and to transform from planned economy to market economy, its focus has been to give market the major role in allocating resources. The process has gone through three stages: between 1978 and 1991 — transition from planned economy to market economy, between 1992 and 1997 — initiation of market economic system, from 1998 onwards — the development of market economy and China's entry into WTO.

It is obvious that the role of GFL has been gradually enhanced with the establishment and amelioration of China's market economic system. In the initial stage, GFL is chiefly observable in notional and systematic innovation, which is followed by institutional and technological innovation, when market economic system has taken shape.

The reason that government can perform foresighted leading is that regional government has dual functions. On the one hand, regional government represents the central government and exercises macro-level administration and regulation of local economy, thus playing the role of "quasi-central government". On the other hand, regional government represents local non-government organizations, implements national policies, solicits national support and competes with other regional governments for the purpose of maximizing local economic interests, thus playing the role of "quasi-business".

In performing GFL in economic activities, regional government must try to avoid the tendency of blindly exaggerating government role and amplifying government functions. Government behavior will have long-term impacts upon economic development, but emphasis on government role does not mean that it should take care of everything. Inappropriate government intervention may hinder the normal development of market and consequently lead to increasing government intervention.

To put it in a nutshell, government intervention, which complies with market mechanisms and responses by measured proportions, will help to realize social goals and promote market maturity. There should be measured balance and degree in handling the relation between government and market. The failure of government may be either due to its doing too little or doing too much, as commented by the economist William Arthur Lewis (1915–1991).

It is of paramount significance to handle well the relation between government and market in order for government to perform foresighted leading in economy. Government should do what it should and let market deal with what it should do. Three important points need to be observed in order to strike a good balance between government and market in foresighted leading: operative resources (private assets) should be handled through market mechanism, non-operative resources (pure public assets) should be supplied by government, and quasi-operative resources (quasi-public assets) should be handled in different ways, depending on the status of government fiscal strength and private business operation, through capitalizing on market allocation of resources and the operation and technological advantage of private businesses in accordance with the principles of government promotion, business participation and market operation.

0.6 Government foresighted leading and innovation in economic theorization

The study of China's economic development shows that regional government plays a key role in regional economic development. Regional government can make an effective allocation of resources, foster leading edge and enhance sustainable development of regional economy by adopting market rules and market mechanism, guiding investment, consumption and exports, capitalizing on economic and legal means, and employing various innovative measures. The economic theory that stems from the facilitation of GFL in regional scientific development comes under the general heading of mezzoeconomics.

The conceptualization of GFL signifies a major innovation in and an important contribution to the theoretical configuration of economics. In between microeconomics represented by businesses and macroeconomics represented by central government resides mezzoeconomics represented by regional government, which not only offers an explanation of China's continuous economic growth but enriches and ameliorates economic theories.

Just as market economic theory lays the foundation for microeconomics and Keynesian theory divides economics into microeconomics and macroeconomics, so the GFL theory further classifies economics into microeconomics, mezzoeconomics and macroeconomics. This conceptualization fills the gap in the configuration of economic theories, indicates the direction for the reform of economic systems, creates multilevel markets by integrating regional economy and regional government into economic theories and thus strengthens the stability of national economy.

From a practical perspective, the regulatory system of mezzoeconomy plays an indispensable part in the whole of national economic system. Mezzoeconomy can serve as the test field for macroeconomy through its part in innovation and first trial and can effectively reduce excessive vibration of macroeconomy through its stabilizing and coordinating functions. In addition, mezzoeconomy can help to ameliorate the monitoring system of national economy and divert risks of central monitoring.

From a theoretical perspective, economics studies the relations of production that are determined by the productive force and correspond to its level of development, i.e. economic structure. The economic base determines the superstructure. As a result, the economic base also determines economic theories. The type of economic base determines the type of economic theories. Speaking from the perspective of historical materialism, a new theory is bound to replace or to help improve existing theories like microeconomics and macroeconomics so as to accommodate and promote the development of new productive forces when they fail or cannot adequately explain new developments in productive forces and production relations.

The proposition of mezzoeconomics, in the light of the GFL theory, embodies both chance and certainty. Mezzoeconomics greatly helps ameliorate modern economic theories and construct, together with microeconomics and macroeconomics, a completely new economic superstructure. It will play a better role in promoting and serving production relations and eventually enhance the development of productive forces.

The road of China's scientific development shows that it has brought about noteworthy economic development and breakthroughs in economic theories which are concomitant with economic development, as is manifested by the progression from GFL to mezzoeconomics. Government of all levels in China has done their bit to make contributions to the economic miracle, and so have Chinese economists, who have come up to meet the challenges of traditional economic theories and made their theoretical contributions.

June 2013

1 The inception of government foresighted leading

The financial crisis that started in the United States in August 2007 raged all over the world and stirred the nerves of the international community.

What caused the crisis? Was it the visible or the invisible hand? Was it due to market malfunction or government malfunction?

The crisis set economists rethinking about economic issues.

Market malfunction occurs despite liberal economics. So does government malfunction despite Keynesian theory. Chinese economy has been "enjoying the landscape here beyond comparison", to put it in a Chinese saying. The sharp contrast sets economists rethinking about traditional economic theories. They need innovation and breakthrough. The developmental experience in developed countries and regions like Singapore and that in China and its regional cities manifest that government should not only implement in-process and post-process regulations but exercise pre-process foresighted leading as well.

The proposition of GFL enables government to exercise foresighted leading in economic activities, make up through the visible hand the defects and margins caused by the invisible hand by resort to the foundation, mechanism and rules of market economy, and reduce government malfunction by giving full play to the competitive role of regional government in mezzoeconomy.

1.1 The theoretical background for conceptualizing government foresighted leading

Debates have been going on for several hundred years regarding the relation between government and market and the economic function of government. Four schools of thought can be identified on the basis of credibility. The first is represented by Marxism, which has a complete negation of capitalist market and a high commendation of planned economy. The second is represented by Keynesianism, a theory of market defects that advocates moderate government intervention. The third is neo-liberalism, with the monetarist, supply-side and rational expectation theories as its representatives. This school believes that government intervention may cause market malfunction and eventually lead to ineffective government regulation and that excessive government intervention in economic activities should be avoided. The fourth is new classical economics represented by the Austrian economists. Ludwig von Mises (1881–1973) and Friedrich August Hayek (1899–1992), the representative economists of this school, hold that government intervention in economy is equivalent to making economy enslaved and that full play should be given to market so as to fulfil complete market economy.

Though various schools of thought exist regarding the relation between government and market, two key theories stand at the core – the liberal economic theory proposed by Adam Smith and the theory of government intervention proposed by John Maynard Keynes.

The liberal economic theory and the theory of government intervention, which have played their role and guided socio-economic activities in various periods of economic development, have become guiding principles for nations of market economy to formulate economic policies and have even been accepted as economic paradigms in some nations. With the development of market economic practice, these two conflicting theories have integrated each other's elements into their own conceptualization and generated new innovations and developments in economics, such as neoclassical macroeconomics represented by Milton Friedman (1912–2006) and Robert Lucas, and neo-Keynesianism represented by Paul A. Samuelson (1915–2009), Franco Modigliani (1918–2003), James Tobin (1918–2002) and Robert Merton Solow and the others.

1.1.1   The emergence and development of theories of free economy

Prior to Adam Smith, mercantilism dominated Western Europe in its transition from feudalism to capitalism, and mercantile capitalists superseded feudal gentry and eventually became the main force of social development. Mercantilism believes that trade generates wealth and government should encourage trade by means of protectionism and that gold and silver currency is the real wealth of a nation. The only means to achieve national wealth is to increase the amount of gold and silver currency, promote foreign trade, accumulate profitable balances so as to facilitate the inflow of gold and silver currency from foreign countries and forbid its outflow. In its initial period, mercantilism pursues the doctrine of "selling more and purchasing less" so as to increase the difference of currency, prevent the outflow of gold and silver, and accumulate more gold and silver, hence bullionism or money balance theory.

In the late stage, mercantilism gives great emphasis to the relative difference in merchandise trade, advocates favorable trade balance and supports domestic handicraft production so as to create profitable balances. Mercantilism demands government intervention, holding that government should monitor and control national economy by exercising its power to accumulate wealth and strengthen national competitiveness through damaging and diminishing opponents.

Mercantilism occurred in the transitional period from natural economy to commodity economy, which brought about the changes in social castes. Former nobility became merchants. They sought more rapid growth of commodity production, the accrual of commodity capital and the accumulation of currency. Mercantilism helped to establish the relation between commodity and currency and promote the development of handicraft production and eventually created favorable conditions for the emergence of capitalism.

The invention of the Spinning Jenny in 1765 marked the beginning of the Industrial Revolution in Britain. In the middle of the eighteenth century, James Watt (1736–1819) invented the steaming engine, which ignited a series of technological innovations and led to the great leap forward from manual labor to machine production. Britain became the "world factory". The Industrial Revolution gradually spread to the European continent, North America and the rest of the world. It immensely enhanced productivity.

Following the outbreak and flourishing of the Industrial Revolution, machines began to replace manual labor, and factories were built to replace handicraft workshops. Capitalist production completed its transition from handicraft industry in workshops to machine production and its transformation from traditional agricultural to modern industrial society. Productivity was unprecedentedly facilitated and emancipated. The practice of mercantilism restraining free trade was incompatible with the new socio-economic transformation, under which case Adam Smith proposed his theory of free economy that brought mercantilism out of the historical scene.

Adam Smith, the initiator of economics, is the pioneer of classical political economy and the founder of Western liberal economics. His book *The Wealth of Nations* (1776) summarized and developed economic ideas and theories of the previous century and established the first coherent theoretical framework for modern political economy and turned political economy into an independent discipline, as Karl Marx (1818–1883) remarked in his work.

Adam Smith's economic theory has rich implications, covering such issues as labor division, currency, value, allocation and capital accumulation, but its focus is on liberal economic ideas.

1.1.1.1 The justification for economic liberalism from the perspective of human rights

Ideas of economic liberalism originated from scholars in Western Europe, which predated Adam Smith's theory. John Locke (1632–1704), a British scholar, held that every individual is by nature entitled to his own being, his labor and the products of his labor and that these inherent rights should never be infringed upon. François Quesnay (1694–1774), who epitomized the achievements of the physiocratic school, proposed the theory of natural order, believing that socio-economic life should follow natural rules and should go independently, without national intervention.

Adam Smith inherited the findings of his predecessors and went further to theorize his economic thinking from the perspective of human rights. According to him, labor ownership is the major foundation of all other ownership rights and can never be violated. What a poor being possesses and inherits from his ancestry is his right and labor skills. It is obviously an offence of his divine possession not to let him do what he thinks fit and not to allow his use of body and skills without damages to other beings. It is an infringement upon personal freedom and human rights, according to Adam Smith, to forbid the general mass to produce what they can and make the best use of their belongings and labor in the ways that they think most appropriate, to forbid manufacturers to trade their products and to impose restrictions upon the flow of labor and freedom in employment relations.

1.1.1.2 The proposition of "economic being"

The motivating mechanism of free market economy that opposes government intervention and advocates economic freedom will inevitably shift the impetus of development upon every individual of economic activities. Adam Smith did not clarify the notion of "economic being", but he is the first to advocate the idea and make it the starting point and base for his *The Wealth of Nations*.

Claude Adrien Heluétius (1715–1771), the French enlightenment philosopher, described egoism as the natural features of human beings and the driving force for social progress. Adam Smith developed this idea and gave it the flavor of economic theorization. He thought that human beings are rational and have the nature of being an egoist. Consequently, the motivation and purpose for economic activities are to pursue maximized economic benefits, but this goal can be fulfilled only when they provide service for others and trade their labor for others.

Adam Smith believed that human beings, under almost all circumstances, need their fellow people to provide assistance and that it never works for them to rely solely upon themselves. It will be of great benefit if they can motivate others' egoism and tell them it will benefit them if they make contributions to others, and it will be easier for human beings to realize their ultimate goals. In other words, to benefit themselves individuals will have to take others' well-being into consideration, and goals can never be achieved if damages are done to others. Only when others' egoist motivation is stimulated can individuals make others beneficial to themselves. It is this egoist motivation that human beings are subject to propensity for exchanges, and it is this propensity that leads to division of labor. As a result, the realization of egoist objectives is contingent upon the smooth exchange of benefits and the smooth flow of production factors.

1.1.1.3 The economic operational mechanism — the invisible hand

How does the pursuit of maximized economic benefits on the part of the "economic being" align with the interest of the general community? Adam Smith reasoned that individuals, when trying to utilize their resources to seek maximum benefits, do not generally target at promoting public interest or know to what extent they can. What they are concerned about is their own security and benefits.

However, under the impacts of the invisible hand, individuals bring forth an unexpected result. In seeking their own interest, they are in a better position to promote social well-being. There is a self-regulating mechanism, under the seemingly chaotic free market, that determines the variety and amount of products that society needs most. For instance, when there is shortage of supply of certain products their prices will automatically rise, and the rise of prices will give manufacturers higher profits. The high profits allure more manufacturers to produce these products. The increase in production will ease off supply shortage, and competition between manufacturers and the increase of supply will lower prices to a natural level, i.e. the production cost. In this process, no one contributes intentionally to the society through the easeoff of shortage supply.

In Adam Smith's words, every individual wants to gain their own benefits, but at the same time, an invisible hand leads each one to realize goals he is unaware of. However, he does promote social welfare, and the results will turn out to be better than expected. It follows that the invisible hand is the automatic effect of market mechanism. In Adam Smith's view, the "natural order" that conforms to natural law and rules will be established as long as full play is given to market mechanisms.

Adam Smith opposes government intervention and advocates free market competition. He thinks that government may grant individuals or businesses the right of monopoly, which will give rise to insufficient market supply due to inadequate stock of products and will not meet effective demands, which will eventually enable monopolistic prices to appear that far surpass their natural costs. Industrial monopoly formed through exclusive privileges of industrial groups will also create monopolistic prices. In addition, government intervention may hinder the free flow of labor and capital, causing some to develop and some others to decline, hence uncoordinated development. On the contrary, free competition can not only inspire the initiatives of every individual but promote the reasonable allocation of factors of labor and capital across departments.

Adam Smith thinks that in order to increase national wealth and public interest, the best economic policy is to give individual economy absolute autonomy, let it develop on its own and practice free competition and trade. He opposes national intervention in economic activities and confines government roles to the following three aspects: (a) strengthen national defense and guard against foreign invasion, (b) set up legislation and justice organizations to maintain social law and order, (c) undertake public causes and facilities and compensate for inadequacies of private enterprises. Moreover, he favors government administration of postal services, reasonable monitoring of interest rates, standardized national education, etc.

Adam Smith attaches great importance to free economy, but he does not deny the role and function government performs in economic activities. He focuses exclusively on its part as the provider of public products and as "night watchman" of market economy. He thinks that government of the least administration is the best government and that government should not intervene in economy as government intervention may cause damages to the natural balance of economy. He advocates small government and big market. Government should take responsibilities for such issues as national security, social stability and order and legislation, which are indispensable external conditions for a nation's economic development. Moreover, government should build such public infrastructure as roads, bridges and canals necessary for economic development and provide public education to the majority of its citizens.

Subsequent to Adam Smith, economists like David Ricardo (1772–1823), Jean Baptiste Say (1767–1832) and Alfred Marshall (1842–1924) further contributed to the theory of economic liberalism and created a coherent framework for classical economics. David Ricardo also believes that market mechanism has the function of self-regulating and self-balancing. He advocates that liberalism should be practiced for domestic economy and foreign trade, assuming that agriculture, commerce and manufacturing will prosper without government intervention.

Jean Baptiste Say inherits liberal ideas of economy from Adam Smith and makes a systematic introduction of them into the European continent. In his *Traité d'économie Politique*, he proposes his well-known laws, i.e. supply will automatically create demand. He believes that market possesses inherent self-balancing mechanism, that government intervention is unnecessary and even detrimental in economy, and that government role should be restricted to maintaining market mechanism, protecting consumer interest, securing personal assets and safety, and so on.

The liberal economic theory dominated economics from the publication of *The Wealth of Nations* to the 1930s, accompanied by the development and perfection of Adam Smith's and his followers' ideas. *The Wealth of Nations* is considered "the Bible" for economic studies. Not only did the liberal economic theory dominate the economic ideology but exercise profound influence upon economic practices. The public came to recognize liberal economic ideas. Free competition and the concept of market economy began to take root in the public mind. European countries began to implement liberal economic policies, which sped up Britain's Industrial Revolution, enabled it to achieve rapid prosperity, and turned it into the world's number one superpower and an empire on which the sun never set.

Britain began to implement liberal economic policies towards the end of the eighteenth century. Domestically, government made no interference with market operation, and the regulation of economic activities depended solely on market forces. Internationally, rigorous measures were taken to practice free trade policies. All this further eliminated obstacles to the development of market economic systems and emancipated labor forces thanks to technological advances the Industrial Revolution brought forth. Meantime, Britain used military power to force open foreign countries' doors for international trade. The practice of liberal trade policies created for Britain immense international market. Had it not been for the foundation the Industrial Revolution had laid, liberal economic policies would not have burst out such forceful power, and had it not been for liberal economic policies, the Industrial Revolution would not have created the worldwide cutting edge for Britain. For some time liberal economic policies became the guidelines for Britain's policy making. The British Prime Minister William Peter Jr. was once reported to have said "We are all your students" to Adam Smith, which is an adequate manifestation of its influence.

The United States followed the example of Britain and adopted the system of private economy and free competition. The invisible hand was also employed to guide economic practice. Government did not intervene in economy and practiced free trade policies, which contributed to America's rapid economic development and prosperity and made it another superpower in the early period of the twentieth century.

The reason that liberal economic theory was able to exercise such profound influence in economic activities was its conformity with social development. Over that period, after the Industrial Revolution, capitalist economy was on the rise, and its development demanded continuous expansion of domestic and international market so as to digest the productivity generated by technological revolution. However, mercantilism imposed a lot of restrictions upon economy, including protectionist measures for limiting exports, which curbed economic development. Liberal economists believed that only by allowing economy to develop freely and letting the invisible hand of market guide economic activities could market economy maintain balanced development, productive forces be emancipated, and national economy achieve sustainable development. Only under that socio-economic background did liberal economic theory gain its domination and promoted prosperity in Britain and the United States.

1.1.2 The inception and practice of theories of government intervention

With further development of capitalist economy, pitfalls of the laissez-faire economic mode gradually emerged, resulting in vicious competition and monopoly. Market economy suffered from extremely unbalanced development. Monopolistic enterprises spoiled the good environment for complete competition, with the unemployment rate remaining high, which showed that the free operation of market economy did not strike a so-called natural balance. The consequences brought about by these imbalances aggravated socio-economic contradictions. Between 1929 and 1933, the worldwide disaster broke out in the capitalist countries, resulting in the first economic depression of the capitalist world.

During that period, the total volume of the world's industrial output went backwards by nearly 20 years, and numerous people went out of work. The liberal economists were quite at a loss as to what caused the disaster and continued to ascribe it to the lack of effective incentive mechanisms for production. They insisted that the rational solution to the problem was the reduction of labor cost to a level that could merely meet the need of survival. Once prices decreased the purchasing power would regain and employment would rise. It was their firm conviction that market economy could self-regulate and remedy its imbalance. Economic crises should not have happened, and the system could put it right even if temporary market imbalance could occur. It was also their conviction that government could only serve as "night watchman" and should not interfere with economy. Under the grave circumstances, the continuation of liberal economic policies would only sharpen contradictions rather than wiping them out.

The 1929–1933 economic depression was the first and the most serious in the history of Western economy with widespread and far-reaching impacts. In fact, it signified the failure of laissez-faire economic theory and radically changed people's perception of a nation's economic function and policies. It marked a major turning point in the development of Western capitalism and economic theorization. Economists came to realize that market is not omnipotent and that market may also malfunction. In market economy, free competition may lead to monopoly, affect market efficiency and give rise to serious concussion of economic cycles, which will cause uneven distribution of wealth and income and aggravate social contradictions.

In 1936, Keynes published his book *The General Theory of Employment, Interest and Money*, which first offered a systematic and complete account of the theory of government intervention and relevant policies and formulated the theoretical foundation and basic principles of government intervention. The book gained immediate popularity among economists and became the "new orthodox" for Western economics. The theory of government intervention became the mainstream theory of economics, laid the foundation for modern macroeconomics and marked an important transition of economics from micro-level classical economics to macro-level Keynesian theory of national intervention.

The book elaborated upon such major economic issues as effective demand and employment, three basic psychological laws (i.e. marginal propensity to consume, law of diminishing marginal efficiency of capital, liquidity preference), multiplier principle, wages and price, and crises. Its core is the theory of effective demand. It is Keynes' view that the general level of production and employment determines the level of aggregate demand. He pointed out that market of complete competition as proposed by classical liberal economists does not exist in real life and that capitalism that solely relies on market regulation will never lead to the balance of social demands, which may, on the contrary, cause insufficiency of effective social demand and economic crises. The concept of "effective demand" was employed to analyze and explain unemployment and production surplus.

According to Keynesian theory, previous propositions of adequate employment equilibrium is founded upon Say's laws, i.e. supply will create its own demand so that the aggregate social supply and demand reach equilibrium. However, this proposition is wrong, as the functional analysis of aggregate supply and demand shows that due to inadequacy of effective social demand, it is impossible for aggregate supply and demand to reach equilibrium unless it is on the level lower than adequate employment, i.e. in the case of economic contraction.

Traditional economists think that balanced employment can be achieved through self-regulation of labor market, which is contrary to Keynes' view that unemployment cannot be eliminated through self-regulation of labor market. The root cause for the existence of equilibrium between involuntary unemployment and less sufficient employment resides in the lack of effective demand. As there is no major changes in aggregate supply over a short period of time employment is determined by aggregate demand and inadequacy in demand will cause involuntary unemployment and in sufficient employment.

Inadequacy in effective demand shows that income has not all generated demand, which is the result of impacts from the three basic psychological laws: reduction in marginal propensity to consume causes inadequate consumption demand, the diminishing marginal efficiency of capital, and liquidity preference leads to inadequate investment demand. These three basic psychological laws explain why the crisis of production surplus in the capitalist society cannot be avoided and why market cannot by itself solve the problem of insufficient effective demand. Therefore, government must exercise intervention in economic activities.

No government intervention is equivalent to letting inadequate effective demand, unemployment and crises continue. Government must make strenuous efforts to stimulate consumption and investment in order to promote economic development by fiscal rather than monetary means. It is particularly important to create a favorable investment environment, build up investors' confidence and elevate demand to the level of adequate employment.

The core of Keynesian theory is government intervention in economy by means of which to stimulate effective demand (i.e. consumption and investment). In terms of fiscal policies, measures should be taken to reduce taxation and increase fiscal expenditures, when aggregate demand is lower than aggregate supply, so as to increase investment and consumption, and when aggregate demand is greater than aggregate supply, measures should be taken to increase taxation, reduce fiscal expenditures so as to reduce investment and consumption.

In terms of monetary policies, measures should be taken to increase currency supply and lower interest rates in periods of economic depression so as to stimulate investment, and in periods of high economic growth, measures should be taken to reduce currency supply and increase interest rates so as to restrain investment. It is Keynes' view that inadequate effective demand is the basic factor that hinders economic development. Therefore, he proposes policies of financial deficit from the perspective of inadequate effective demand, which means that financial deficit can occur as long as the increase of government expenditures can facilitate economic growth and increase individual income. He advocates economic regulation by adjusting government expenditures and revenues.

Keynesian theory replaced classical liberal economics. Western capitalist governments advocated and practiced the theory and accepted it as the guideline and the foundation for their economic policy making. The typical case is the New Deal the American government implemented in 1933 under Franklin D. Roosevelt's administration. Between 1929 and 1933, the most catastrophic economic crisis happened in the American history. The flourishing American economy was gradually overshadowed by the distressing overstock of products, unemployment of workers, close-down of businesses. The whole American economy fell as backwards as 1913.

After Roosevelt took office as president, he took a series of measures and policies aimed at overcoming the economic crisis, known as "the New Deal". It was implemented through two phases: between 1933 and 1935 focus was on readjusting and recovering economy through emergency measures, and government intervention so as to put an end to economic chaos, stabilize the society and get out of the crisis; between 1935 and 1939 focus was on reform which, after successful trial, brought forth a series of transformative policies regarding finance, industry, agriculture and labor so as to consolidate and develop the existing accomplishments. Hence, the New Deal was summarized into 3R – i.e. recovery, relief and reform. The concrete measures include the following:

(a)   Readjusting banking and financial system

In March 1933, the Emergency Banking Act was passed to permit individual examination of banks and issue permits to banks. Meanwhile, government forbade the stock and export of gold in order to secure bank reserves and prevent gold outflow. The Glass-Steagall Act made a strict division between investment banking services and commercial banking services and introduced American finance into an era of separation of banking from securities. It announced the separation of gold from dollars, depreciated dollars and abandoned the gold standard. All these measures consolidated the economic status of America and its international competitiveness of products and turned out to be highly powerful in stabilizing the situation and calming down the general public.

(b)   Recovering industry and agriculture

The Congress passed the Agriculture Adjustment Act and the National Industrial Recovery Act. Government requested that factory owners abide by the rule of fair competition and lay down specifications of production scale, price, sales, minimum wages and maximum work hours, etc. so as to curb monopoly and ease off the intense class contradictions. Government granted the blue eagle medal to those businesses that obeyed the laws and rules with the words such as "We do our duty". In order to stabilize agriculture, government granted subsidies to those farmers whose yield decreased so that the price of agricultural products was heightened and stabilized. By taking all these measures, government strengthened its control and regulation of industrial and agricultural production and prevented production surplus which might have appeared as a result of blind competition.

(c)   Increasing unemployment relief, investing in public facilities and fueling demand and employment

In the initial stage of Roosevelt's administration, over 17 million unemployed workers and their families survived on the relief and charity from the state government, the municipal government and private charity organizations. All this almost came to nothing, considering the large army of unemployed workers. Facts proved that only the federal government had the ability to solve the problem. The federal government provided direct help through industrial rescue organizations, urged the Congress to pass the Federal Emergency Relief Act, founded the federal relief organizations, clarified the proportion of the federal and the state government and laid down preferential policies to encourage local government to provide direct relief to impoverished people and unemployed workers.

During the New Deal period, a great number of industrial rescue organizations were set up. They created numerous job opportunities. That became a good example of the stimulating and driving force of government investment in private consumption and individual investment.

(d) Labor legislation and intervention of labor market

In 1935, the Social Security Law and the National Labor Relations Act were passed, followed by the Fair Labor Standard Act in 1938. Social security system, minimum wages and maximum work hours were part of legislation, which improved the economic and political environment of laborers to some extent, avoided social disorder and even revolution, and made enormous contributions to saving the economy and stabilizing the society.

(e) Readjusting the tripartite political system

In 1937, the Federal Supreme Court of the United States was founded to expand the limits of the executive power into the economic area and secure the freedom of the general public. More executive organizations were set up to take care of budgeting, national resource planning, personnel administration, etc. and to work for the executive office of the president, which were very much like today's Office of Administration, Office of Management and Budget, Council of Economic Advisers, etc. All these measures were the result of making wise use of the legislation concerning the presidential power and obligations stipulated in the U.S. constitution and removed the obstacles to government intervention of economy. The New Deal signified the victory of a promising government and legalized the expansion of presidential powers.

Up to 1939, Roosevelt's New Deal turned out to be a huge success. Almost all the economic indexes steadily rose up, and the public confidence in national system was recovered, which helped to avoid great social turmoil in America. Close to the end of the Second World War, a great proportion of production and wealth of the world concentrated in America. American economy entered into a new era of development and prosperity.

Roosevelt's New Deal radically changed government functions and strengthened national intervention in economy while retaining the foundation of free economic system. It implemented a series of regulative measures for chaotic production, created a new model of national intervention in economy and transformed America's economic system from private capitalism to a new system of national intervention.

Economically speaking, Roosevelt's New Deal is the largest-scale trial of Keynesianism. It laid a great practical foundation for the eventual formation and perfection of Keynesianism, which developed Keynesian ideas into a complete coherent theoretical system and established the status of Keynesianism in economics.

1.1.3 The confrontation and development of theories of free economy and government intervention

Keynesian economics saved the Western world form the serious economic crisis, facilitated the economic growth in the Western world for some period of time and brought the Western economy into a golden period of growth. Keynesianism reached its prime period of development from the Second World War to the 1970s, occupied the orthodox status in economics and became the theoretical basis for governments of Western countries to formulate economic policies and develop their economy.

However, with the further development of economy, the drawbacks of government intervention in economy began to surface. The stagflation in the 1970s pushed Keynesian theory into a crisis. Different ideas and theories were derived from the absorption and development of the findings of serious explorations centring on the two opposing systems of laissez-faire economy and government intervention.

1.1.3.1 Neo-liberalism and its development

Subsequent to the Second World War, all major capitalist countries followed and practiced Keynesianism. The policies of expanding aggregate demand and relaxing monetary policies contributed to some extent to the rapid growth of economy, the decrease in unemployment, the lessening of and shortening of economic crises. However, there coexisted stagflation, unemployment and economic depression in the 1970s.

Confronted with a new cycle of economic crisis, economists began to rethink about the problems, to find that one of the causes for stagflation was the excessive exercise of Keynesianism and the overemphasis on the role of government intervention in economy. Consequently, the role of market itself was disregarded, which led to a series of problems, such as the destruction of market effect, the low efficiency of government, etc. New theories and proposals were put forward. Economists of neo-liberalism treated Keynesian theory of government intervention as the major target and criticized Keynes for his overemphasis on government intervention. They suggested less government intervention in economy and more reliance on market.

New liberal economics inherited Western classical liberal economics as its basis and was characterized by opposing and resisting Keynesianism. It satisfied the demand of new transformation of Western economy. There are relations and differences between neo-liberalism and classical liberal economic theory.

New liberal economic economics stemmed from a great debate concerning the relation between market and government planning in the 1920s and 1930s and began to attract worldwide attention. The Austrian economists Ludwig von Mises and Friedrich August Hayek, the neo-liberalists, led the debate on one side, and on the other side, there was the Italian economist Enrico Barone (1859–1924) and the Polish economist Oskar Lange (1904–1965), the market socialists. The debate became a milestone for neo-liberalists to get onto the historical stage. Numerous thoughts and theories were derived from almost one hundred years' evolution of neo-liberalism.

Neo-liberalism can be distinguished in the narrow and broad sense. In the narrow sense, neo-liberalism mainly refers to neo-liberalism represented by Friedrich August Hayek, and the broad-sense liberalism covers not only the London school and neo-Austrian school but also the Chicago school with Hayek, Milton Friedman, George Joseph Stigler (1911–1991), and Ronald H. Coase (1910–2013) as its main representatives, the monetarism represented by Friedman, the rational expectation school represented by Robert Lucas and Robert Joseph Barro, the school of new institutional economics represented by Coase, the school of public choice represented by James McGill Buchanan (1919–2013), the supply school represented by Arthur Betz Laffer and Martin Feldstein, and so on, among which the London school, the monetary school and the rational expectation school are the most influential.

The London school holds that freedom is the ultimate political goal and is the guarantee for the pursuit of the ultimate goal of civilized society and the security of personal life. According to the principles of liberalism, full play should be given to initiatives rather than coercive forces to handle things. It emphasizes that private ownership is the most important assurance of freedom and that personal initiatives can be most stimulated only on the basis of private ownership. The restraints and management of private property by means of government intervention rather than market mechanism will result in damages to efficiency, the frustration of personal initiatives, the imbalance of resource allocation and eventually totalitarianism and the "enslavement" of individuals.

Monetarism emerged in America in the 1960s. Its leader Friedman believed in maintaining free market economy and the old doctrine that the idealist economic system should follow the principles of free market. He is ranked as the strongest advocate of the laissez-faire theory of economics. He thinks that the instability of the economic system stems from the interference in currency. So he believes that currency is the most important and the sole primary factor that determines the output volume, employment and price. There should be no government intervention in personal economy and full play should be given to market mechanism. The economic system can be steady by itself as long as full play is given to market mechanism.

The rational expectation school thinks that human beings are rational and are always in the pursuit of maximum personal gains. They will make the best use of their wit and resources available to make possible speculations about the changes in economic variables in the light of their knowledge and experience, as they are related to their personal choice and benefits. As a result of the effects of rational expectation, market mechanism can maintain balanced full employment. Policies of government intervention are totally unnecessary, as they will either come to nothing or aggravate economic turmoil.

Therefore they come to the classical conclusion that government will not do better than individuals or enterprises, and that the mechanism of free market competition remains to be the best mechanism of economic development. Lucas, professor of Chicago University and the representative of this theory, adopted the model of monetary cycles by using theories of rational behavior of "economic beings" and rational expectation as the starting point and the foundation, to expound the rationale for economic fluctuations and prove the ineffectiveness of Keynesian policies and unnecessariness of government intervention. He attaches great prominence to the stability and continuity of economic policies. His ideas caused a great stir of "rational expectation" in the economic field.

New institutional economics gained rapid growth over that period, and its representative theory — Coase's property theory — won worldwide popularity in the economic arena. For some time the notion that the privatization of property is the most efficient and economical policy arrangement was regarded by most as the economic doctrine. Coase's theory of property eventually became the theoretical guide for privatization reform and liberalization of market in many Western countries.

The appearance of neo-liberal economics was confronted with the 1929–1933 economic depression that raged through the whole Western world. There came into being a new type of Keynesianism, which advocated the increase of government expenditures to create demand and the promotion of economic growth through government intervention. Roosevelt's New Deal demonstrated the effectiveness of Keynesianism through putting it into operation and turned it into the mainstream of Western economics. Keynesianism led economic operation for as long as 40 years in the Western countries. That period was termed the "Keynesian era", and new liberalism was overlooked.

Neo-liberalism had a turning point in the early 1970s, when the outbreak of two oil crises brought the whole of the capitalist world into stagflation, and Keynesian policy makers could do nothing about it. New liberalists attributed it to excessive government intervention, too much government expenditure and the failure of government policies caused by the public rational expectation. Neo-liberalism dominated mainstream economic thinking in Britain and the United States, after the wake of negating Keynesianism, and with Ronald Wilson Reagan (1911–2004) being in office as U.S. president and Margaret Hilda Thatcher (1925–2013) as Prime Minister in Britain. The opposition of government intervention was elevated to a new level of theoretical generalization.

Meanwhile, in most of the developing countries and socialist countries in East Europe, which depended on planning and nationalization to accelerate their capital accumulation and industrialization and adopted the strategy of export replacement, there appeared various problems and contradictions in its economic operation, and their economic development almost came to a halt. In sharp contrast, the so-called Four Asian Tigers (Singapore, Hong Kong China, Korea and Taiwan China), which remained highly open to the outside world, attached great importance to market mechanisms and adopted the strategy of export orientation, achieved remarkable economic success.

That situation enabled the ideas of free economy to exercise more extensive and profound influence in developing countries. The economic reforms in Latin

American countries further consolidated the mainstream status of neo-liberalism in Western economic theorization. The Washington Consensus signified that neo-liberalism began to transform itself from its theoretical and academic nature to the political, ideological and paradigmatic nature. It became an important part of the theory of globalization of market economy that Western countries like Britain, the United States tried to promote.

1.1.3.2 Neo-Keynesianism and its development

Neo-Keynesianism was developed from the writings of John Maynard Keynes and absorbed some ideas and concepts from non-Keynesian thought. Keynesian economists formalized and synthesized neo-Keynesianism to cope with the Keynesian economic theory in the 1970s. In the late period of the 1970s, efforts were made by economists like Stanley Fischer, Edmund Phelps and John Taylor to lay foundations for neo-Keynesian economics. In 1977, Fischer published his "Long-Term Contracts, Rational Expectations and the Optimal Money Supply Rule" in the *Journal of Political Economy* (February 1977, 191–206), which was reprinted in *Rational Expectations and Econometric Practice* (R. Lucas and T. Sargent (eds.), University of Minnesota Press, 1981), and Stabilizing Powers of Monetary Policy under Rational Expectations, which made the first attempt to integrate the hypothesis of rational expectation theory.

In the 1980s, a group of young scholars in the United States tried to create a solid microeconomic foundation for the Keynesian economic theorization and established a theoretical framework that used theories of wages, price stickiness, non-market-clearing price and rational expectation as the microeconomic foundations. The representatives include George Arthur Akerlof, Janet Louise Yellen, Nicholas Gregory Mankiw and Ben Shalom Bernanke.

Neo-Keynesianism inherited the basic concept of government intervention in economy from traditional Keynesian economists and landed macroeconomics upon solid microeconomic footing. It tried to explain macroeconomic fluctuation by employing such theories as incomplete competition, information inadequacy and relative rigidity of price under the general framework of principles of maximization of benefits and hypothesis of rational expectation.

Neo-Keynesianism differs from traditional Keynesianism in that it attaches greater prominence to the microeconomic foundation of macroeconomics and employs the notion of actual market incompleteness as the key to explaining economic fluctuation. Neo-Keynesian economists think that owing to the existence of price stickiness, incomplete competition and information inadequacy, the complete laissez-faire operation will lead to the inefficiency of equilibrium, i.e. market malfunction. They believe that relative to the impacts arising from demand, wages and price adjustment takes place at a relatively late time, and it takes a longer time for economy to return to the state of actual production output equating with normal output, hence market non-equilibrium. Asymmetrical information exists in modern market economy, and there is stickiness to wages and prices. There will occur inadequate effective demand, as deviation from the rate of natural unemployment will materialize over a short period of time. So policies of demand management are necessary and will play their due role.

The aggregate supply curve is vertical in the light of the classical theory based on the hypothesis of complete wage elasticity and complete market competition. Under such circumstances, no matter what changes take place in aggregate demand, the production output will remain stable, and the performance of currency keeps neutral. Friedman, a neo-liberalist, thinks that owing to the factors such as rational expectation the long-term aggregate supply curve is vertical, that is the long-term neutrality of currency performance. Lucas' model also shows that under the hypothesis of rational expectation the prediction of inflation can be quickly adjusted. So the long-term aggregate supply curve is vertical. The output will be affected only when the performance of currency is not predicted. Currency will not exercise long-term effects upon output.

David Romer, a new Keynesian economist, also finds that the short-term aggregate supply curve goes up rightwards, which approximates to Friedman's and Lucas' conclusion, but he emphasizes that due to cross-pricing, menu cost and incomplete competition, monetary policies remain effective even if they can be precisely predicted. The existence of these three factors will result in the stickiness of wages and prices, and when the general price level goes up labor supply that is determined by the predicted price cannot be rapidly adjusted, because of the effects of wage stickiness, which is similar to the original Keynesian theory. According to neo-Keynesianism, the aggregate supply curve goes up rightwards, and the changes in aggregate demand will affect both the price level and the actual production output.

It follows from the above analysis that neo-Keynesian economists think that the policies concerning aggregate demand management remains effective, that government can play a better role in remedying market malfunction, and that economy can recover, after the shocking impacts of aggregate demand, to the extent of the equilibrium of employment

Another feature of neo-Keynesianism in guidelines for fiscal policy making is its belief in "moderate" national intervention. Neo-Keynesian economists recognize the neoclassical macroeconomic view that frequent intervention in economy will result in stagflation. They accept the hypothesis of benefit maximization of economic beings and rational expectation, attach greater importance to the role of market mechanism than traditional Keynesianism and advocate sketchy regulation of economy. Compared with traditional Keynesianism, which focuses on the "quantity" regulation of economy and overlooks the actual microeconomic operation, neo-Keynesianism extends the regulation of fiscal policies into economic operation and emphasizes the "quality" regulation.

New Keynesian economics persists in government intervention in economy, but it also absorbs the findings of rational expectation school and the view of predictable failures of macroeconomic policies. Neo-Keynesianism does not just stop at traditional Keynesian theory of short-term demand management but gives special emphasis to the view of the supply school about economic regulation by means of supply. It considers economic policies from a long-term perspective and from the angle of supply.

Neo-Keynesianism inherits the basic view of national intervention in economy from traditional Keynesian economists. It not only integrates the reasonable ideas and policies of neoclassical economics but also develops the theory of national intervention in economy, on the basis of experience and lessons from the macroeconomic operations from the 1980s, and pushes the policy system of national intervention in economy to a new level.

Subsequent to the 1990s, under the guidance of neo-Keynesianism, developed countries, especially Britain and America, not only exercised moderate intervention in economy but also emphasized the regulative function of market competition mechanism, thus establishing an integrated model of government and market relations characterized by both government intervention and market regulation.

1.1.4 The defects of theories of free economy and government intervention

According to Adam Smith's theory of free economy, microeconomic operation solely depends on the competitive market regulative mechanism to achieve the self-regulating and balancing of resources, which is an effective way of optimizing the allocation of resources. However, market malfunction may materialize due to the spontaneity, blindness, hysteresis and externality of market, thus giving rise to the unfair allocation of income and wealth, market monopoly, imbalanced regional development, inadequacy of public products, economic fluctuation, etc.

When market malfunction occurs, market cannot play an effective role in allocating commodities and labor forces. In addition, market mechanism may not satisfy the needs of public interest. Four factors may cause market malfunction: market forces, incomplete information, externality and public products. The defect of the allocation of resources by means of market mechanism is reflected in the unfair allocation of income and wealth, external negative effect, competition failure and the formation market monopoly, imbalanced regional economy, the insufficient supply of public products, the excessive utilization of public resources, etc.

To remedy market malfunction, Keynes proposed the theory of government intervention in economy and advocated administrative, legal, fiscal and monetary measures to overcome market malfunction, stimulate economy, and guarantee steady and smooth economic development, but the stagflation of Western economy in the 1970s turned Keynesian legend into bubbles. It was found that government is not omnipotent and that government intervention may create government malfunction, such as miscalculation of public policies, inefficiency of bureaucratic organs, power peddling, corruption, and so on.

Samuelson (2006) describes government malfunction as occurring when the measures taken by means of government policies or collective efforts cannot improve economic efficiency or the income distribution recognized by moral standards. Charles Wolf (1827–1918), after a careful analysis of government malfunction from the perspective of non-market limitation, defines it as the high cost, low efficiency and unfair allocation in terms of government operation that are determined by the internal deficiencies of government organizations and government supply and demand. Government malfunction is mainly reflected in the failure of government policies, the expansion of government organs and public budgeting, the low efficiency of public product supply, government power peddling, and so on. The causes for government malfunction include the lack of competition between government departments, the lack of precise information for intervention, the hysteresis of intervention, the lack of reasonable rules and regulations that constrain government conduct, the lack of effective supervision and monitoring, etc.

In short, government malfunction means the inability of government to effectively optimize the allocation of social resources due to the limitations of government conduct and the restrictions of other factors in intervention of socio-economic activities. Under modern market economic system, market regulation and government intervention are intertwined with free competition and macro-regulation. They are closely related and are all indispensable.

Many valuable economic theories are derived from discussions concerning the relation between government and market. Different theories guide and dominate economic policies and practice over different periods of socio-economic development. Market malfunction is inevitable in the traditional theory of free economy, and government malfunction cannot be eliminated in Keynesian theory of government intervention. During the economic depression, Keynesianism occupied the dominating position. In the period of stagflation, neo-liberalism reclaimed the dominating position, which had been taken by neo-Keynesianism.

No matter what changes may take place, these theories are innovations and developments under the general framework of Adam Smith's theory of free economy and Keynesian theory of government intervention. They either focus on the primary role of enterprises and individuals in microeconomy or the in-process and post-process intervention of government in macroeconomy. Almost nothing is touched upon concerning pre-process intervention and the role of regional government in mezzoeconomy. Inadequacy in researches on the foresighted-leading role in pre-process government intervention and the role of regional government in mezzoeconomy is a huge blank left by microeconomics and macroeconomics since their establishment as a discipline and an enormous drawback in the existing economic theoretical generalization. It is for lack of appropriate theoretical guidance that the efficiency of market economic system and the effectiveness of government intervention are seriously reduced. The financial crisis starting from 2007 is a good example to illustrate this.

In the light of the GFL theory, government can exercise foresighted leading by means of market economic foundation, mechanism and rules and make up the margins left by the invisible hand with the visible hand and remedy market malfunction. It can also lessen government malfunction and minimize the cost of remedying malfunction and errors by giving play to the competitive role of regional government in mezzoeconomy and exercising pre-process foresighted regulation.

1.2   The practical background for conceptualizing government foresighted leading

1.2.1   Lessons from international financial crises

The outbreak of America's sub-prime crisis in August 2007 dragged America into the most serious financial crisis since the economic depression of the 1930s. The crisis raged over most of the world and deteriorated into the most serious international financial disaster since the 1930s. It triggered off, to varying degrees, international economic and social problems.

There is still a great deal of controversy concerning the cause of this crisis. Was it caused by the invisible or the visible hand? Some ascribe it to the pursuit of benefits and greed of the Wall Street and the anticipatory excessive spending of the American public, some to the abuse of financial derivatives and the unconstrained financial innovation, and others to the effective regulation and monitoring of the Federal Reserve and securities regulative organizations and the mistakes of monetary policies.

Most regard market malfunction as the root cause of this crisis, a result of economic liberalization. As a matter of fact, after the outbreak of the crisis, Keynesian policy of government intervention in economy started to display its prowess to the fullest. Western countries such as America tried to shift their liberal strategy to policies of injecting capital, nationalization, increasing fiscal deficit, increasing investment, etc. so that economists began to call it the retrogression of liberalism.

It is worth noting that there existed problems of government malfunction in this crisis. For almost ten years before the crisis, the Federal Reserve implemented the policy of low interest rate and credit expansion so that market information and signals were twisted and the bubbles in real estate and securities foamed up rapidly. With the twisted signal of interest rate by the U.S. government, the pricing mechanism, whether financial or tangible assets, began to lose its due effect. In addition, owing to the fact that the U.S. government provided guarantee for real estate market credit, moneylenders were no longer worried about the borrowers' credit status and their financial ability. Borrowers began to borrow money without worrying about their solvency after they knew about government guarantee. That increased the moral risk on the part of borrowers and aggravated the crisis.

This crisis shows that free market theory embodies market malfunction and that government malfunction resides in government intervention theory. In addition to the above defects, Keynesianism that focuses on in-process and post-process intervention must face the problem of high costs in remedying government malfunction, which is exemplified by the huge losses this crisis caused to the world economy.

According to a statistic report by Jeffrey Sachs, professor of Columbia University, this crisis brought about an evaporation of 15,000 billion worth of assets. The post-process interventional measures the U.S. government took for market rescue and economic stimulation will create an enormous fiscal deficit of thousands of billions of dollars in the years to come.

1.2.2 China's economic growth under adverse conditions

China has maintained a high rate of continuous economic development over the past three decades of reform and opening up and has been enjoying "the landscape here beyond comparison" against the background of successive economic crises, such as the 1997 Asian financial crisis and the 2007 American sub-prime crisis. Foshan, Guangdong Province, under the guidance of GFL, quickly and successfully broke out of the crisis and accomplished its transformation of economic restructuring, hence "a beautiful overtake at the bend".

It can be concluded from the market malfunction of liberal economic theory, the government malfunction of Keynesianism and China's economic growth over the past 30 years or so, particularly the development of regional economy that government should not only exercise in-process and post-process intervention but also be capable of pre-process foresighted leading. China's well-known economist and Professor Li Yining also held similar views. Early in 2010, he pointed out that in order for Chinese economy to get out of the vicious cycles of investment impulses and capital bubbles government cannot stop at post-process regulation only. It should take pre-process regulative measures and set up early warning systems.

With over 30 years' reform and opening up and the continuous rapid growth of Chinese economy, the world economic centre is gradually shifting to the Asian region with China standing at the centre. In 2010 China surpassed Japan and became the second largest economy in the world with its GDP (gross domestic product) amounting to 5,878.6 billion U.S. dollars, while Japan's GDP stood at 5,474.2 billon U.S. dollars. Japan occupied the second place from 1968 and for the first time, it retreated to the third place.

According to *The World Economic Outlook* (2011) released by the International Monetary Fund (IMF) and based on the purchasing power parity, China's GDP will reach 19,000 billion U.S. dollars by 2016 if it grows at the rate in 2010. In contrast, America's GDP will increase from 15,200 billion U.S. dollars to 18,800 billion U.S. dollars, which will be a little bit lower. Also by 2016, changes will take place in the percentage roles China and America will play in the world economy. China's percentage will go up from 14% to 18%, while America's will go down from nearly 20% to 17.7% and takes the second place, next to China's. As indicated by America's CNN, the IMF report predicts that the American era will end in 2016, which will mark the Year Zero of China.

It is certain that the IMF is not the first to make such predictions regarding when China will surpass America in terms of GDP. The Nobel Laureate in economics, Robert William Fogel (1926–2013), once prophesied that China will have the largest economic aggregate in the world by 2020. In subsequent years scholars and research institutions made similar predictions. Britain's prestigious journal the *Economist* assumed in 2010 that, in the ten years to come, if the growth rate of China's and America's GDP is 7.75% and 2.5%, respectively, the rate of inflation 4% and 1.5%, and the rate of appreciation for the exchange of Chinese yuan with U.S. dollar stands at 3%, then China will replace America and become the largest economy in 2019. Specialists estimate that Chinese economy will surpass America and the European Union and become the largest economic market by 2030.

The Chinese economic circles have so far remained quite low-key about these predictions and estimates. They have even thought of them as a kind of early warning. It cannot be denied that the world's economic attention has been gradually turning towards China and towards Asia with China as its core, no matter whether these predictions are accurate or not and no matter when these predictions can turn into reality. It is just against this background that the American president Barack Hussein Obama implemented his strategy of U.S. "pivot" to Asia. China's economic growth has been recognized as a most significant economic phenomenon of the world economy. It follows naturally that the findings and the theorization of China's economic development are deemed to be an essential part of world economic researches. As indicated by the American economist Milton Friedman, whoever can offer a clear explanation of China's reform and development will likely be a winner of the Nobel Laureate in economics.

Over the past years, many economists of international renown, like Joseph E. Stiglitz — a Nobel Laureate in economics and University Professor at Columbia University, have paid special attention to Chinese economy. Quite a few Nobel laureates are frequent visitors to China. Chinese economists have also contributed to the study of the Chinese economic phenomenon in the light of Western economic theories. Various monographs and studies have appeared in large numbers and have attempted to explain and reveal the secret of China's economic development.

It is the view of the mainstream economists with neo-classicalism as its theoretical core that China's economic success has mainly benefited from a series of favorable initial factors, internal conditions, market mechanisms and the advantages of post-development. Jeffrey Sachs, professor of Harvard University, is the representative of this view. He does not attribute China's success to the special role of gradualism. He thinks (2003) that what really matters is to allow sufficient economic freedom so as to make the best use of China's economic structure. He holds that China's success can be ascribed to two factors: the structural difference between China's economy and that of the former Soviet Union and east European countries and the relatively stable finance.

In the initial stage of reform and opening up, the state-owned organizations in China accounted for 18% of its total labor force, and 70% were in the rural areas. China's reform is a typical case of structural transformation from the agricultural sector of low productivity and autonomy to the industrial sector of relatively high productivity. It is easier to develop economy by following normal steps than to restructure economy. A huge amount of surplus labor force did not enjoy the privilege of national subsidies and was eager to mobilize. These people provided workers for the newly emerging non-state-owned businesses. If the percentage of the labor force that was employed by the state-owned organizations had not been 18% but 80 or 90% like in Poland and the former Soviet Union, then reform in China could not have gone ahead smoothly. Another factor that helped to explain

China's success was its financial stability in the initial stage of reform and opening up and the absence of heavy foreign debts.

Many more scholars think that China's success lies in its taking a road of gradual reform and therefore in its adoption of right strategies. Professor Barry Naughton of The University of California thinks (1994) that the reform strategy China has adopted is the key factor for its success. He characterizes China's reform as the employment of the double-track system, the shift of economic performance index from quantity-oriented to benefit-oriented type, gradual transformation from planned economy to market economy, the initial macro-level stability, the impacts of continual macro-level fluctuations upon long-term marketization of economy, the increase of private savings that maintained the high level of savings and investment, etc.

Economists attach great prominence to the double-track pricing system. They thought that the double-track pricing system was a compromise between the retention of planned allocation and the absorption of the increased proportion of output into the market system. By so doing, i.e. turning huge concussions into small concussions, the risks of economic reform were reduced. The track of the increased proportion of output also enabled and facilitated the price reform and business reform. Professor Ronald McKinnon of Stanford University believes (1993) that in the initial stage of reform, China implemented the double-track pricing system in state-owned businesses that made it possible for China's reform to stay away from the "inflation tax", and this double-track system should also be employed in other transitional economies.

Shen Hong, a Chinese economist, also mentions (1991) that the double-track system could be regarded as the basic mode of China's reform, which allowed the old part of the system to remain unchanged and the increased part to be absorbed into the new system and gradually reformed the old part when the proportion of the increased part became bigger and bigger and accounted for a greater part of the system, eventually completing the transition from the old system to the new system. So the double-track system reform is also called the "incremental reform" or "out-of-system reform". The incremental reform approximates to Pareto improvement or Kaldor improvement.

Zhang Yu, professor of Remin University of China, holds (1997) that the road of reform from outside the system to within the system is an important experience of China's achieving success through gradual reform. It has many apparent advantages. The reform outside the system is the basic driving force for promoting marketization. It is obviously easier to achieve breakthroughs in reform from outside the system than from within the system. Under conditions where normal socio-economic order remains unharmed, the development of non-state-owned economy may strengthen economic vitality, increase the efficiency of resource allocation and national income, create more job opportunities, facilitate both reform and development, lessen the hindering force of reform and avoid the economic consequences of "shock therapy".

However, some economists raise their suspicion concerning the incremental reform. Chinese economist Wu Jinglian refutes the view and insists (1996) that "gradualism" cannot fully explain China's strategy of reform. China's mode of reform is manifested in its strategic principles, which give priority to out-of-system reform and then turn to the state-owned economic system itself. The strategy for China's reform is not gradual but radical. For instance, the rural contracting system was put in place within two years, the reform of the pricing system within five years, etc. Chinese economist Li Xiaoxi holds (1996) that China's reform is a process combining gradualism and radicalism and that gradualism is one of the many characteristics of China's reform but not the only one.

Regarding China's success in economic development, Chen Siqing (2009) thinks of four reasons: (a) the creation of reproductivity in the process of transformation and restructuring, (b) the emancipation of human initiatives brought about by transformation, (c) the wave of industrial creation brought about by transformation, and (d) the amalgamation of policies in transformation. Zheng Jingping summarizes the following reasons for China's economic miracle: (a) the successful transformation from planned economy to market economy and from semiclosed economy to open economy, (b) the stability of systems and the gradual transformation that fully enjoyed the dividends of transformation, (c) the best use of the opportunity of globalization.

Researches are still going on, and many more findings are published almost every day, but no consensus can be reached so far. However, the consensus has been reached among many economists that the current mainstream economic theories cannot fully explain China's success in economic reform.

In the early stage of China's implementation of the double-track pricing system, many mainstream economists believed that the shock therapy that is based on privatization should be practiced in the reform of socialist countries. They held the view that the successful operation of an economic system must be backed up by institutional policies, including the sole determination of prices by market, small government, etc. the former U.S. treasurer and economist Larry Summers once mentioned that economists may differ in many issues and that there is surprising consensus that reform should be conducted in planned economy.

Quite unexpectedly, China's GDP increased by 9% annually between 1978 and 1990 and 9.9% between 1990 and 2005. No sign of economic breakdown appeared, as predicted by the then economists. On the contrary, no economic boom happened, as expected by the mainstream Western economists, in the former Soviet Union and eastern European countries where the shock therapy was practiced, and there was serious economic recession. Their economy has begun to recover to some extent, but there is still a sharp contrast between China and those eastern European countries.

A brief retrospection of previous observations and researches show that many economists then, including those master economists, made wrong judgments and predictions about China's economic transformation, chiefly due to the existing deficiencies of current economic theories. The incapability of existing theories to explain current economic phenomena does not mean that they cannot be analyzed by theoretical means. Theoretical innovation always emerges from the new phenomenon that cannot be expounded by existing theories, and China's economic development is filled with such new phenomena. Chinese economists are in a better position than their foreign counterparts to more fully understand China's economic reform and have the advantage of always standing at the forefront of China's economic reform. China's economic experience over the past 30 years implies great opportunities for Chinese economists to promote theoretical innovation. With China's continuing development and the steady rise of China's international status, it is likely that China will create world-class economists in the near future.

1.2.3 Theoretical innovations in Chinese economics

A careful reexamination of China's 30 years or so of economic reform and development and its theoretical generalization clearly demonstrates that both China's economic policies and the Chinese economic academics have followed a clear line of development going from "feeling the stones" to "active construction" and from "explanation" to "leading".

Prior to the reform and opening up in 1978, almost no Chinese economists had any knowledge of modern economics, and what most of them did was strive to publicize and explain government economic policies in the light of Marxist, Leninist and Stalinist theories. There was no exchange of economic theories with their foreign counterparts. At the time that China began to implement the policies of reform and opening up, Chinese economists were mostly devoid of modern Western economics, to say nothing of the basic logics of market economy and a specialist team armed with modern economic expertise.

The reform and opening up were basically guided by high-level government leaders' strategic visions and direct experience. The Third Plenary Session of the Eleventh Central Committee of CPC in 1978 formally declared the implementation of reform and opening up by adopting the strategy of "crossing the stream by feeling the stones", i.e. "moving one step and looking one step farther" without any predetermined goals, models and plans". It is understandable to adopt this strategy under such a special background of economics.

The reform measures over that period are mainly as follows. First, in the vast rural region, the collectively-owned land was "leased" to farmers, thus the privatization of the agricultural sector and the flourishing of township enterprises. Second, the fiscal responsibility system was resumed so as to delegate power to lower levels of government, i.e. the provincial and the county governments, and practice budgeting at different levels and revenue sharing, thus setting up a pattern of competition between regional governments and supporting the development of non-state-owned enterprises in their respective regions (province, county and township). Third, the policy of opening up to the outside world was implemented, thus breaking the state monopoly of international trade, lowering trade barriers, permitting direct foreign investment and joint ventures.

The strategy of "crossing the stream by feeling the stones" did produce some good results in the beginning stage, but a lot of problems ensued as a result of no predetermined goals and "moving one step and looking one more step farther" only. There occurred between 1979 and 1988 three waves of inflation, the power peddling resulting from the double-track system, corruption, etc., which caused great social dissatisfaction and turmoil.

Meanwhile, the Chinese economists speeded up their steps in theoretical configuration and launched the campaign of "going west for Buddhist scriptures" (i.e. learning from modern economists). Universities in China started to provide courses in Western economics, and a large number of scholars were sent overseas like Europe and America for further studies, especially Western economics. All this enabled Chinese academics to merge into the world' mainstream economics. By the middle of the 1980s, a considerable number of economists appeared in China with comprehensive economic expertise. They worked together with their foreign counterparts to explore the goals and models of China's reform and participated in government policy making.

In October 1992, the Fourteenth National Congress of CPC decided upon the goal of "socialist market economy" on the basis of numerous research findings both at home and abroad and passed the general plan for marketization reform—Decisions Concerning Various Issues of Establishing Socialist Market Economy, thus the blueprint for establishing market economic system, which can be summed up as follows:

(a) establishing the market system, including commodity market, labor market and financial market
(b) practicing the system of current account convertibility and promoting comprehensive opening up to the outside world
(c) implementing the strategic restructuring of national economic layout through reforming state-owned enterprises and encouraging private businesses
(d) practicing "letting go small businesses", i.e. turning hundreds of thousands of small state-owned businesses and township businesses into different forms of privatized enterprises
(e) establishing and perfecting the macroeconomic administrative system chiefly via indirect regulation
(f) establishing new social security system
(g) transforming government functions
(h) enhancing legal system construction

This round of reform implied, in a strict sense, theoretical construction and policy guidance in the Chinese economic circles. It enabled China to set up the general framework for socialist market economy, emancipated labor forces and contributed considerably to China's rapid sustainable development since the 1990s.

Between the end of the twentieth century and the beginning of the twenty-first century, the world economy experienced the 1997 Asian financial crisis, the 2000 Internet bubble and the outbreak of the international financial crisis starting from 2007. The economy of the Four Asian Tigers gradually lost their former glory. The Japanese economy was still in its sluggish state, and the American economy was dragged by heavy debts and high unemployment rates. Risks were latent in the European economy. However, the Chinese economy successfully overcame difficulties and got over the crisis and maintained a high rate of rapid development. Some regions beautifully transformed themselves by restructuring and upgrading their industries and accumulated more momentum for further growth. Foshan, Guangdong Province is one of such models in China.

When the wave of the financial crisis spread to Foshan in 2008, there were widespread worries and even panic about possible economic downturn in China. It was a different case with Foshan, which had foresighted planning for its industrial restructuring and implemented the "Triple-Three Strategy", namely three categories of industry (the coordinated development of the primary industry, the secondary and the tertiary industry), three pillar lines (no less than three pillar lines to be supported within each category of industry) and three leading enterprises (within each pillar line of industry, no less than three locomotive enterprises to be nurtured).

Foshan took the lead among regional governments in industrial restructuring by transforming from simple industrial manufacturing and export orientation to new pillar industries with self-developed technology. Consequently, Foshan stood the test of the financial crisis and was the first of the nine cities in the region of the Pearl River Delta, Guangdong Province, to have broken out of the crisis and maintained economic growth. Even under the high pressure of the international financial crisis and China's macroeconomic regulation, Foshan's GDP rose from 382.7 billion yuan in 2007 to 701 billion yuan, at the annual rate of 10.6%, and it turned out to be the fastest in the Pearl River Delta cities. Its per capita GDP reached 96 534 yuan, which stood very close to that of developed countries.

Why was the Chinese economy able to maintain a high rate of development and successfully resist the impacts of several international financial crises? Why could Foshan turn crises into opportunities? Behind all these significant economic phenomena has resided an important economic theory — GFL.

A truly successful economic system implies that government must exercise foresighted leading by the aid of the foundations of market economy, its mechanisms and rules and employ the "visible hand" to overcome the defects and make up the margins caused by the "invisible hand". Meanwhile, government can avoid the post-process cost of remedying errors the method of "crossing the stream by feeling the stones" brought about by exercising foresighted leading. GFL, particularly on the level of regional government, enables mezzoeconomics to play its role in between microeconomics and macroeconomics and regional governments to play their role in between businesses and the state, thus constructing a complete and coherent economic system.

By comparison with the great nature, microeconomics is like streams, macroeconomics is like seas and oceans and mezzoeconomics is like rivers. Streams merge into rivers, and rivers flow into seas and oceans. Rivers play their role of connecting streams and seas and oceans and coordinate and regulate their relations so as to prevent possible draughts and floods. The same can be said of a nation's economy. Some laws and rules can be discerned in the development of some regions from the perspective of foresighted leading and mezzoeconomics. An investigation of the rate of socio-economic development and social welfare in different countries and regions will reveal that what lie behind them are not only natural resources, systems, technological factors, etc. but also the roles and functions regional governments fulfill and their effects.

Foshan is situated in the inland of the Pearl River Delta region. It neither borders upon coastal areas nor boasts natural resources, with only ordinary natural resources and geographical location. But in fighting against the 2007 international financial crisis, it played a leading role among all the Pearl River Delta cities. One of the most forceful explanations is that its municipal government performed wonderfully in exercising GFL.

Singapore can also be cited to illustrate this. Over less than half a century, Singapore has transformed from a small fishing village without resources into a developed country, owing to the foresighted leading of its government in industrial policies, talent development strategy and the creation of favorable environments, etc., which is another fine example of universal significance and application that the GFL theory embodies.

1.3 Government foresighted leading: Its implication

1.3.1 Government foresighted leading: Its definition

GFL means giving full play to government functions, particularly those of regional governments, in economic guidance, regulation and warning and taking the lead in promoting scientific and sustainable growth in regional economy with recourse to market rules and forces, by means of investing, pricing, taxation, legal and other measures and through innovation in organization, system and technology.

Several key issues are worthy of special attention in understanding the implications of GFL:

1.3.1.1 Regional government and regional economic development

Under market economy, regional government should not only administer public affairs and provide services but coordinate and promote economic development as well, such as formulating economic norms, maintaining market order, stabilizing macroeconomy, providing basic services, nurturing market system, reallocating income and social wealth, contributing to social equality, etc. The dual function of regional government stands for both micro-level and macro-level of market economy, the latter referring to the central government leading and regulating economic development on the macro-level.

Businesses and government are the dual components of competition in market economy. On the micro-level, the sole body of market competition is businesses, but on the macro-level, in addition to businesses, there is also the regional government. Competition on these two levels is the "dual driving force" for China's rapid continuing economic development over the past three decades.

In the 1980s, China resumed the implementation of "the fiscal responsibility system" so as to delegate power to lower levels of government, i.e. the provincial and the county governments, and practiced budgeting and revenue sharing at different levels, thus setting up a pattern of competition between regional governments. Consequently, economy developed, but tax revenues decreased. From the early 1980s to the early 1990s, the percentage of fiscal revenues in GDP and of fiscal revenues of the central government continued to decline, which significantly diminished the control of the central government upon the entire national economy. In 1994, the reform was launched to implement the tax-sharing system, which changed the fiscal responsibility system to the tax-sharing system. As a matter of fact, no matter whether it was the fiscal responsibility system or the tax-sharing system, both had contributed enormously to the momentum for regional economic growth, as part of reginal government's efforts.

In his book *China's Economic Policy* (2009), Steven Cheung regards the central government's delegation of power to the county-level government and the competition between county-level governments as the secret of China's economic growth. He thinks that it was unusual for county-level governments to enter into fierce competition and that it was the main reason that China could achieve rapid growth under such difficult circumstances. Around 2004, the Vietnam followed China's practice, and its economy started to take off. Local government competition is the main cause of China's economic growth, as remarked in an article carried in *The Washington Post* on September 6, 2010.

During this process, the performance of regional government determines regional economic development. Judging from the actual situation ranging from the central government to the local government of different levels and from the coastal region to the inland region, imbalance can be detected in the relation between the performance of regional government and the development of regional economy. In the frontier regions of reform and opening up, where regional government, in accordance to the internal demands of market economy, underwent quick functional transformation and went one step ahead so that they grasped the priority for development and took the lead in performing foresighted roles in exploring and practicing market economy, their socio-economic development went far ahead of regions where regional government was slow in transforming its functions with backward ideology and had a poor understanding of market economy so that regional economic development was seriously hindered.

1.3.1.2 Government foresighted leading and market mechanism and rules

In the age of planned economy which was a highly centralized economic system, all resources were coordinated and allocated according to plan, and market was basically excluded from economic activities. The role of government, especially the central government, was boundlessly expanded to take charge of everything and replace almost all the rights and opportunities of policy making and choices on the part of economic entities. Under such circumstances, local government was turned into a transferring point for the central government and did not have their own independent economic interest, responsibilities, rights and obligations. All their rights and activities were strictly confined within the limits laid down in the central government documents. They had no chance of playing an active role in economic activities, let alone exercise foresighted leading. Businesses became government affiliations. The government made policies regarding production, supply and marketing, and their related resources such as labor forces, capital and assets. What businesses could do was fulfill the production quota according to government planning. They did not need to take market and benefits into consideration. They were by nature the organizers of production rather than the actual economic entities. The consumers' opportunity of choosing market also fell into the hand of government, like employment arrangement, the supply of daily necessities, etc.

Under market economic system, the allocation of resources is realized through price mechanism. Under ideal conditions, market can automatically regulate supply and demand on its own so as to achieve equilibrium between supply and demand. However, there exist in real economic life such factors as incomplete information, monopoly, and public products that affect market clearing so that market malfunction may occur, exemplified by lack of transportation facilities, social order and security, social services, unemployment, inflation, imbalance of income distribution, social inequality, polarization of the rich and the poor, etc. The occurrence of market malfunction is an effective justification for government involvement in economic life and is the fundamental basis for the formulation of government functions.

It must be made clear that the emphasis of government role does not mean that government will have to be involved in everything. Inappropriate government intervention may hinder the normal development of market so as to bring about more government intervention. On the contrary, moderate government intervention will contribute to the realization of social goals and facilitate market nurturing. So government should exercise moderate and appropriate intervention. As indicated by the developmental economist William Arthur Lewis (1915–1991), the failure of government may be either due to its doing too little or due to its doing too much.

Then what is the right extent of government intervention, and how can its control be measured? The answer lies in effective resource allocation and leading-edge formation by means of market rules and mechanism, through effective leading in investment, consumption and export and by employing economic and legal means and various innovative measures.

1.3.1.3 Government foresighted leading and sustainable development

Various metaphorical expressions are in use concerning government roles — Adam Smith used "night watchman", Keynes "visible hand", and Friedman "servant" government in his *Free to Choose: A Personal Statement* (1980), and so on.

Over the past decade, in order to meet the need of investment attraction, local government in different regions of China proposed that they act as "nanny" and provide nanny-type service to businesses, investors and projects. It should be noted that their proposal displayed their respect for market economic system and their commitment in serving businesses, but in practice, harm may be done to business operation and economic development, owing to excessive service and blind service. Too "enthusiastic" involvement in business affairs and too "thoughtful" nanny-type service may easily cause government dislocation. Government "pampering" of businesses will also cause unfavorable consequences upon business operation and economic development if government grants approval to business demands, no matter whether they are right or wrong, whether they conform to legal regulations, social equality, the long-term industrial development or the long-term business interest. This kind of "service" must be avoided.

What is indeed the government role? Neither "servant" nor "nanny" is enough to cover its full implication. It may be more precise to use the term "leading", which indicates the guiding, regulating and early warning function of government and its role in employing such measures as investment, pricing, taxation and law by means of market forces. Shunde District, Guangdong Province, for instance, was the first county in China whose GDP surpassed 100 billion yuan and remained for several successive years on the top of "China's top 100 counties" list. The root cause for its remarkable achievement is the extraordinary role of its successive governments in exercising foresighted leading, which is well worth serious study and attention.

In the early 1980s, Shunde District government proposed a strategic "three-based" economic system, consisting of publicly-based economy, industry-based economy, and mainstay enterprises-based economy, with a view to promoting industrialization in rural areas. By the early 1990s, the output ratio of industry and agriculture amounted to 98:2, indicating that Shunde became basically industrialized within only ten years. After 1992, Shunde District government pioneered system innovation in the area of property rights, which instantly emancipated the productive forces of enterprises and nurtured a large number of enterprise groups and famous brand products.

In 2005 another industrial development program was put forward, called the "Triple-Three Strategy", namely three categories of industry (the coordinated development of the primary industry, the secondary and the tertiary industry), three pillar lines (no less than three pillar lines to be supported within each category of industry) and three leading enterprises (within each pillar line of industry, no less than three locomotive enterprises to be nurtured). Meanwhile, strategic programs for industrialization, urbanization and internationalization were implemented in Shunde, with the hope of promoting its sound and rapid development. By 2006, Shunde's GDP exceeded 100 billion yuan, and that figure became 254.5 billion in 2013.

Similar examples are found in other parts of Guangdong and many more regions in Jiangsu and Zhejiang provinces, whose regional governments have played an active role in regional economic development, and the practice of foresighted leading has yielded the desired results. China's development has got over the period of "crossing the streams by feeling the stones" and it is high time to enter into the stage of foresighted leading. In the early stage of low-level development, it was necessary to "cross the streams by feeling the stones", but it becomes a must for government to guide, lead and plan economic development when it moves into corresponding stages.

1.3.2 Government foresighted leading: Its key component and categorization

1.3.2.1 The key component of government foresighted leading

Competition is the core of market economy. Viewed from the global perspective, there exists a double-component entity in market competition — businesses and government.

Businesses form the sole entity of market competition on the microeconomic level, but on the macroeconomic level, there is another key component of market competition—regional government. For instance, competition exists between nations when viewed from the global perspective, and between regions when viewed from the perspective of national economy. It is this double-component competition that has created the miracle of China's economic growth and has generated the driving force for regional (national or municipal) GFL. Take America for example. Regional competition covers competition between states and between cities. In China, regional competition covers competition between provinces, cities and counties, and so on.

In terms of competition between regional governments in China, Steven Cheung defines it within county-level competition in his book *China's Economic Policy* (2009). He holds that the greater the economic power the fiercer the regional competition and that the economic power mainly resides within the county, rather than within the city, the province or the central government in today's China. He reasons that the right to utilize land lies in the hand of the county, which gives it strong economic power, and the strongest county-level competition ensues.

We, however, think that as far as regional government is concerned, competition mainly takes place between municipal governments, which therefore become the real entities that should exercise foresighted leading.

First, the municipal government enjoys greater power in economic development, and as a result, competition is the fiercest. In China, the central and provincial governments provide guidelines for land employment and other economic policies and retain the power to appoint government officials and reallocate fiscal revenues. Of the factors of market economy, capital is mainly controlled and regulated through monetary policy of the central government, and labor is mainly determined by market. Only the power to supply and utilize land remains within the authorities of the municipal government.

Second, the city's economic independence and government interests are closely related to economic development. The fiscal revenues of the municipal government, the economic performance of officials and the status of fiscal revenues are all contingent upon project construction, investment attraction and regional growth.

Third, within a region, cities may vary only slightly in natural resources, and there is a high degree of comparability, but within a province or a state, cities may vary greatly, as they may have different locations like in the coastal or inland areas and different natural resources, and therefore there is a relatively low degree of comparability. Comparison can be made between cities with similar natural conditions.

Finally, the number of cities in China is great. They are in most cases of large scale and possess the sufficient environment and conditions for competition. According to the Chinese Constitution, the hierarchy of China's administrative government goes from the central level to the provincial level and then to the county level and down to the level of township, but another level comes in between the provincial and the county level – the municipal level. So in reality, China practices a five-level administrative hierarchy.

It must be noted that the so-called city here is a relative concept to the countryside, so the "municipal government" is opposite to the "rural government". The concept of "city" may refer to the administrative division of a city and the geographical location of a city.

By establishing the contractual competition ties like the tax-sharing system and the binding competitive relations with the higher level of government and the investors, government of different levels is unanimous in economic development and attempts to satisfy their political appeals and economic benefits by developing economy so as to increase tax revenues and their own share of disposable income. It is commonplace that provincial government may be directly involved in competition of inter-province investment-soliciting projects and even in project biddings on the municipal and county levels.

1.3.2.2 The categorization of government foresighted leading

From the developmental perspective of an economy, institution, organization, technology, notions are all important factors. Accordingly, GFL is classified into institutional, organizational, technological and notional categories.

Institutional foresighted leading means giving full play to the role of government, particularly regional government, in innovation of systems by creating new and more incentive policies and standards to increase the efficiency of resource allocation and the sustainability of socio-economic development and reform. Its core part is innovation in social, political, economic and administrative systems, in regulations of human conduct and interrelations, and in organizations and relations of its external environment.

Its direct consequence is the inspiration of human creativity and enthusiasm, the creation of new knowledge, the fair allocation of social resources and the continuous creation of social wealth, which ultimately promotes social progress. Only when there is innovative government can institutional foresighted leading be realized and innovative systems and policies be formulated.

Organizational foresighted leading means the innovation of government, particularly regional government, in such areas as organizational structure, organizational mode and organizational regulations with the aim of strengthening foundations for economic and industrial development and eventually facilitating innovations in policies and technology.

Technological foresighted leading means giving full play to the advantage of government in allocating social resources and enabling government to participate in and lead technological innovations directly or indirectly so as to promote scientific and technological advancement and strengthen the capabilities of cities and businesses to perform scientific and technological innovation.

There are two aspects to technological foresighted leading. On the one hand, government should create a favorable environment for businesses to enhance the capabilities to perform technological innovation, for example the construction of systems for patent application and protection and product standardization. On the other hand, government should implement effective economic measures and policies to encourage businesses to take the initiatives for technological innovation, for example granting fund to support research and development in key technologies, establishing technological fund, recruiting leading experts, and so on.

Notional foresighted leading means that in the course of exercising authorities and power, government should conduct foresighted investigation, rational analysis and theoretical thinking concerning newly emerged issues and problems, foresee new social and economic phenomena and generalize work experience and push it to a theoretical elevation so as to guide innovation and advancement in economic systems and institutional structuring.

In the new phase of economic development, only by continuously transforming and upgrading government notions, such as notions of civilian community, restrained government, open government and government efficiency, can government innovate administrative systems, behavior, methodology and technology and provide right value guidance and boundless innovative incentives.

The focal points of GFL may vary with economic systems, phases of economic development and economic resources. In countries where economic transformation is in progress, economic system remains to be improved and mode of economic growth is extensive, it is of special significance for government to exercise foresighted leading in institution, organization, technology and notions, which has been amply exemplified by China's experience in reform and opening up over the past 30 years.

In the forefront regions of China's reform and opening up, like Shunde and Jiangyin of Jiangsu Province, government conducted foresighted explorations and practices of its role in market economic development and took the lead in innovations of economic systems and restructuring. For instance, in the early 1980s, Shunde District government proposed a strategic "three-based" economic system, i.e. publicly-based economy, industry-based economy, and mainstay enterprises-based economy, with a view to promoting industrialization in rural areas. Jiangyin decided upon the development guidelines of "no prosperity without industry, no stability without agriculture, and no vitality without commerce" and determined to set up factories to boost industry. After 1992, Shunde became the first again to conduct ownership reform under the guidance of institutional innovation.

The institutional, organizational, technological and notional foresighted leading on the part of regional government endowed these regions with temporal advantages in reform competition and enabled them to have the initiatives for development. That is why their socio-economic development went ahead of others. Over the 30 or so years' reform and opening up, Shunde had always been taking the lead in China's county development and became the first to surpass 100 billion yuan of GDP and remained on the top of "China's top 100 counties" list for several successive years. Jiangyin was also exceptionally remarkable for its township enterprises and successfully transformed from an agricultural county to an industrial county, hence a "Model of South Jiangsu", as generalized by sociologist Fei Xiaotong (1910–2005).

1.4 Government foresighted leading: A major breakthrough in economic theories of government functions

1.4.1 Government foresighted leading and theories of free economy: Similarities and differences

Adam Smith's theory of free economy emphasized market mechanism. In his famous work *The Wealth of Nations*, he believed that under market economy every individual regards it as their goal to pursue personal interest, and the choices they make for the pursuit of their interest will naturally optimize the allocation of social resources by means of regulative market mechanisms and under the guidance of the invisible hand. The free economic theory advocates free competition and free trade and opposes government intervention in economic activities. Government can only perform the function of providing public products and act as the "night watchman" for market economy.

The GFL theory focuses on giving full play to government functions, particularly those of regional governments, in economic guidance, regulation and warning and taking the lead in promoting scientific and sustainable growth in regional economy with recourse to market rules and forces, by means of investing, pricing, taxation, legal and other measures and through innovations in various aspects. The GFL theory attaches great importance to giving full play to government functions, particularly the economic role of regional government, and involving government, on the basis of market mechanism and with the optimization of resource allocation as its main goal, in promoting economic development.

1.4.1.1 Differences

Liberalists hold that market mechanism can perform the function of self-regulation and self-balancing. They advocate the policies of laissez-faire economy domestically and free trade internationally and oppose government intervention. According to Say's law, supply will create its own demand, and the crisis of production surplus can be avoided. This law further reinforces the theory that market has inherent self-balancing mechanism. It is liberalists' view that the government that administers least is the best and that government had better not intervene in economy, as intervention will damage the self-balancing of economy. They believe in small government and strong market and the confinement of government role to maintaining market mechanism, protecting consumer interest, protecting personal and property security, etc.

The GFL theory holds that government should play its part not only in public affairs and services but also in the coordination and promotion of economic development. It is particularly the case with regional government, whose dual function represents the micro-level of market economy but also the macro-level of government leading and regulation of economic development. It emphasizes that under market economy regional government has the status of quasi-market economic entity. Regional government can effectively exercise its leading role by means of investment, land, tax, legal policies, guide industrial development, participate in regional competition and promote regional economic development through competition between regional governments. The role regional government plays in economic activities determines regional and even national economic development.

According the theory of free economy, only businesses and individuals are market entities of economy, and government can only serve as "night watchman". In the GFL theory, government, in particular regional government, has the feature of being quasi-market entity and play a key role in regional economic development.

In the theory of free economy, government function is limited only to the provision of public products, and government intervention in economy is ineffective or even detrimental. In the GFL theory, the role of government, particularly regional government, covers not only the provision of public products and the administration of public affairs but also the participation, coordination and promotion of economic development. China's 30 years' economic practice proves that government involvement in economic development and the participation of regional government in market economic competition may remedy the defects of market malfunction and facilitate regional and national economic development.

1.4.1.2 Similarities

Liberal economists follow the mechanisms of market and free competition, encourage the inspiration of individual initiatives, promote the reasonable allocation of factors of labor and capital in different categories of industry and attaches primary importance to the role of market in allocating resources and in determining the prices of various factors of production.

Like the theory of free economy, the GFL theory also attaches great importance to the role of market mechanisms and the effective allocation of resources according to market rules and by means of market mechanisms. Under ideal conditions, market may also self-regulate supply and demand by its own forces and achieve the equilibrium between supply and demand. In actual economic life, however, due to various factors that affect market clearing, such as incomplete information, monopoly, public products, etc., market malfunction may occur, for instance, inadequate transportation facilities, social disorder, lack of social services, unemployment, inflation, unfair income distribution, the polarization of the rich and the poor, social inequality, etc. In case market malfunction occurs, government must exercise foresighted leading and effective allocation of resources by means of market rules and mechanisms.

The theory of foresighted leading focuses on relying on the foundations, mechanisms and rules of market economy and making up the defects and margins left by the invisible hand with the visible hand. The GFL theory is significant "Pareto improvement" upon the market economic theory proposed by liberal economists and major innovation in theories of market economy.

1.4.2 Foresighted government leading and Keynesianism: Similarities and differences

Keynesian theory, which is based on three psychological rules, suggests that there naturally exists the problem of insufficient demand and that it is difficult to recover economy through the self-regulation of market. It opposes the traditional idea of laissez-faire economy and advocates active government intervention in economy. The core of Keynesian theory is national intervention in economic life through which to stimulate effective demand, i.e. consumption and investment, chiefly by adopting fiscal and monetary policies. The theory of foresighted leading, on the other hand, focuses on the role of government, especially regional government, in the guidance, regulation and early warning of economy and the effective allocation of resources with the visible hand of government by means of market rules and mechanisms.

1.4.2.1 Similarities

The Keynesian theory and the GFL theory have in common the following points. First, both think market cannot clear itself and therefore market malfunction may occur. According to liberal economists, market economy can self-regulate and operate on its own. There is no chance of crises occurring, and it can remedy by itself even if temporary malfunction takes place in market.

The Keynesian theory holds that complete market competition in the hypothesis of free economic theory does not exist and that sole dependence upon market regulation cannot bring about equilibrium of social demand and will cause the inadequacy of effective social demand and eventually economic crises. The GFL theory also holds that there exist the problems of monopoly, incomplete information, externality and public products, and etc. in market economy, which makes market unable to effectively distribute commodities and labor, i.e. the phenomena of market malfunction, in the form of unfair allocation, inadequacy of public product supply, imbalanced regional development, monopoly, the twisted resource prices, etc.

Second, both believe in government intervention in economy, which may make up the defects of market malfunction and facilitate economic growth. According to Keynesian theory, it is hard to recover economy through market self-regulation. It advocates active government intervention in economy. Government should adopt expansionary fiscal policies rather than monetary policies. Government should increase direct investment so as to give full play to the multiplier effects, as a certain amount of government investment will attract more concomitant private investment and one job will create more employment opportunities. Debt financing, in particular national debt, may raise more funds for investment. There should be no worry about inflation as long as the issued currency can bring idle factors of production into play so that more products are manufactured and supply is greater than demand. In addition, as the marginal propensity to group consumption on the part of low-income consumers is strong, there should be a redistribution of income by means of taxation and transferred payments so as to heighten the consumption propensity of the whole community.

The GFL theory holds that market regulation is generally post-process regulation and that a certain degree of time gap may exist from pricing, signal feedback and then to product output. Regulation may cause fluctuations as described in "cobweb analysis". This is more apparent in industries of long production cycles, like agriculture. As it boasts the obvious advantages of macro-level information, social resources accumulation, and the status of being quasi-market entity, particularly on the part of regional government, government stands in a better position to formulate macro-level economic policies from a comprehensive and longer-term perspective and makes effective allocation of resources by means of investment, pricing, taxation and legal measures so as to provide anticipatory guidance, regulation and early warning for micro-level policy making.

Finally, the emphasis of both theories on government role does not negate the basic role and status of market in microeconomy. The 2007 international financial crisis has led to unparalleled government intervention in market. Governments in different regions started to appeal to Keynesianism and implemented policies of intervention. Some have even come to suspect whether government should replace market. The answer is in the negative.

The relation between government and market is a basic issue in economics. In the history of Western economic theories, there are two different lines of economic philosophy regarding this issue – economic liberalism and government interventionism. Over the past 200 years or so of economic theorization, at least five theoretical confrontations occurred, and Keynesianism turned out to be the winner twice. The first time was the "Keynesian revolution" subsequent to the 1920s to '30s economic depression, during which period President Roosevelt's New Deal was practiced and the theory and policies of national intervention were established. The second time is the ongoing international financial crisis, which sets us rethinking about the effectiveness of free market competition and reemphasizing the necessity of government intervention in economy.

Underneath all those long-term debates and confrontations, no matter which school of economic philosophy it is, and no matter what position is taken, there is no denying that market mechanism is the basic mode of resource allocation. It is Keynesian view that macro-level government intervention is necessary, as there exist on the micro-level market such problems as externality and monopoly, which will cause certain degrees of distortion of resource allocation. Although Keynesianism emphasizes that malfunction may exist in free market competition, it does not deny the basic role of market and focuses on government intervention on the basis of recognizing market mechanism. It does not want market to be replaced by government.

New Keynesian economics, which relies on microeconomic foundation, lands macroeconomics upon a solid microeconomic footing. It explains macroeconomic fluctuations under the hypothesis of the maximizing principle for the benefits of economic beings and rational expectation and from the perspective of the actual market incompleteness, such as incomplete competition, information inadequacy and relative rigidity of price. It attaches greater importance than traditional Keynesianism to the role of market mechanism, advocates "sketchy" regulation and "moderate" intervention in economy, gives prominence to internal structural adjustment of economy and focuses on the quality of economic regulation.

The GFL theory also confirms the basic role of market mechanism and emphasizes the effective resource allocation by means of market rules and mechanisms. Regional government is supposed to play a leading role in promoting regional economic development through effective industrial guidance, participation in market competition, and the optimization of resource allocation via market competition. In its participation in market competition, regional government should also follow the supply-demand law of market and act according to market signals in terms of prices and interest rates. Without the support of the basic role of market in social resource allocation, regional government will lose its foundation for playing a leading role in economy and foresighted leading on the part of the government will be a castle in the air.

Instead of denying the basic mode of resource allocation via market mechanism, the GFL theory attaches greater importance to the basic role of market mechanism in market competition, particularly in regional competition. Rather than being retrogression of market economic system, this theory is enrichment and perfection of market economic system.

1.4.2.2 Differences

Some may ask, is the GFL theory a reproduction of Keynesianism, like old wine in new bottles? A careful analysis of the implications of the two theories will reveal their major differences. Keynesianism adopts the theoretical framework for macroeconomics and the macro-level perspective. Its regulation is mainly conducted by macro-level means and through in-process and post-process intervention. The GFL theory adopts the theoretical framework for mezzoeconomics and the mezzo-level perspective. Its regulation is mainly conducted by means of pricing, taxation, exchange rate, interest rate and legal measures and through innovation in institution, organization, technology and administration. It focuses on pre-process regulation as well as in-process and post-process regulation.

(a) Differences in research objects and perspectives

Keynesianism focuses its attention on macroeconomics and state and adopts a macro-level perspective for the analysis of national economy. It explains economic crises and macro-level regulative policies in the light of the relation between aggregate demand and supply. In the Keynesian view, the insufficiency in effective demand is the normal state of a nation's economy. Therefore, he proposes the fiscal deficit policy and thinks that the increase of government expenditures will facilitate economic growth and that fiscal deficit does not matter even if it occurs. He believes that macro-level policies should be employed to stimulate demand and increase investment and consumption.

The GFL theory focuses its attention on regional economy and regional government and adopts a mezzo-level approach to regional economy. This theory holds that regional government is an important and indispensable quasi-market economic entity whose role exercises profound influence upon regional economic development. Market competition takes place not only between businesses but also between regions, and that is where GFL can take effect.

(b) Differences in policy orientation

The Keynesian theory centres around macro-level fiscal and monetary policies as it regards the aggregate demand and supply of a nation's economy as its main object of research, including income and production, currency, pricing, employment and international trade, etc. In the Keynesian view, the insufficiency in effective demand is the normal state of a nation's economy, and expansionary economic policies should be employed on the macro-level to achieve balance between supply and demand by regulating interest rates and tax rates, and by increasing government expenditures, etc.

In employing macro-level policies, Keynesianism focuses more on the control of total capacity and overlooks the structural diversities in industries and regions. When the aggregate demand is smaller than the aggregate supply, Keynesian economists propose tax reduction and fiscal expenditure expansion so as to stimulate investment and consumption, and when the aggregate demand is greater than the aggregate supply, they propose the increase of taxes and fiscal expenditure reduction so as to control investment and consumption. In terms of monetary policies, they propose the increase of currency supply and the reduction of tax rates so as to stimulate investment in times of economic depression and the reduction in currency supply and the increase of tax rates so as to control investment in times of economic boom.

The GFL theory, however, adopts a mezzo-level approach to regional economy and the economic role of regional government and attaches great importance to the role of regional government as quasi-market entity in the economic system so as to exercise foresighted leading in regional economy. Therefore, its policy orientation goes towards regional economy and regional government. As regional government can perform foresighted leading functions and roles in regional economy, this theory gives full play to the economic function of regional government and its foresighted leading role in terms of investment, pricing, taxation, exchange rates, interest rates and legal means. Its policy range is far more extensive than the pure category of fiscal and monetary policies.

As is known to all, China's economic development was once bothered by unbalanced development of regional economy, exemplified by the typical dual structure of urban and rural areas, the three-grade economic scale marked by eastern coastal economy, central economy and Western regional economy, the static and dynamic imbalance, etc. The causes for such unbalanced development are manifold, including factors such as distribution, location, history, demographical quality, macroeconomic policy making, and so on. The eastern coastal region enjoyed the privilege of location and preferential policies and its economy developed at a faster rate. Compared with the eastern coastal region, the central Western region was backward in infrastructure and transportation and did not enjoy preferential policies, and its economy was lagging behind.

In policy making, if no thought is given to regional differences, e.g. simply by adopting Keynesian control of total capacity, the same macro-level policies may be good for some regions but unfavorable to others. The results may be contrary to the initial expectations. The GFL theory, starting from the diverse economic reality, pays special attention to the structural differences between regions and between industries in mezzoeconomy, requires regional government to develop economy in line with local conditions, and gives full play to the leading role of regional government in economic guidance, regulation and early warning so as to effectively allocate resources and promote the scientific development of regional economy.

(c)   Differences in the timing of policy effects

Judging from the practical effects of Keynesian theory that focuses on in-process and post-process intervention, there is obviously the problem of policies and measures lagging behind the economic reality, i.e. the stimulating fiscal and monetary policies will not be put into operation unless economic recession occurs in national economy. Monetarists like Friedman assume that Keynes' macroeconomic policies have the problem of hysteresis, as a series of measures are to be taken when problems have actually occurred in economy, and it takes time to put each of the measures into operation and for them to take effect. Thus it takes a long period of time before substantial effects can be achieved. These intervening measures and policies with the problem of hysteresis will not have the effects of pacifying macroeconomic fluctuation. On the contrary, they may aggravate economic fluctuation.

The GFL theory focuses more on pre-process regulation and economic guidance. Its regulative measures include institutional, organizational, technological and administrative innovation, in addition to investment, pricing, taxation, exchange rates, interest rates and legal means. As the term indicates, "innovation" means creation and updating and implies foresighted leading and guidance. Joseph Alois Schumpeter (1883–1950) mentions in *The Theory of Economic Development* (1982) that innovation is a new combination of new factors of production and conditions of production that integrates them into the production system.

The Keynesian intervention has the feature of anti-cycles and abnormality, i.e. immediateness, while the regulation implied in GFL has the feature of sustainability and normality, i.e. stability. "Leading" is active, while "intervention" is passive. It is self-evident whether government function should be "intervention" or "leading".

1.4.3 Government foresighted leading: An important innovation in economic theorization

The 2011 Nobel Prize was awarded to Thomas J. Sargent and Christopher A. Sims for their empirical research on cause and effect in the macroeconomy. Their focal point was the impacts of policy factors upon economy and the role of policies in macroeconomic operation. The Nobel Memorial Prize in Economics of The Royal Swedish Academy of Sciences announced that Sargent and Sims were awarded for their research on cause and effect in the macroeconomy. The theories they published independently in the 1970s and 1980s explained how temporary increase in interest rates and tax reduction made impacts upon economic growth and inflation. For long, Western economists tended to conduct researches on "what causes what" by means of mathematical models. This logic thinking seems to have uncovered the key analytical instrument for expounding diverse economic reality, but it is far short of the complexity of the real economic world.

With the increasing cognition of the general world, human understanding of the natural world and the economic reality has been greatly improved. After the publication of Adam Smith's *The Wealth of Nation* in 1776, economists began to have a complete picture of market economy and established the theoretical system of microeconomy. In the subsequent 160 years or so, economics evolved around microeconomics, and no serious doubt about free economic theory was raised until the world economic depression in the 1920s–1930s. The proposition of government intervention via the visible hand by Keynes in 1936 identified economics into microeconomics and macroeconomics, which have developed for nearly 80 years.

The world stagflation in the 1970s and the international financial crisis that started in 2007 demonstrate that market malfunction and government malfunction may coexist. Neither the microeconomic theory advocating liberalism nor the macroeconomic theory of government intervention can offer a fully convincing explanation of these economic phenomena. Meanwhile, China's economic growth set economists thinking about whether new theories can be developed in addition to the traditional macroeconomics and the classical economic theory of microeconomics.

The GFL theory marks a major innovation needed for the amelioration of economic theorization. The creation of mezzoeconomics represented by regions in between microeconomics represented by enterprises and macroeconomics represented by the state can offer a theoretical explanation of the causes for China's continuing economic growth, in addition to the enrichment and amelioration of economic systems. Just as market economic theory lays the foundation for microeconomics and Keynesian economics divides economics into microeconomics and macroeconomics, the GFL theory puts mezzoeconomics in between microeconomics and macroeconomics, which not only fills the blank in researches on economic theorization and signifies important orientations for economic system reform but creates a multilevel market by integrating regional economy and regional government into the economic system, hence strengthening the stability of national economy. It imposes a serious challenge to the theoretical system of economy that has been in existence and in use for almost a hundred years and is a major innovation of modern economic theorization.

2 The theoretical foundations of government foresighted leading

The foresighted leading role of regional government is contingent upon its dual function: one of representing the national government and serving as "quasi-state" to exercise macro-level administration and regulation of regional economy and the other of representing non-government social organizations and serving as "quasi-business" in the region to solicit national support, allocate regional resources and compete with other regional government through institutional, organizational, technological and notional innovation so as to maximize the economic benefits of the region.

In performing the role of "quasi-state", regional government can take advantage of its public and coercive features to promote the build-up and maintenance of regional market order, protect the free and fair transactions between market entities and intensify the output and income of the whole community. Regional government can exercise influence upon economic development via fiscal expenditures, effectively allocate resources and nurture cutting-edge advantages so as to achieve foresighted leading in the scientific and sustainable development of regional economy.

In performing the role of "quasi-business", regional government should actively propel infrastructural project construction and try possible means of attracting investment, etc. as there is strong regional economic dependence and the need to satisfy regional government's income demand and the need for its officials' economic and eventually political accomplishments. Naturally, regional government will have a strong propensity for institutional and technological innovation. Viewed from the global perspective, regional development is, to a greater extent, determined by the foresighted thinking and the audacity for reform on the part of regional government administrative teams. The team members can, in a sense, be classified as "entrepreneurs" and possess the same entrepreneurship as business people.

2.1 The active role of government in establishing market order

National government can impose impacts upon the construction and maintenance of a nation's market order by means of its publicity and coerciveness. Similarly, regional government can stand for the national government and take advantage of its public and coercive forces granted by the national government to enhance the construction and maintenance of regional market order, hence the role of "quasi-state".

2.1.1 The publicity and coercive forces

Government, businesses and individuals are all the key parts of economic activities, but government distinctively differs from the other two in its publicity and coercive forces. The government emblem or logo of some countries is the lion or eagle, which reflects the government's coerciveness. As an organization of public and coercive nature, government can contribute to constructing and maintaining market order and has the natural advantage of remedying market malfunction, typically in the case of national government and regional government.

An organization of coercive nature means that it can employ coercive forces to exercise control upon its members, such as the state, the army, the prison, the reform centre, etc. Non-coercive organizations, such as companies, associations, clubs, etc. employ economic or other means, rather than coercive forces, such as pay increase or decrease, bonus adjustment, prize awarding, and so on to inspire and lead their members.

In non-coercive organizations, an individual can make free choices to become a member of an association or company though his or her choices may incur certain economic costs or losses, for example, membership fees, the payment for breaking a contract, etc. An individual unwilling to work for a company any longer has the right to quit, although he or she will have to pay for the possible losses incurred to the company as a result of his or her resignation. The right to resign from his or her post is a striking feature of all voluntary organizations. The transactions are by nature voluntary, except for coercive organizations like government.

However, any individual, no matter whether he or she has a job or belongs to a certain company, association and club, is coercively affiliated to a state as long as he or she lives in a certain country and must abide by its laws and regulations.

2.1.2 Maintaining market order and remedying market malfunction

Under normal conditions, individuals voluntarily trade with each other to gain their benefits and are willing to conduct such transactions to increase their benefits as long as transaction costs surpass benefits, which is a kind of "Pareto improvement" to the social community. However, without a government endowed with social coercive forces for control and protection, the rational party of the transaction may sometimes resort to threats or even direct force in order to realize its goals. This takes place not only between individuals but between countries, which is commonplace when viewed from the historical perspective of world trade and the current economic patterns of the world. For lack of an organization that could exercise forceful and binding control, military powers and economically developed countries used to resort to threats, monopoly and even wars to plunder resources from small and weak or underdeveloped countries by rather unfair means or at extremely low prices and costs.

Under the direction of the invisible hand of market, the rational self-interest can bring about mutual benefits via voluntary exchanges and thus increase social productivity. However, without constraints, this kind of self-interest is inclined to lure people into using force to coerce others, hence the dark side of force, as commented by Jack Hirshleifer (1925–2005).

Only under the supervisory mechanism of a third party with coercive force can market mechanism and voluntary exchanges play their due role. In cases where there occur conflicts between the trading parties or contract violations, the coercive organizations, such as the court and the police, will help the party that suffers losses to recover losses and penalize the party that breaks the contract. Such being the case, the party that is inclined towards contractual violation will have to assess its benefits of practicing the contract and the cost of breaking the contract, which will enhance the likelihood of voluntary and fair trading. Just as Thomas Hobbes (1588–1679) said, "covenants, without the sword, are but words and of no strength to secure a man at all". As a last resort, there must be a third party that can assure the implementation of the contract, like the underground gangs in some period of history that played similar roles.

As Mancur Lloyd Olson Jr (1932–1998) once pointed out, a state can never establish peaceful order by means of voluntary social contracts. The existence of coercive forces like the court, the police and the military is an inevitable choice for the assurance of market order of voluntary transactions.

The universal coercive power of government in economic activities is displayed in many aspects, such as laws and tax collection. All individuals must abide by the laws and regulations of the country where he or she lives, or he or she will be penalized. All individuals must pay taxes in line with the requirements of national government, which is another example. Government may also require economic entities to be involved in certain economic activities, such as the obligatory social insurance system for enterprises and their members, the preventive policies, the policies for special permission, etc.

The universal coercive power of government in economic activities greatly enhances the construction and maintenance of market order, protects and facilitates the fair voluntary transactions between market entities and increases the output and income of the whole community. In addition, it gives government the natural advantage of remedying market malfunction through laws and regulation, taxation policies, industrial policies and other coercive measures so as to continuously ameliorate market mechanisms, improve market order and direct market orientations.

Suspicion may arise as to whether government that possesses the natural, universal and unbinding coercive power may strip the general public of their wealth, do harm to the economic order of market and the benefits of the community. It is undeniable that such cases may exist under some circumstances, but governments of quite a lot of countries are able to make good use of their coercive power and maintain a good balance of co-existence between market and government.

Even though it has the universal coercive power, such as tax collection, government as a rational economic entity, whether national or regional, may not necessarily use its coercive forces to exhaust social resources and collect taxes relentlessly and boundlessly from the general public. Rational government will adopt appropriate and necessary policies for tax arrangement and taxation orientation and create more tax sources through long-term economic growth for future development.

2.1.3 America's antitrust policies and their practice

It is known to all that competition is an important proposition in economic theorization. Only under complete competition can market mechanisms and their role be brought into full play. Monopoly is regarded as its opposite and is likely to do damages to social well-being.

According to economic principles, supposing that the average cost equates the marginal cost, market can achieve, under the condition of competition, the equilibrium at point D where the price and quantity curves of P_c and Q_c cross each other, and thus the triangle of AP_cD forms consumer surplus, which goes to the consumer. However, supposing that monopoly occurs, the equilibrium will appear at point B, where P_m crosses Q_m, the extended line of point C in AC=MC, in which case the marginal income MR equates P_m. In this case the previous consumer surplus covered by AP_cD is divided into three parts: the uppermost AP_mB remains with the consumer surplus, the middle square part of P_mBCP_c goes to the manufacturer, and thus the former consumer surplus becomes the manufacturer surplus. A comparison with the original situation of competition shows that the small triangle of BCD is the so-called deadweight loss (abbreviated as DWL) resulting from monopoly, as shown in Figure 2.1.

The analysis of DWL shows that that part of consumer surplus which should go to the consumer has gone to neither the consumer nor the manufacturer and has been lost, which has resulted from monopoly. Therefore, microeconomists think that monopoly may cause the loss of social welfare, suppress the full play of competition and eventually affect the operation of market mechanism.

Prior to the American Civil War, the American economy mainly consisted of small businesses, merchants and farmers, and there were no such issues as economic problems caused by monopoly. After the industrialization of the second half of the nineteenth century, America rapidly grew from a local agricultural economy into an industrial nation. During the Civil War and its subsequent reconstruction, American capitalists accumulated huge amounts of wealth at an incredible speed and set up, through merger and acquisition, a large number of industrial empires that were due to exercise extensive and profound influence upon American and even the world economy.

The Carnegie Steel Company and The Rockefeller Standard Oil Co. Inc. are classical cases. The industrialists adopted the strategies of horizontal and vertical integration, in the form of "trust", to manipulate market prices. They divided

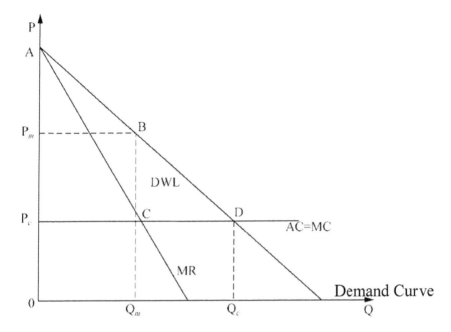

Figure 2.1 Monopoly and the welfare analysis of competition

markets, relentlessly pursued private interest and gradually gained economic and political control upon the American society, with the consumers and workers under their exploitation. As remarked by the American president Stephen Grover Cleveland (1837–1908) in a speech, the industrial groups, which should be strictly bound by the law and public servants by nature, had become masters of the general public.

Monopoly seriously affects the production and creation of the society and shakes the political foundation of democracy. For the first time, the American government strongly felt the fundamental threat of monopoly to its free market economy and free political system and formulated a series of antitrust laws by means of the coercive instrument of state, which dealt heavy blows to monopoly, reestablished free market order, brought vigorous vitality into American economy and turned America into a super economic power in the world.

From the late part of the nineteenth century, America passed dozens of antitrust laws and laws of economic regulations (see Figure 2.2), but only three turned out to be most effective in antitrust and economic regulation. The most prominent one that has won worldwide recognition as a landmark federal statute on United States competition law is the Sherman Antitrust Act(1890), followed by Federal Trade Commission Act (1914) and Clayton Antitrust Act (1914).

Table 2.1 America's major antitrust laws

Laws	Time of Passage	Main Contents
AnAct to Protect Trade and Commerce Against Unlawful Restraints and Monopolies	1890	Abbreviated as Sherman Antitrust Act, which prohibits certain business activities deemed to be anticompetitive, requires federal investigation of trusts, companies and organizations suspected of being in violation and still forms the basis for most antitrust litigation by the United States federal government.
Federal Trade Commission Act	1914	Abbreviated as the FTC Act, one of President Woodrow Wilson's major acts against trusts, the FTC was authorized to issue "cease and desist" orders to large corporations to curb unfair trade practices.
Clayton Antitrust Act	1914	Enacted to add further substance to the U.S. antitrust law regime by seeking to prevent anticompetitive practices in their incipiency.
Robinson-Patman Act	1936	Prohibiting anticompetitive practices by producers, specifically price discrimination and acting as an amendment to the Clayton Antitrust Act.
Celler-Kefauver Act	1950	Passed to reform and strengthen the Clayton Antitrust Act of 1914 and to close a loophole regarding asset acquisitions and acquisitions involving firms that were not direct competitors.
Hart-Scott-Rodino Act Rodino Antitrust Improvements Act	1976	A set of amendments to the antitrust laws of the United States, principally the Clayton Antitrust Act.

Source: The U.S. Antitrust System and Recent Trend in Antitrust Enforcement, *Journal of Economic Surveys*, Vol.14, No.3 (2000)

According to America's antitrust laws, once suspected of monopoly, businesses will be faced with penalties like fines, imprisonment, compensations, civil sanctions, forced dissolution and demolition and distribution. The Department of Justice can directly lodge civil and criminal action against businesses suspected of monopoly. The U.S. Federal Trade Commission can also bring direct civil and criminal action against those businesses. In addition to civil actions, businesses and individuals that suffer losses can also demand compensations of three times that of their losses.

America's antitrust laws, which are basically oriented toward economic efficiency and use it as the basis for its value judgment, are intended to maintain free competition order and regulate and remedy market disorder through legal precedents and jurisdiction. For instance, the Standard Oil Company, which was run by the Rockefeller brothers was charged with ruling out competitors through predatory pricing and preventing competitors of crude oil suppliers by purchasing oil supply lines and was pronounced guilty of monopoly. It was eventually divided into 34 independent companies based upon geographical locations. Toward the end of the twentieth century, the Department of Justice sued Microsoft for monopoly through packaging sales of Internet applications. Despite long legal prosecutions, Microsoft fortunately escaped the fatal fate of dissolution but had to pay a heavy fine of 0.75 billion dollars to its competitors to guarantee fair competition opportunities for browsers, such as Firefox, Safari, Chrome, and so on.

2.1.4 Fallacies of the Coase theorem and the fundamental non-decentralizability theory

Ronald H. Coase won the Nobel Prize in economics in 1991 for his outstanding achievements. He elaborated upon transaction costs, provided the key insight that it is unclear where the blame for externalities lies and explained the important role of property rights in economic institutions and business activities.

His representative views were published in two of his major publications : *The Nature of the Firm* (1937) and *The Problem of Social Cost* (1960) and were summarized as the Coase Law. A popular view goes like this concerning the Coase Law: as long as the property right is well defined and the transaction cost is naught or very limited, the final result of market equilibrium is efficient, and the Pareto optimality of resource allocation can be achieved no matter whom the property right is granted at the beginning.

It is also believed that the Coase Law consists of three rules. George Stigler explains the first rule as follows: if transaction cost is naught, no matter what the property right arrangement is at the outset, the negotiations between the relevant parties will lead to the maximization of wealth, that is to say the market mechanism will automatically bring resource allocation into Pareto optimality. The second rule goes like this: in the real world where the transaction cost is greater than naught, once the transaction cost is taken into account, the initial delimitation of legal rights and the choice of forms of economic organizations will exercise influence upon the efficiency of resource allocation. The third rule goes as follows: because of the transaction cost, different rights delimitation and their distribution will bring different benefits of resource allocation, and so the design of property rights systems is the basis of resource allocation optimization (Pareto optimality).

In Coase's view, as long as transaction cost is naught, the distribution of the legal ownership of property will not affect the efficiency of economic operation. Coase's theory of property rights is regarded as the "property rights legend" with two-fold implications: property ownership privatization and non-government intervention, under which case market can effectively allocate resources.

2.1.4.1 Property ownership privatization and efficiency

According to Coase, the property rights under privatization are most clearly iden-
tifiable. The system of free property rights best suits the need of market economic
development and can bring forth the greatest efficiency. As the Coase Law indicates, as long as the property rights are clearly clarified any way of property rights
distribution will result in Pareto optimality. Even in such a case, different ways of
property rights distribution may give rise to different income allocation, the consequence of which has been overlooked in the Coase Law. Coase also holds that
market is efficient no matter who owns the property rights as long as the property
rights are clearly defined and are transferable and there is no transaction cost.

However, there is no chance of these hypotheses existing altogether simultaneously due to natural factors, the internal structure of economy and the external
environment of economy, so all the property rights that are hypothesized in the
Coase Law are clearly definable and transferrable, and the resource allocation
can achieve Pareto optimality and the greatest efficiency, which can only exist in
hypotheses but not in reality. In addition to its being too much idealized, there are
other serious problems with Coase's theory of property rights, such as the identification of property rights and the rights of operations and the understanding of
the driving force of resource allocation, which lead to the wrong oversimplified
conclusion that ownership privatization will bring efficiency.

Joseph E. Stiglitz holds similar views. In *The Economic Role of the State* (1989),
he pointed out that the Coase Law consists of fallacies. In 1994, he reiterated that
in the Coase Law, what needs to be done to guarantee economic efficiency is to
clarify property rights, which is absolutely wrong. He called this theory of property rights with their clarification as its core the property rights legend, which
misled those countries transforming from planned economy to market economy
to concentrate upon ownership privatization.

Stiglitz commented that no economic theories have exercised such great influence upon human perception and behavior than the property rights legend, which
holds that what needs to be done is to allocate ownership so as to guarantee efficiency, and it does not matter how it is allocated . . . This legend is dangerous,
as it has misled many transitional economies to focus on the issue of property
ownership, i.e. its privatization.

According to Coase, what government must do is to clarify property ownership.
Once this is done, economic efficiency will follow automatically. Stiglitz holds a
different view, believing that the clarification and privatization of property ownership does not necessarily generate efficiency, and vice versa. Market reform can
be successfully conducted without the privatization and clarification of property
ownership. Privatization is not almighty and cannot guarantee the effective operation of economy, and there is no scientific justification for privatization to be the
prerequisite for the success of state-owned enterprises.

In *The Economic Role of the State* (1989), Stiglitz cites cases of publicly owned
enterprises being inefficient and points out that privately owned enterprises are
no exception. The case of Canadian National Railway, as he cited, demonstrates

that its cost and efficiency are tantamount to those of private enterprises. Government of Singapore Investment Corp (abbreviated as GIC) and Temasek Holdings (abbreviated as Temasek) are also examples well-known for their efficiency in the world. In *Privatization, Information and Incentives* (1987), David E. M. Sappington and Joseph E. Stiglitz proposed a fundamental principle for privatization: under normal circumstances there is no guarantee that private enterprises are necessarily better that public enterprises and that an ideal business run by government is better than a private one.

Regarding the questions of why public enterprises are lacking in efficiency and under what circumstances or conditions they can achieve greater efficiency, Stiglitz proposed that the lack of private ownership is not a crucial issue and that the crux of the matter is lack of competition, incentives and ownership distribution. Both large public and private enterprises have the problem of inefficiency, and it is even worse in public enterprises run by government organizations, why is that? If the agent system is popular with both public and private enterprises, the pressure from fairness and morality will seriously whittle down the power to make judgments on the part of administrators and debilitate the incentive structure that spurs them to work effectively. Moreover, the problem becomes deteriorated due to the non-competitive nature of many public enterprises and the manifold organizational goals which make administrators pursue greater space for their own interest.

Economic reforms started almost at the same time in the 1990s in China, the former Soviet Union and eastern European countries. In the former Soviet Union and east European countries, Coase's theory of private ownership was advocated, and the shock therapy was applied for complete privatization reform with the ultimate goal of transforming the traditional planned economy based on public ownership into market economy patterned after Western European countries and based on private ownership, which later gave rise to a twisted capitalist economy, one without national capital. Instead of promoting productivity, privatization turned out to be detrimental to economic development in eastern European countries, and their economy went into retrogression in terms of economic and social indicators.

In contrast, China adopted the strategy of gradual reform. While maintaining the main body of its socialist public ownership, China started its reform in market economic system and state-owned enterprises. Market became the fundamental force in resource allocation and competition between economic entities was enhanced, owing to the introduction of market competition, share-holding system and modern business management technologies into reform. Meanwhile, scientific incentive and punitive mechanisms were introduced to promote the initiatives of business managers. All this not only prevented economic retrogression in China but enhanced its rapid growth into the world's second largest economy. A comparison between China and the former Soviet Union and eastern European countries shows that privatization does not necessarily generate efficiency and that competition proves more important than privatization.

The greater the degree of production socialization, the greater unlikelihood of means of production being solely owned by individuals and private owners. In

Western developed countries, enterprise ownership is gradually transforming from the traditional sole proprietorship into a modern form of ownership like share-holding companies. Under the system of modern enterprises, no matter whether the shareholders are private or public, there must appear such problems as entrust-agency relations, corporate governance, moral hazard and internal control.

Besides, the initiatives for economic activities are not just affected by property issues but other factors as well. Under modern corporate system, business managers are quite often not owners but managers employed or appointed by the board of directors. Whether they work wholeheartedly for the interest of the corporation is contingent upon competition between businesses and between business managers and the reasonable scientific incentive, punitive and authorization mechanisms between business owners and managers rather than the distribution of business ownership or the private and public nature of the business.

If businesses and their managers share common interest, then their managers are entitled, to some extent, to business property distribution, though they are not business owners. Under such conditions, if competition exists between business managers (i.e. labor markets) and between businesses, rational managers must make full use of market to allocate resources and give full play to business initiatives so that they contribute to business interest, and there will not appear such negative conduct as low efficiency, idleness, corruption, power peddling, etc. that used to exist in traditional state-owned businesses.

Therefore, privatization does not necessarily bring economic efficiency. Just as there are both efficient and inefficient state-owned businesses, so there are both efficient and inefficient privately owned businesses. The crux of the matter lies in competition rather than ownership. Competition counts much more than ownership. Publicly owned businesses can gain sufficient economic momentum through reform.

2.1.4.2 Government intervention and effective resources allocation

As Coase argues, if property rights are clearly defined, people will voluntarily cooperate to resolve any problem of inefficiency, bargaining between the stakeholders will bring about the arrangement that maximizes social welfare, and market mechanism will lead to Pareto efficiency of resource allocation. All this has been known as the Coase Theorem. This theorem oriented the radical economic reforms in the former Soviet Union and eastern European countries with much emphasis laid on setting up private ownership and removing government intervention. However, the result of these reforms has revealed serious defects in such economic reasoning.

Some embracers of the Coase Theorem may take it for granted that property rights are unimportant and do not affect efficiency only if transactional cost is naught. Steven Cheung also holds that under such circumstances how property rights are allocated is absolutely unnecessary. Some even go so far as to conclude that there is no need for government intervention and that the market will automatically settle the problems of externalities and achieve the optimal allocation of resources.

Nonetheless, there will be market failure due to such problems as externalities, which can hardly be resolved by collective actions voluntarily organized by separate individuals. In this case, the government may play a crucial role in establishing a mechanism to remedy market failure associated with the problems of externalities and transactional cost. From this perspective, the government can be regarded as a collective organization to fulfil this duty.

Market and government are not entirely independent of or opposing to each other. They should not be opposing sides. Instead, a proper balance should be struck between them. Resource allocation through market or prices is in many cases inefficient and is likely to cause market failure, which then requires government intervention. Stiglitz, an economist in public economics, attaches special importance to the active role of government intervention in economies. He thinks that the "normal state" of market is information asymmetry and market imperfection, and the market failure related to public products, the externalities and monopoly defines where the government should play a role. Pareto efficiency is hardly achieved in the real world, and the cause of market failure is usually the absence of government intervention. So it is reasonable to have government intervention in case of market failure to increase welfare.

In their famous article *Externalities in Economies with Imperfect Information and Incomplete Markets* published in 1986, Stiglitz and Greenwald proposed the fundamental non-decentralizability theory: under normal conditions the efficient allocation of market resources cannot be achieved without government intervention. They criticized Coase's view that the efficient allocation of market resources can be automatically achieved without government intervention. According to their argument, the government has power that private organizations usually do not have, which helps to improve the efficiency of market resource allocation. In particular, Stiglitz adds that the role of government should be reshaped and regulated rather than crippled in the countries whose planning economies are being reoriented towards market economy.

Stiglitz identified two types of resource allocation, pricing allocation and non-pricing allocation. The former is focused on resource allocation according to the traditional Western economic theories. Stiglitz, however, does not agree with that. He thinks that the price (and the market) can play only a limited role in resource allocation and that non-pricing mechanism is more important. He criticizes marketism by arguing that it only focuses on the price and market and turns a blind eye to the important role of non-pricing mechanism in resource allocation. In addition, he emphasizes that the government could be more efficient in promoting large-scale investments by avoiding production surplus that is often seen in market economy.

The problems like externalities and incomplete information impede the optimal allocation of resources through market. In this case, the government, particularly the local government, can not only create the necessary legal and policy environments for market transaction but also remedy market failure by using pricing and non-pricing policy instruments, such as ownership distribution, investment, price adjustment, taxation, laws, policies, education, etc. By doing this, the government plays its role of foresighted leading in economy.

2.2 The importance of government role in social resources allocation

Not all government behavior involves resource allocation, but the great part of it leaves impacts upon social resources allocation as can be seen from the ever-increasing public expenditures of government. Government may exercise great influence upon economy in areas of production and consumption, like how to manufacture products, what to produce and for whom to manufacture them, etc. The central government can regulate social resources allocation by such means as central fiscal expenditures, and regional government can exercise enormous influence upon regional resource allocation by such means as investment, taxation and law, which is a manifestation of the role of "quasi-state". The analysis of government role in social resources allocation usually starts with government expenditures.

2.2.1 Government expenditure: Definition and classification

Government expenditure, also known as public expenditure, is the spending of public finance, i.e. the spending government needs for providing market with public service. In addition to the full play of government functions and the fulfillment of government economic roles, public expenditure can facilitate the formation and growth of market economy in the market economic society as well. The proportion of government expenditure reflects government capabilities of directly mobilizing social resources and the degree of its influence upon socio-economic activities over a period of time. Public expenditure is generally classified into purchase expenditure and transfer expenditure.

2.2.1.1 Purchase expenditure

Public expenditure is also known as exhaustive expenditure. The cash flow of this category of public expenditure imposes direct purchasing demands upon market and results in corresponding products for procurement or labor activities. Purchase expenditure may go into pure public goods and private products for the general public. The former refers to the products provided by the government for common public consumption, like military defense, and the latter to the products individuals can manufacture and provide, like education and medical care. Purchase expenditure basically reflects the proportion of social resources and factors of production that government can directly allocate and consume and therefore is a direct manifestation of the role of government in social resources allocation:

(a) Purchase expenditure directly leads to the allocation of social resources and factors of production. Its scale and structure basically correspond to the scope and intensity of direct government intervention in resource allocation and reflect the degree of fulfillment of the efficiency function of public finance. Whether purchase expenditure meets the basic requirement for market efficiency rules signifies the efficiency of government activities.

(b) Purchase expenditure directly causes changes in the contrast between market supply and demand and affects economic cycles. It is therefore one of the basic instruments for government fiscal policy making and is the direct demonstration of how public finance performs in stabilizing economy.

2.2.1.2 Transfer expenditure

Transfer expenditure refers to the spending activities of government transferring public finance to beneficiary recipients. It is mainly made up of expenditures of social security, fiscal subsidies, and so on. Its cash flow does not impose direct purchasing demand upon market and does not generate product or labor purchasing activities.

Money supplied by means of transfer expenditure goes directly to individuals and businesses rather than being directly spent by government. It is up to individuals and businesses themselves whether they use the money and how they use it. Government may lay down some binding rules, but these rules will not determine their purchasing behavior. Government can indirectly influence social resources allocation through transfer expenditure distribution so as to exercise impacts upon resource allocation on the part of recipients.

(a) Transfer expenditure causes the flow of cash income and indirectly affects the allocation of resources and means of production.
(b) Transfer expenditure is a means of affecting the efficiency of social resources allocation and more importantly, a key means of government performing its function of doing justice to the society. By transfer expenditure, government increases the cash income on the part of the recipients and practices its policies of social equality through income reallocation.
(c) Transfer expenditure is also an important means of public finance of fulfilling the function of stabilizing economy. It helps to increase the disposable income of beneficiary individuals and businesses and thus indirectly increases social purchasing power and affects the operation of macroeconomy. It is worthy of special notice that the expenditure that goes into aiding the poor and social insurance can change its direction of flow, depending upon macroeconomic operation, and become the automatic stabilizer of macroeconomic operation.

The proportion that purchase expenditure and transfer expenditure account for in a nation's total expenditure is determined by the level of its economic development. Generally speaking, in developed countries, government seldom gets directly involved in production, there is ample fiscal revenues, and fiscal functions are more inclined toward income distribution and economic stability, so their transfer expenditure accounts for a larger proportion or is approximate to purchasing expenditure or increases at a faster rate than purchase expenditure. Stiglitz's research findings show that two-thirds of the U.S. government (federal or state) expenditure is used for procurement and one-third for transfer reallocation. The transfer reallocation of the federal government accounts for 60%, and purchase expenditure 40%.

In developing countries where government gets more directly involved in production, its fiscal revenues are relatively less sufficient, so its purchase expenditure takes a larger proportion, and its transfer expenditure a lesser proportion.

2.2.2 Government expenditure growth from global perspectives

In general terms, two indicators are used to measure the scale of government fiscal expenditure: absolute index and relative indicators. The former, i.e. the absolute amount of public expenditure, can visually show the status and changes in public expenditure, but it cannot reflect various complicated factors that may affect fiscal expenditure, which is its drawback. The latter refers to the ratio of total amount of public expenditure to other relevant economic indicators, like GDP and personal dispensable income. The structural characteristic of fiscal expenditure growth can be observed from the ratio of major expenditure items to GDP. In addition, there are other indicators that may reflect the changes in the scale of government fiscal expenditure, such as the increase rate of fiscal expenditure, the elasticity of fiscal expenditure increase, the marginal propensity for fiscal expenditure increase, etc.

The increase rate of fiscal expenditure is used to measure the degree of changes in fiscal expenditure. The computational formula goes as follows:

$$\Delta G(\%) = \frac{\Delta G}{G_{n-1}} = \frac{G_n - G_{n-1}}{G_{n-1}}$$

The coefficient of fiscal expenditure increase elasticity is used to indicate the relation between the increase rate of fiscal expenditure and the growth rate of national economy. The computational formula goes as follows:

$$Eg = \frac{\Delta G(\%)}{\Delta \text{GDP}(\%)}$$

The marginal propensity for fiscal expenditure increase is used to measure the ratio of GDP growth to fiscal expenditure increase. The computational formula goes as follows:

$$\text{MGP} = \frac{\Delta G}{\Delta \text{GDP}}$$

A careful historical analysis of Western public expenditure increase may reveal the following characteristics: (a) the huge expansion of the absolute amount of public expenditure, (b) the massive increase of the relative scale of public expenditure, (c) the substantial expansion of the contents and scope of public expenditure, and (d) public expenditure has been on the gradual increase though periodical fluctuations appear.

A look at the historical statistical figures shows that the scale of public expenditure in Western countries has evolved from small sizes to large sizes. Public expenditure was on the increase in industrial countries between the 1870s and the mid-1990s on account that in the early stage of capitalist economy the function of the state was basically limited to maintaining social order and defending national security and therefore the public expenditure was of relatively smaller proportion. In later stages, government increases investment to meet the requirement of maintaining economic development and the ever-increasing public needs. In addition, the growth of GDP and the strengthening of measures of raising public income added to the expansion of public expenditure in terms of financial sources.

Let us take the United States for example. In 1870, government expenditure accounted for only 7.3%, but in 2005 it amounted to 36.6%. In 2013, America's GDP totaled 16,695 billion dollars, and in 2012, the federal government fiscal expenditure budget reached around 3,800 billion dollars, that of the state government 17,00 billion dollars, and that of local government 2,100 dollars, totaling 7,600 billion dollars and accounting for 45.8% of its GDP, which means nearly half of its GDP went into public expenditure.

A comparison between the figures of other Western developed countries demonstrates the general tendency toward the continuing increase of government expenditure from the long-term and whole perspective though negative increases were also detected in some countries and in some periods. Owing to the fact that they were in different stages of economic development, the scale and proportion of government expenditure in developing countries turned out to be lower than developed countries, but their scale was also on the continuous increase.

Prior to transformation into market economy, government in socialist countries had under its control huge amounts of economic resources, but its public expenditure began to show similar inclinations and tendencies to developed countries subsequent to their transformation. The increase in China's fiscal expenditure, for example, was characterized by the tendency of changes in the ratio curve of fiscal expenditure and GDP from the initial downturn to the later upturn, which is typical of economic transformation in transitional countries, as indicated in Figure 2.2.

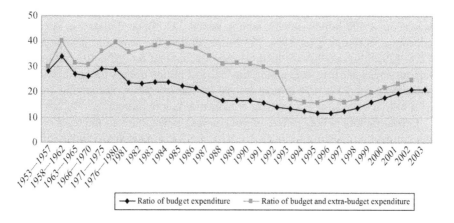

Figure 2.2 Changing proportions of China's fiscal expenditure

In the 1950s to the 1970s, China was still under planned economic system and was about to initiate economic system reform, and government was the main body of resource allocation, with the ratio of government expenditure to GDP amounting to 40%. The high ratio of government expenditure to GDP was due to the then planned economic system. On the one hand, the policy of low wages and high employment rate was implemented, and on the other hand, the profits the state-owned enterprises earned were almost totally handed over to the state.

In the 1980s to the mid-1990s, China implemented the policy of reform and opening up to the outside world and started its transformation from planned economy to market economy. Government began to take gradual steps to transfer its dominating power of resource allocation to market and practice the policy of "authority delegation and profit sharing", i.e. the distributional tendency of national income being inclined more towards the general public, which resulted in the decrease of proportion of government expenditure to GDP since the reform and opening up. From 1996 onwards China basically completed its establishment of market economic system. With its economic growth, however, the social demand for public products has been on the rise, and the proportion of government expenditure has been again on the track of gradual upturn.

A further examination of the structure of government expenditure will reveal great structural differences in government expenditure on different levels. Take the United States for example. The great part of government expenditure on the federal level goes into national defense and medical care. In 2010, the U.S. federal government fiscal expenditure budget was about 3,500 billion dollars, among which 149.5 billion dollars was spent for education, accounting for 4%, 754.1 billion dollars for pensions, accounting for 21%, 846.8 billion dollars for medical care, accounting for 24%, 871.9 billion dollars for military expenditure, accounting for 24%, 419.6 billion dollars for social welfare, accounting for 12%, 55.7 billion dollars for civil justice administration, accounting for 1.5%, 106.9 billion dollars for transportation, accounting for 2.9%, 25.6 billion dollars for government organizations, accounting for 0.7%, etc.

The great part of government expenditure on the state level goes into medical care and education. In 2010, the U.S. state government fiscal expenditure budget was about 1,400 billion dollars, among which 273 billion dollars was spent for education, accounting for 18%, 173 billion dollars for pensions, accounting for 12%, 429 billion dollars for medical care, accounting for 29%, 103 billion dollars for social security, accounting for 7%, 152 billion dollars for social welfare, accounting for 10%, 104 billion dollars for transportation, accounting for 7%, 34.8 billion dollars for government organizations, accounting for 2.3%, etc.

Education took a lion's share of government expenditure on the level of local government, accounting for 40%. In 2010, the fiscal expenditure budget of local government was about 1,800 billion dollars, among which 692 billion dollars was spent for education, accounting for 37%, 40 billion dollars for pensions, accounting for 2%, 131 billion dollars for medical care, accounting for 7%, 192 billion dollars for social security, accounting for 10%, 92 billion dollars for social welfare, accounting for 4.9%, 114 billion dollars for transportation, accounting for 6%, 68.8 billion dollars for government organizations, accounting for 3.6%, etc.

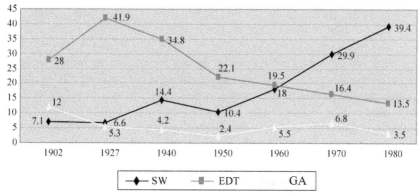

(SW: social welfare EDT: economic development and transportation GA: general administration)

Figure 2.3 Proportional tendency and changes of major items in the U.S. fiscal expenditure

The proportion of social welfare and economic development in the total expenditure is contingent upon a nation's economic development and the phases of its economic development. Generally, in the early stage of economic development or in underdeveloped countries, the primary goal of government expenditure is to support economic development, and therefore only a small proportion goes into social welfare. However, in the late stage of economic development or in economically developed countries, government seldom gets directly involved in production, and its fiscal revenues are ample, and consequently its fiscal function is more inclined toward income distribution and economic stability, hence a greater proportion of social welfare in the total expenditure, which is evident from the tendency and changes in the U.S. fiscal expenditure over the past hundred years or so, as indicated in Figure 2.3.

Due to differences in stages of economic development and economic systems, China differs from the United States in government expenditure structure and tendencies for changes, and its proportion has remained far higher than that of the United States though there has been an obvious decline over the past decade.

2.2.3 Theoretical explanations on the growth of government expenditures

Many scholars have conducted research on the continuous expansion of government expenditures and have proposed different theories to explain it, including Wagner's Law, the gradient gradual growth theory, the growth theory of government official behavior, the theory of the stages of economic growth, etc. Among them, Wagner's Law, which was named after Adolf Wagner (1835–1917), a German economist of the nineteenth century, might be the most noteworthy.

2.2.3.1 Wagner's Law

Wagner's Law, also known as the expansion theory of government activities, was proposed by Adolf Wagner, a leading scholar of the German school of social policy. After investigating the industrialization of America, France, Germany, Japan and other countries during the British Industrial Revolution, he offered an explanation on the increase of fiscal expenditures from the perspective of the expansion of government functions. It is unclear whether the increase of public expenditures mentioned in Wagner's Law refers to an increase in the proportion of public expenditures in GDP or only to that of absolute amount. However, according to R.A. Musgrave, a famous American economist in public economics, it should refer to the former.

Wagner's Law tells that when the domestic income increases, the public expenditure will increase faster, so the proportion of government expenditures in GDP increases with income per capita, which is called the relative increase of fiscal expenditures, as shown in Figure 2.4.

As Wagner argues, the modern industrial development will promote social progress, which will in turn result in the increase of government activities. He summarizes three factors that contribute to the increase of government expenditures as follows: the political factors, the economic factors and the income elasticity of demand for public expenditures.

The political factors indicate that with the industrialization of economy, the relations between the expanding market and its participants become increasingly complicated, which gives rise to the demand for commercial laws and contracts

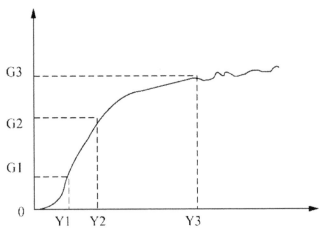

Figure 2.4 Wagner's law

as well as the establishment of judicial authorities for the implementation of these laws and contracts. More resources are thus devoted to guaranteeing public security and providing necessary judicial facilities.

The economic factors mean that the industrialization promotes urbanization, and the more concentrated population gives rise to external problems like overcrowding, environmental pollution, etc. Government intervention and regulation thus become more necessary.

In addition, Wagner ascribes the increase of public expenditures spent on education, entertainment, culture, health care and welfare service to the income elasticity of demand. The underlying logic is that the increase of disposable income is bound to generate demand for more and better public service, thus leading to the continuous increase of public expenditures in the aforementioned areas where social benefits are hardly evaluated economically, with the increase rate going up faster than that of GDP.

There is no doubt that all theories have their limitations, and so is Wagner's Law. First, his theory was formulated under the special historical background of industrialization. Industrialization is not only the engine of economic growth but also supports the expansion of fiscal expenditures. The question is how to explain the expanding tendency of fiscal expenditures even when the economy grows mature or stays in the stage of stagflation? Second, the theory fails to take into account such factors as the political system, cultural background and in particular public choice. If the public choice results in privatization, the fiscal expenditures are very likely to decrease with the per capita income, no matter whether they are measured by the absolute scale or the relative scale. Finally, Wagner's Law explains the increase of fiscal expenditures only from the perspective of demand, but it fails to examine the other force that drives up fiscal expenditures, say, the supply of public service (Guo Qingwang 2002). In *Public Spending in the 20th Century: A Global Perspective* (2000), Vito Tanzi and Ludger Schuknecht stated that Wagner's Law could not explain why there was no increase in government spending from 1870 to 1913.

2.2.3.2 The gradient gradual growth theory

Put forward by Alan T. Peacock and Jack Wiseman, this theory was reckoned as the best-known analysis of the time-series models for public expenditures. In *The Growth of Expenditure in the Kingdom* (1961), Peacock and Wiseman identified both internal and external factors that drive the increase of public expenditures. On the basis of Wagner's Law, they studied the growth of the British public organizations from 1890 to 1955, and found that the external factors accounted more for the faster growth of public expenditures than GDP. Their analysis was based on the hypothesis that the government tends to spend more while the public prefer fewer taxes. The government should thus pay special attention to the reaction of the public when it decides to collect taxes to support public expenditures, that is to say, the highest tax amount tolerated by the public lays down the *de facto* upper level of government expenditures. Normally, tax collected at a given tax rate will rise when the economy grows and the income increases, so the government expenditures will be linearly related with GDP. This is called the effect of internal factors.

However, the government will have to collect more taxes if the external conflicts occur such as a war, and in general the public will accept such an increase in the taxes as a response to the emergencies. This is the so-called substitution effect that the public expenditure will replace private spending under emergencies, resulting in an increase in the proportion of public expenditures. But the problem is that the public expenditure will hardly return to its previous normal level when the period of emergency is over. In general cases, there will be a huge amount of national debt to be paid after the war, so the public expenditure will maintain a high level. This is called the effect of external factors.

Moreover, unexpected events usually unveil many social problems, and lead the public to recognize the importance of solving these problems. In such cases, the public will accept higher taxes for this purpose with greater willingness. This can be called the "inspection effect".

Under normal circumstances, the division of expenditure responsibilities between the central and the local government is clear and stable. However, during social turmoil, the public are likely to accept that the central government should pool more fiscal resources to financially support the expansion of its functions. This in turn usually leads to more taxes and expenditures, and we call this the "concentration effect".

2.2.3.3 The growth theory of government official behavior

William Arthur Niskanen (1933–2011), a major contributor to the public choice theory, proposed this theory. The key idea is that an individual is always seeking to maximize his personal benefits. A government official, like other individuals, also pursues the maximization of his personal benefits, like salary, the number of staff subject to him, reputation, extra payment, decent offices, facilities, public activities spending, etc. In order to maximize their power and thus their personal benefits, the officials tend to expand the organizations as much as possible. Compared with the private sector providing personal products, the public sector providing public products is characterized as follows: (a) there is a lack of competition in providing public service, leading to low efficiency; (b) government bureaucracies do not seek profit maximization, resulting in no constraints upon the costs of public service; (c) there are difficulties in measuring and evaluating the efficiency of the public sector as the public good is not usually supplied at a market price.

2.2.3.4 The theory of the stages of economic growth

The American economists Richard Abel Musgrave (1910–2007) and Walt Whitman Rostow (1916–2003) proposed this theory, and the main idea is that the meaning and contents of public expenditure vary with the stages of economic development. An analytical description of the phenomena of fiscal expenditure growth is provided in such works as Musgrave's *Fiscal Systems* (1981) and in Rostow's *Politics and Stages of Growth* (1971). They attempted to analyze the reasons for public expenditure growth by examining different stages of economic development and the correlations between public expenditure and different stages.

In the early stage of economic development, the government investment accounts for a great proportion in the aggregate investment, and the public sector provides necessary social infrastructure for economic development, such as roads, transportation systems, environmental and hygienic systems, law, health, education, human resources investment, etc. This investment is crucial for the economy to "take off" in the early stage of social and economic development.

The government investment should continue in the middle stage of economic development, but it plays only a supplementary role to private investment. Market failures occur in both the early and middle stage of economic growth as the obstacles to further economic development. The government intervention must be strengthened in order to overcome market failure and defects. Musgrave believes that in the whole process of economic development, the proportion of aggregate investment in GDP is on the rise, but that of the government investment in GDP will decline.

In the mature stage of economic development, income per capita will increase substantially. With the hope for a better life, the public impose more duties upon the government and forces it to provide healthier environment, more convenient transportation, more accessible communications, better education and healthcare, etc. Consequently, the public investment will pick up its pace again to grow up.

In addition, market failure tends to be more serious with economic development, so the government has to devote more to dealing with pervasive conflicts by making laws, increasing investment and providing various services, which in turn will result in expanded public expenditures. To sum up, the expansion and contraction of public expenditures are contingent upon the different stages of economic development as well as the income elasticity of public service.

Recalling the comparison between the fiscal expenditure structure of China and that of the United States that has been aforementioned in this book, we agree that Musgrave and Rostow's theory of the stages of economic development is of strong guiding significance in understanding the real world. The United States can be reckoned as being in the mature stage of economic development, so the government allocates more expenditure to such public service as national defense, education, healthcare and pension, etc. On the contrary, China is still in the middle stage of economic development (some of its provinces are still in the early stage), so a higher proportion of its government expenditures should go to improve economic growth.

Musgrave and Rostow's theory tells that the growth in fiscal expenditures in fact reflects the multi-roles of the government in economic development. The government provides fiscal resources for infrastructural facilities and social investments, and it also tries to correct market failure, especially in the areas where the market force is absent. It implies that the government, in particular the local government, can shape more or less the structure and level of economic development by adjusting its fiscal expenditures, making foresighted leading possible in economy.

2.3 The role of government in innovating and leading economic growth

In addition to its influence upon market order and social resources allocation by means of its popularity and coercive forces, government, in particular regional government, is also the key force for innovations in institution, organization, technology and administration. It can play a leading role in economic development through innovation, and that is particularly conspicuous with regional government. Local government, which serves as the non-main-body government representative in a region, will actively seek national support so as to maximize the economic benefits of the region and compete with other regional governments through innovations in institution, organization, technology, etc. so as to lead its economic and social development, which embodies the "quasi-enterprise" role of regional government.

As the saying goes, innovation leads development. The benefit requirements of regional government in the capacity of "quasi-enterprise" – due to its economic independence, such as government income and economic performance – are intimately related to economic development. The impetus for innovation in organization and technology is strongly inherent in regional government itself. Viewed from the perspective of global economy, regional development is to a larger extent determined by the audacity of reform and foresighted thinking on the part of regional government officials, who can also be reckoned as "entrepreneurs" and also possess the "entrepreneurship", as is called by Schumpeter.

2.3.1 Joseph Alois Schumpeter's theories of innovation

2.3.1.1 The development and characteristics of innovation theories

The concept of innovation was first interpreted from the angle of the combination of technology with economy and technological innovation was integrated into economic development. However, Schumpeter is the first to have made a systematic exposition of the concept, and because of that he is awarded the title of the initiator of modern theory of innovation and the major representative. Schumpeter, an influential Austrian economist (but not a member of Austrian school), was born in Austria, traveled far and wide in Germany and moved to settle down in America. He taught in Harvard University, acted as head of American Economic Association, formed his own theory and was held in high esteem by economists like Paul Samuelson (1915–2009).

In 1911, Schumpeter published one of his early works—*Farsighted Visions on Economic Development*, which gives a full description of the theory of economic innovation based on technological advancement. In 1942, he published probably his most popular book in English—*Capitalism, Socialism and Democracy*, which showed sympathy to Marx's theory and believed that the capitalist system would collapse as a result of an internal conflict that bolstered hostilities within itself. He borrowed the phrase "creative destruction" and made it well-known by using it to describe a process in which the old ways of doing things are endogenously destroyed and replaced by new ways. He stuck to his theory of innovation and expounded his ideas of philosophy, politics and economics. Due to his theory being regarded as too much of heresy and the limitations of the times, Schumpeter's ideas were not widely recognized by the main stream economists until after the Second World War, when the role of science and technology was becoming more apparent in economic development. Since then ideas of technological innovation have gained wide approval by scholars, entrepreneurs and government officials.

Economists such as Nobel Laureate Solow further expounded and developed his theory of economic innovation, which eventually led to the theory of national innovation system put forward by the British economist Friedman in the 1980s. Schumpeter was thus accredited with the title of the pioneer of the school of innovative economics. Although his theory did not gain such wide popularity as Keynes' in his lifetime, Schumpeter's unique theory of economic innovation laid a solid foundation for his position in the history of economic theories.

Schumpeter's theory is characterized by its theoretical analysis of capitalism from the angle of "pure economic features" on the level of productive forces while putting aside production relations. In his view, the issues involved in the classical economist Adam Smith's research, like division of labor, the origin of land private ownership, the ever-increasing control upon nature, economic freedom, law and security, etc. are more of sociological problems than economic problems and can be categorized into economic sociology or even historical sociology. The reason for Schumpeter's emphasis of economics on economy itself is his firm belief that real economic development is the result of internal changes inherent in economy itself instead of external factors imposed upon economy. Without such changes, economy is dragged on by the changes in the surrounding world, and then economy itself does not change, the reason for changes must be sought from outside the category of factors described by economic theories.

Schumpeter's theory is also characterized by his dynamic analysis. It is his view that stative analysis is not enough to explain the "productive revolution" in economy. He adopts the historical approach to analyze innovation and capitalism and create the core of his theory of economic development — theory of economic innovation. He goes on to further enrich his theory of economic innovation on the basis of transformation of productive technology and methodology by examining credit, capital, profit, interest rate, economic cycle, etc. and comparing development with cyclic circulation. He holds that capitalism is by nature a form or method of economic change and has never been and is never static. This economic change is qualitative change, "creative destruction" or "abrupt industrial change" and a transformation of productive technology.

2.3.1.2   The basic views of innovative theory

In Schumpeter's writings, innovation, invention and creation are not entirely similar. He suggests on several occasions that innovation should be distinguished from invention and experimentation. Creation is a new artificial apparatus or process and can be granted patent. Experimentation is a scientific practice and can create new knowledge. Invention and experimentation are of a scientific nature and can produce knowledge. Innovation, on the other hand, is economic behavior aimed to gain better economic and social benefits and is a process of creating and executing new programs. Invention can become innovation only when it is applied to economic activities, so innovation is not a technical concept but an economic concept.

Schumpeter thinks that innovation is to create a new set of production functions, i.e. the recombination of factors of production, which means the introduction of the new combination of factors of production and production conditions that have never existed into production systems so as to realize the recombination of factors of production or production conditions. The role entrepreneurs should play is to achieve innovation and introduce new combinations. The so-called economic development is in fact a process of continuously realizing these new combinations on the part of the whole social community, or to put it in another way, it is the result of continuous innovation, the objective of which is to gain potential profits or to gain maximum extra profits. The discontinuity and imbalance of innovation is the root cause of cyclic economic fluctuations, and different innovations exercise varied influence upon economic development, which result in economic cycles of different time lengths. Innovation is the impetus for economic growth and development, and capitalism will not develop without it.

Schumpeter further categorizes innovation into five cases, which correspond respectively to product innovation, technological innovation, market innovation, resource allocation innovation and organizational innovation (or institutional innovation). In the light of his categorization of innovation, Schumpeter's major followers gradually formed two innovative theories: theory of technological innovation with technological innovation (cases 1 and 2) and market innovation (cases 3 and 4) as its research object and theory of institutional innovation with transformation of organizations and administration as its research object.

(1) using a new product, i.e. a product that consumers are not yet familiar with or a product with new features
(2) employing a new method of production, i.e. a method that has not been examined and tested in the manufacturing sector, which does not need to be based on a new discovery but can exist in the new mode of handling a product in commerce
(3) opening a new market, i.e. a market that the manufacturing sector in a country has not entered into before no matter whether this market has existed or not
(4) opening up or utilizing a new source of raw material supply or semi-finished product supply, no matter whether this source has existed or is newly created
(5) forming a new industrial organization, e.g. forming a monopolistic status (like in the form of trust) or breaking an existing monopoly

Schumpeter's theory of innovation embodies the following basic viewpoints: innovation is inherent in production process, innovation is a revolutionary change, innovation means destruction, innovation must create new values, and innovation is an irreversible campaign in history.

Schumpeter attaches great prominence to the role of entrepreneurs. In his view, the role of entrepreneurs is innovation in its purest sense. No matter what type he or she belongs to, he or she can be called an entrepreneur only when he or she realizes the new combination in reality and will lose this qualification once he or she sets up the enterprise and settles down to operate it, just as others do, which is a natural law. Therefore, almost no one can always retain the title of entrepreneur in his or her several decades of business life. Innovation is making decisions concerning the formulation and execution of innovative strategies rather than routine work in daily business administration. Schumpeter refuses to accept the definition of entrepreneur approved by the majority of scholars represented by Alfred Marshall (1842–1924), i.e. treating the role of entrepreneur as "administration" in its broad sense. Schumpeter thinks that the entrepreneur is one who achieves the new combination, on which point regional government officials have something in common.

The history of the development of world economy from the end of the eighteenth century, to some extent, demonstrates the importance and profundity of Schumpeter's theory of economic innovation. Numerous experiences and lessons tell us that change and development are eternal and that a nation or a country can accommodate itself to changes and development and hold its position in the world merely through continuous adjustment and innovation. Nowadays, innovation is still an old and new theme, and the ways that a nation adopts the strategy of innovation to allocate its resources and formulate relevant policies determine its future competitiveness in the global economy.

Innovation is of paramount importance in the age of information technology. Information technology has been rapidly transmitting, spreading and penetrating into almost every sphere of world activities, which has gained forceful momentum for the restructuring of global economy. Due to the more intense globalization and penetration of informationalization than industrialization, the speed of technological revolution of information has greatly surpassed that of any industrial revolution in the history. Government in developing countries are most privileged to take advantage of this trend to improve their innovation in technology, organization and institution, protect and enlighten entrepreneurship, give full play to late-arrival advantage and catch up with developed countries.

2.3.2 The government's role in innovation of technology and institution

2.3.2.1 Government – the propeller of technological innovation

The history of world economic development proves that whichever country can take the lead in the competition of innovation will have the advantage of development priority and the initiatives of economic development. Britain led the first industrial revolution and then became the first superpower of the world. America predominated over the information technological revolution and its economy has been occupying the dominating position in world economy. The same can be said of enterprises. Google became a large-scale world enterprise through its search engines in just a few years, and Apple became the enterprise with the greatest market value in the world through its product refinement and technological innovation.

In the 1980s, the British economist Friedman put forward the concept of national innovation system and pushed innovation to the level of national strategy. Over the past three decades, government in different parts of the world has played a key role in encouraging and promoting technological innovation.

(a) American government's hidden force in driving innovation

In 2008, the American scholar Fred Block wrote that over the past three decades, although new liberalism played a dominating role in America's political ideology, the federal government greatly intensified its intervention and provided financial support in the commercialization of new technology. However, the partisan opposition and the ideology of new liberalism overshadowed the important role of the American government in promoting technological innovation in public debating. Block added that unlike developmental bureaucratized states such as Japan and South Korea, America is a developmental network state, which pays greater attention to original creation rather than imitation and intervenes in a more decentralized and flexible mode rather than in a highly centralized mode, thus creating an environment more favorable to "one hundred flowers blossoming", as the Chinese saying goes.

In 2009, Fred Block and Matthew R. Keller reached a surprising conclusion that after 1970 American government was the major driving force for technological innovation. This article draws on a unique data set of prize-winning innovations between 1971 and 2006 and documents three key changes in the U.S. economy. The first is an expanding role of inter-organizational collaborations in producing award-winning innovations. The second is the diminishing role of the largest corporations as sources of innovation. The third is the expanded role of public institutions and public funding in the innovation process. The American government played an important part in overcoming network failures and remedying collaboration malfunction and in providing critical funding for the process of research, development and innovation.

Over the past 20 years or so, the majority of prizes for innovation went to the laboratories and universities that are affiliated to the federal government and the derivative companies funded by the above laboratories and universities. Among the 100 prize winners selected by the journal of *Research & Development* through public appraisal in 2006, the number of prize winners that were funded by the federal public finance rose from 14 to 61, in addition to 16 "private" prize winners that were indirectly funded by the federal government. The total number of prize winners went from 37 in 1975 to 77 in 2006. Even in the critical period of innovation that was dominated by the Fortune Top 500, they largely depended upon the financial support of the federal government for innovation. History would have to go back to the days before the Second World War, if innovation that solely relied upon private funding rather than federal support had to be found. The number of prize-winning enterprises over the 40 years after the Second World War demonstrated that the primary role of government in innovation got increasingly intensified. In earlier times, America's industrial and technological policies were solely monopolized for military purposes and for space development programs. Over the recent decades, a great number of non-defense institutions have been involved in the research and development of private enterprises. Currently these institutions mainly include the Department of Commerce, the Department of Energy, the Department of Agriculture, the Department of Homeland Security, the National Science Foundation and the National Institutes of Health.

(b) Germany's national innovation system

Over the last 20 years of the nineteenth century and the beginning 10 years of the twentieth century, Germany made great strides in economic development, and there appeared a number of self-initiated innovations and large innovative enterprises represented by Siemens. Made in Germany was a substitute name for good quality products. The manufacturing industry in Germany was well-recognized by the international community. In 2007, Germany, with a small population of 83 million, boasted 969 billion euros of exports, more than one-third of its GDP, and became the world champion in commodity exports, ranking before China, the United States and Japan. Of its total exports, 87% came from manufactured goods in 2006. At present, Germany's most important industrial sectors include vehicle manufacturing, electronics, chemical industry and machinery manufacturing. The key to the international competitiveness of these industrial sectors resides in technological innovation. In 2012, Germany spent 79.5 billion euros into scientific and technological research, which accounted for 2.98% of its GDP. The greatest part of that expenditure, which reached a new height in the German history and ranked on top of the European countries, went into the R & D of its manufacturing sector (86%), and the spending on such areas as electronics and mechanical engineering also rose substantially. Early in 2004, the number of patents Germany registered in the European Patent Office reached 23,044, accounting for 18% of the European Patent Office patents, far more than other European countries.

As a late-arrival industrial country, Germany has gained a profound understanding of the part that technological innovation can play in the catch-up process. Technological innovation in industries enabled Germany to rapidly industrialize itself and to surpass Britain and turned Germany into the second largest industrial country in the world, only next to the United States. In this process, the German government's coordination, entrepreneurship and educational system played an important role. The role of government is particularly noteworthy.

First, Germany's market economic system created a good legal and institutional framework for innovation in the manufacturing industry. Second, governments at all levels laid down their own policies and carried out the national policies for research and technological innovation. Support was given to all aspects of technological innovation of enterprises. The German government formulated a series of beneficial systems and policies with a view to promoting the transfer of knowledge to industry, including the support of universities in scientific research, the promotion of the transfer of scientific research findings to economic application and scientific research independent of universities. In addition, the German government also granted support to the development of local business networks so as to promote the transfer and transmission of knowledge and technology.

As is obvious from the German experience, the advantages the German manufacturing industry has gained are closely related to Germany's national innovation system. The German government, drawing on the traditional manufacturing base and the national innovation system integrating production, government, learning and research into a unified whole, has led technological innovation and enabled Germany to continue its leading role in the world's modern manufacturing.

(c) The promotion of technological innovation in key areas

According to Schumpeter's innovation theory, technological innovation is the important source of economic growth. In 1990, Paul Michael Romer opened up the study of the growth of the endogenous technological change. His thinking differs from the new classical theory of economic growth in that in the economic growth driven by endogenous innovation, market is not always Pareto optimality, due to the existence of monopolistic profits innovation requires.

The development of new materials and new products is merely one form of research and development. The emergence of new materials or new products will amplify the number of intermediate product categories or the consumptive end product range, thereby expanding the scope of choices of economic entities, continuously improving economic welfare, and bringing monopolistic benefits to new intermediate product developers. Inspired by monopolistic interests, new intermediate product researchers and developers will constantly strive to pursue their new intermediate product research and development. If the new intermediate product researchers and developers are free to enter, they will invest all of their resources into research and development, so long as their net present value is greater than the cost of research and development of new intermediate products.

Government can reduce the utilization cost of intermediate products through subsidies of public expenditures or guarantee the profit level of producers approximating to the social level. For instance, Germany granted electric price subsidies to residents using solar energy so as to develop new energy, and China implemented car subsidies policies to residents who purchase new energy cars. All this can stimulate the demand for intermediate products and pushes economic growth under market conditions to a socially optimal level.

Government can also grant subsidies for private research and development through public financing. Government subsidies can reduce research and development costs so that marginal benefits can be raised for private capital so as to increase the speed of economic growth under decentralization. Government can also invest public spending directly in research and development so as to increase the supply of intermediate products and promote technological innovation.

In *The Long-Run Growth Effects of R&D Subsidies* carried in *Journal of Economic Growth* (2000), Paul S. Segerstrom found another scenario in his survey of economic growth effects of research and development subsidies in an economy comprising two categories of innovation: the effects of research and development subsidies upon economic growth are uncertain, and economic growth is enhanced only when government grants subsidies to more efficient research and development institutions. Therefore, cities can lead economic development only when they take into consideration their natural resources, their economic development status and the long-term development trends of the world economy and science and technology and only when they heighten their own demand for development or possess intermediate products with higher efficiency, i.e. promoting certain areas of technological innovation through public spending policy choices.

2.3.2.2 Government–the engine of institutional innovation

(a)   The implication of systems and institutional innovation

In *Structure and Change in Economic History* (1981), Douglass C. North stated that institutions are "humanly devised constraints that structure political, economic and social interactions", and constraints are devised as formal rules and informal restraints which usually contribute to the perpetuation of order and safety within a market or society. So institutions are the game rules of a society or are in form artificially devised as restraints that shape human behavior and interaction and aim at constraining individual behavior in pursuing common welfare or maximizing benefits. T. W. Schultz defined "institution" as rules of conduct which involve social, political and economic behavior.

In its narrow sense, "institution" is a general term usually referring to rules, regulations, administrative laws, provisions and pledges, etc. Broadly speaking, "institution" covers a wide range of areas, including rules, order, organization, political, economic, cultural and technical aspects of the system, and ethical, ideological and other aspects as well. The fundamental role of institution is to form a certain social order through its incentives to and constraints on individual and organizational behavior.

The institutional effectiveness lies in whether it can stimulate or constrain individual and organizational behavior. It plays a vital role in economic development and the rise or fall of a nation. Once formed, institution has the feature of stability. The society is susceptible to change, but not institutions, the contradiction between the society that is liable to change and the institutional stability. Therefore, institutional reform, i.e. institutional innovation, must predate social changes and reform.

Institutional innovation can be classified into induced and forced types. The former refers to the change or replacement of current institutional arrangements or the creation of new institutional arrangements. One individual or a group of people spontaneously advocated, organized and implemented it in response to certain benefit opportunities. So it is spontaneous, partial, nonstandard and unsophisticated. The latter is characterized by compulsoriness, standardization and sophistication and is mainly implemented by government instead of individuals or groups, and government institutional innovation is not simply driven by benefit opportunities but completed within a short period of time by its coercive power. By so doing, the cost of innovation is reduced.

Institutional innovation has three implementing entities: individuals, groups and government. Viewed from this angle, three types can be identified: individually-motivated, group-motivated and government-driven. Institutional innovation can be conducted on these three levels, but with extremely varied impacts. Owing to the coercive power of government, the government-driven type is conducted on the macro-level, with wide-ranging influence. Individuals and groups may also participate, which is exemplified by Taylor's approach (often referred to as Taylor's Principles or Taylorism). Taylor's approach was a new industrial management system created by the American mechanical engineer Frederick Winslow Taylor (1856–1915) on the basis of traditional management methods in the early twentieth century to bring forth standardized operations and improve production efficiency, thus also known as scientific management. It was widely adopted in enterprises of capitalist countries and considerably raised the efficiency of industrial production.

(b)   The extremely important role of government in institutional innovation

From the perspective of government function, government, on behalf of the state, will naturally become producers and suppliers of institutional innovation, because the state has the comparative advantage of violence, it can maintain the basic social and economic order and promote economic growth and social progress. In addition, the institutional innovation initiated by government is most cost-efficient. Institutional arrangement is a kind of public goods, and the production of public goods by government is more efficient than the private production of public goods. It is more than so with institution as public goods.

Although individuals and groups can also conduct induced institutional innovation, it may be short of supply because of the external effects that induced institutional change will encounter and the problem of "free riders". In cases where this happens, the mandatory institutional change will replace the induced institutional change. Government can exercise its coercive power and ideology to reduce or curb "free riders" so as to reduce the cost of institutional change. When institutional innovation cannot balance the interests of all, or when some benefit and others' interests are hurt, it is the government's responsibility to conduct institutional innovation (Zhang Yuyan 1993).

Government-initiated institutional innovation is a process of government exercising authority and implementing active and enterprising public policies to promote the changes of existing institutions. In this kind of institutional innovation, national and regional governments have a decisive role to play, as the new institution is introduced and executed in the form of mandates and laws (Tang Xinling 1997). Government can take measures to facilitate innovation and economic development by changing the relative prices of products and factors of production. Government can adopt policies to pool human and material resources so as to develop and introduce new technologies and inspire innovation. Government can eliminate artificial barriers between regions to unify the divided domestic market and expand the size of the market. Government can change the existing laws and institutional arrangements so that innovation can move toward more efficiency.

(c) The spontaneity and foresightedness of regional government's institutional innovation

In addition to institutional innovation on the state level, regional government can also play a primary role in institutional innovation. Owing to the fact that there exist long-term structural differences of institutions and the need for competition between regions, local government can acquire monopolistic benefits from institutional innovation over a period of time, and therefore has strong initiatives to carry out institutional innovation.

Take China for example. Since its reform and opening up, China has been transforming itself from the traditional planned economy to market economy, and the key issue is that market has been gradually becoming the main body of resources allocation and that government has been gradually withdrawing from economic decision making. In this process, the central government practiced top-down decentralization of power from within, and local government obtained the relatively independent financial power. Regional governments were pushed into extensive horizontal competition in order to gain greater control upon resources allocation. Competition between regional governments can be ascribed to institutional competition between governments of different regions, and competition on the institutional level is the result of deepened local competition and is in essence competition for institutional innovation.

Since its reform and opening up, China has been following a gradual line of institutional transformation. In order to pursue greater fiscal benefits and faster economic development, local government in some regions takes the lead and gives active support to the induced institutional innovation conducive to their economic development. Nationally, the local government officials who are working in the Pearl River Delta region and the east coastal region of China with broad visions, great audacity and foresightedness, for the purpose of heightening the level of their economy and welfare and out of consideration of their political achievements, have been inspired by the central government's macro-level reform policies and have achieved bold breakthroughs out of the old system and made headway in new institutional innovation, which led to the rapid development of their regional economy in the initial stage of reform and opening up and eventually the institutional competitive advantages that are different from those of the inland regions.

It turns out that the reform process of a region is to a greater extent determined by the audacity and foresightedness of local government officials. These "cannot-wait-any-longer" officials and their governments tend to act as "the first action group" that push forward institutional changes in the region and lead its economic development.

China's institutional innovation has spread "from point to surface and step by step". This is especially true of those transformations involving the overall situation. The central government may decide on one region where trials may be conducted, like the establishment of special economic zones. After success in the pilot areas has been achieved, local governments in other regions will learn and follow the successful patterns through transplantation and imitation, which has made it possible for the transformation of China's economic systems to take place in the whole country. The trial cost of pilot areas of institutional innovation is small. Besides, the strong driving force and competitiveness that regional government displays in promoting institutional innovation shorten the time lag of institutional changes and facilitate institutional innovation and changes in different regions.

The spontaneous and foresighted institutional innovations on the part of regional government have not only brought forth the advanced development of regional economy but will ultimately spur the institutional innovation of a nation as well. They are bound to play a strong and foresighted-leading role in regional development.

2.3.2.3 Government—the main force for national innovation system

No innovation can be achieved in absolute isolation. Technological innovation can promote organizational and institutional innovation, which in turn guarantees technological innovation. If the utility of technological innovations is to be maximized in economy, they require not only the protection of intellectual property right legislation but also capital investment and the support of the soft environment, such as talents. Technological innovation is a complete chain, which includes incubators, public research and development platforms, risk investment, industrial chains centring around innovation, property rights trading, market intermediaries, legal services, logistics platforms, etc. The perfect ecology of innovation should include policies for innovation, innovation chains, innovative talents and innovation culture. Take high-tech industries for example. The developed countries in the world have all established their perfect system of innovation through legislation, taxation, investment, talent education etc. so as to ensure the rapid development of high-tech industries.

(a) Legislation. Laws must be made to protect and promote technological innovation and the development of high-tech industries. Take the United States for example. In order to protect its technology monopoly and market monopoly, America has drawn up such laws as the Technology Transfer Act, the Patent Act, the Act of Computer Software and the Trademark Act; in order to develop small and medium-sized enterprises of science and technology, America has passed laws such as the Equal Opportunity Act and the Act of Small and Medium-Sized Enterprise Technological Innovation. In order to promote technical cooperation and the integration of production, study and research, America has formulated the National Research Cooperation Act and the Act of Production, Study and Research Integration, which have promoted technological innovation and the development of high-tech industry.

Take Japan for another example. Japan formulated the Basic Law of Science and Technology to promote its high-tech development, the Industrial Education Revitalization Act, the Basic Principles for Promoting Production, Study and Research and the Application of Policies Concerning Foreign Exchange Rules, etc. to facilitate the integration of production, study and research. And in Israel, government established the Investment Encouragement Act, the Act of Industrial R&D Encouragement to encourage enterprises to invest in high-tech industry and to promote its development.

(b) Investment and Financing. In order to intensify investment in technological innovation and high-tech industries, the Western developed countries have adopted multiple channels for financing. The first is direct government grants. The Clinton administration issued a statement in 1994, deciding to increase civil research budgeting to 3% of GDP, and the total investment in science and technology in 1996 amounted to 184.3 billion dollars. Japan's total funding for scientific research in 1996 was 13.66 trillion yen, accounting for 2.96% of its GDP. In Germany, government aid policies for enterprises have always inclined toward high-tech enterprises, and its R&D funding for small and medium-sized high-tech enterprises in 1998 amounted to 600 million mark, about one-third of its total enterprise R&D investment. The second is to encourage private companies to increase R&D input. The third is the establishment of risk investment mechanisms to attract money into high-tech industries. Western countries encourage venture capital investment in high-tech industries. In 1996, more than 40% of venture capital in the United States went into high-tech industries, and the proportion rose to 62% in 1997. In Israel, about one-sixth of its high-tech companies started and developed on venture capital, and the rapid development of these companies enhanced the development of the whole high-tech sector.

(c) Taxation. Under market economy, it has proved successful for Western countries to use tax leverage for the promotion of high-tech industries. They share some common characteristics, like encouraging R&D investment, improving their innovation capabilities, and supporting small and medium-sized high-tech enterprises in their "second venture". In Britain, tax subsidies are important means of government support to the development of high-tech industry. Enterprise expenditures for research and development can be used as tax subsidies and can be totally deducted from pre-tax margins. Hi-tech industry and sunset industry differ essentially in R&D investment, and therefore the effects of these preferential policies are obvious. Since 1967, the

Japanese government has also formulated a series of tax preferential policies to promote the development of high-tech industries. In order to encourage enterprises to invest in research and development of high-tech industry, the Japanese government formulated the testing fees accrual and tax deduction system and implemented tax preferential policies for the increased experiment expenditures over previous years. The Israeli government also made policies for attracting capital to promote the development of high-tech industries. In 1994, the policy of "tax rates being set in advance" was formulated, which allowed negotiations between enterprises and tax authorities concerning tax rates after capital investment in high-tech industries produced profits. The Israeli government imposed duty-free policies upon foreign pension fund investment so as to attract foreign pension funds to invest in Israel's high-tech industry.

(d) Planning and Planning Guidance. The United States, in its implementation of innovation strategy, adopted the "triple-spiral" operational mode so as to strengthen cooperation between academia, industry and government and promote the overall coordinated progress. America' National Science Foundation began in 1971 to formulate a series of production-study-research cooperation programs, such as the College and Business Cooperation Program, the Engineering Research Center Project, the Small Business Equivalent Value Research Project, the College and Business Materials Research Cooperation Program, the College and Business Biotechnology and Advanced Computer Research Cooperation Program and so on. The implementation of these plans has closely linked basic research to applied research and to the future development of national industry and opened up more areas, broader scope and more modes for "production-study-research" cooperation. The Japanese government has also paid great attention to strengthening basic research and applied research integrated in 1993, including the Big Industrial Technology Research and Development Program and the Next Generation Industrial Foundation Technology Research and Development Plan into the Industrial Science and Technology Research and Development Plan, leading businesses to strengthen basic research and technical reserves while conducting current application research.

Government policies of science and technology are of vital importance to technological innovation. Government should take the major responsibility for building up a completely innovative ecological environment through science and technology innovation policies and pooling as many high quality R&D resources as possible to generate sustainable innovative capabilities and their ensuing results. In addition, government should protect entrepreneurs and entrepreneurship and expand them.

In Schumpeter's view, innovation occurs as a result of the innovative spirit of entrepreneurs. Entrepreneurs differ from ordinary merchants and speculators, whose only interest is making money, in that personal wealth is at best only part of their motivation, and the most prominent motivation for them is "individual actualization", namely entrepreneurship. Schumpeter believes that "entrepreneurship" includes establishing private kingdoms, harboring passions for victory and delight of creation and cherishing strong wills, which is the source of outstanding entrepreneurs and the intellectual foundation for creative breakthroughs. Entrepreneurs have become the most scarce resources of market economy and the precious wealth of society. The number of entrepreneurs in a country or a region is one of the important indices for its level of economic development. China has been practicing market economy, but for economic, historical and cultural reasons, it has not completely got rid of social shortcomings like seniority, one size fitting all ages, hatred for the rich, etc., and there is still great need for institutional incentive policies for talents and the social atmosphere for risk-taking and failure tolerance. All this will contribute considerably to the nurturing and maturity of China's entrepreneurs.

2.4 The prerequisites for government to exercise foresighted leading

Economists have put forth various theoretical explanations regarding China's miraculous development. In our view, one of the important reasons is the dual role of regional governments and the competition between them. As pointed out by *The Wall Street Journal* on September 6, 2010, the competition between regional governments is the main driving force for China's economic growth. Competition between regional governments is so sharp and has even become such a prominent characteristic of China's social and economic operations that firm believers and advocators of liberal economics like Steven Cheung also think that the mechanism of competition between regional governments, particularly county governments, established after China's reform and opening up, is one of the major causes of rapid growth of Chinese economy over the recent decades. He even went so far as to say on several occasions that China's current economic system is likely to be the best in the history of humanity. What role should regional government play in economic development? Why can competition between regional governments promote economic growth? What kind of regional government can exercise foresighted leading in economy? This section will address these questions.

2.4.1 Regional government and its characteristics

Regional government, also known as local government, refers to the government organization that administers public affairs of a region in a country, which is relative to the central government (in the federal system, federal government, and in Chinese, local government. Apart from special administrative regions, like Hong Kong and Macao, China's regional government is divided into provincial, municipal, county and township levels. In its full sense, regional government is composed of three elements: relatively fixed location, relatively concentrated population and local institutions of governance.

Government as a whole is mainly characterized by its commonality and coercion. Government's commonality lies in its official representative of the whole society and its concentrated manifestation of a tangible organization and it reflects and represents the interests and will of the whole society. As an integrated part of the regional government hierarchy, regional government shares common features of serving the local community, whether it represents the central government or acts as an entity of relative power. In addition to the three super economic coercive powers, i.e. legislative power, judicial power and administrative power, regional government also possesses economic coercive authorities, which are embodied in its power of fiscal resources allocation and of handling public affairs.

Regional government's political power of "super economic coercion" and economic power of "economic coercion" depend on the gaming results between local and central government and their own economic and social strength, so regional governments face two different types of power: political power, namely the power of the quasi-state, typically the use of the state power to ensure public spending and maintain the normal order of market through taxation, industrial and commercial monitoring, market supervision and other measures and to ensure market fairness and openness through administrative legislation and judicial means, and fiscal power, namely the power of the "quasi-enterprise" to rely on its own strength and assets to get their due returns, such as local state-owned enterprises, holding enterprises, joint-stock enterprises and resources like land and minerals.

Relative to the central government and local non-government entities, like residents, enterprises and other organizations, the function and status of China's regional government have two notable features: the dual-role representative of the interests of both central government and local non-governmental entities and the information exchange intermediary and bridge between central government and local non-governmental entities. These dual-role features determine its role as an intermediary agent between central government and local non-governmental entities. On the one hand, regional government acts as representative for central government and plays the "quasi-state" role in monitoring and regulating macro-level administration of regional economy and leading and promoting its development, and on the other hand, regional government also plays the role of "quasi-business" and represents local non-government entities in allocating regional resources, soliciting the support of central government and maximizing regional economic benefits through institutional, organizational, and technological innovation.

Since the central government's administrative decentralization toward regional government through a series of major reforms like the fiscal and taxation reform and the financial reform, regional government has completed its conversion to the relatively independent status with their own interests. After years of market orientation reform, regional autonomy of government and economic strength have been enhanced continuously. In fact, regional government has become a relatively independent economic entity. Such a dual-role identity determines the unique dual status of regional government as leadership and under leadership in social and economic life. On the one hand, as the decision maker of local economy and the quasi-market entity, it stands in contrast with central government and seeks to achieve more economic interests, and as one level of government administration and executor of central government policies, on the other hand, it stands in contrast to market and businesses.

2.4.2 The dual function of regional government and foresighted leading

The economic system reform that started in the late 1970s has pushed China onto a track of institutional transition. Positive changes have taken place in the relations between central government and regional government, and regional government has won a certain degree of financial, administrative and political autonomy in the reform, which has endowed regional government with increasingly important roles in economic development and led to inter-governmental competition between regions.

Since 1980, central government has introduced and at the same time discarded four different income distribution systems and fine-tuned incentive policies for regional government. In 1988, the financial responsibility system was introduced. Negotiations and even bargaining between central government and each provincial government were conducted regarding the proportion of fixed income assignment being turned over to central government, leading to the abolishing of the past income distribution system, the retention of the great part of the new revenues by regional government and eventually the rapid increase of regional government revenues.

Meanwhile, regional government spending increased at a much faster rate than central government spending, owing to different levels of regional government bearing expenditures in areas of social security, infrastructure, education that were previously borne by central government. The Budget Act by central government confirmed and wrote these spending responsibilities for the regional government after the financial responsibility system was in place in 1988. The regional government on the provincial, municipal, county and township levels implements about 70% of China's public spending, more than 55% of which the regional government below the provincial level implements.

The fiscal revenues of regional government were on the rise, while the proportion of total fiscal revenues to central government income continued to decline, which diminished central government's capability to exercise control over the whole national economy. In 1993, central government income accounted for only 22% of total fiscal revenues, and central government power was evidently weakening, which was reflected in the lessening of central government macro-control capability and the "balkanized" resistance to the central power. To cope with this situation, central government took active measures of moderate centralization and stronger macro-level regulation and supervision. The tax reform was launched in 1994 to change the fiscal responsibility system into the tax distribution system.

Under the tax distribution system, the proportion of regional government income declined. However, under both systems, regional government has enjoyed higher autonomy, in comparison with under planned economic system, and has, on the whole, strengthened its economic competitive power.

That reform, characterized by administrative simplification, decentralization and benefit-awarding, was intended to give more decision-making authorities down to regional government and production units and more benefits to local government, businesses and individual laborers, for the purpose for arousing the enthusiasm of regional government and individual laborers. It is quite obvious that the institutional arrangement of decentralization in that reform meant relatively independent benefits and stronger economic administrative authorities, which has given regional government the dual role of both the controlled object in regional balance of the aggregate national economy and the controlling subject with autonomous power in regional economic activities that can exercise direct regulation of regional economy on different levels. The decentralization gives regional government a certain degree of autonomy and responsibilities, which turn inter-government competition between regions into real competition between independent economic entities.

Regional government's economic responsibilities usually go as follows: First, regional government should provide such intangible public products as policies and regulations for local market and the development of regional economic development and such tangible public products as infrastructure. On the one hand, regional government should publicize and explain central government policies so as to execute them and serve local economic and social development, and on the other hand, regional government can, in the light of regional characteristics and development, formulate specific local policies and regulations to fill in the "vacuum" left behind by central government. In addition, regional government should also provide society with non-competitive and non-exclusive physical public goods, such as infrastructure construction, environmental beautification, sewage capacity enhancement, public welfare improvement, etc.

Second, regional government should remedy market malfunction, nurture market and promote social transformation. As is known to all, market has its inherent defects, such as spontaneity, externalities, hysteresis of price regulation, etc. In cases where market malfunction occurs and government regulation and control turn out to be effective, regional government can perform the function of intervention in economy.

Third, regional government should exercise macroeconomic regulation and control on social and economic development and adopt necessary measures to ensure fair and orderly redistribution. There are close interrelations between regional and central government in macroeconomic regulation and control. Central government can only exercise macroeconomic regulation and control from the perspective of the overall national development, and for each region, it is the responsibility of regional government to exercise hierarchical regulation and control. As suggested by Li Yining, government must not do what market can, and central government must not do what regional government can.

Finally, regional government should exercise comprehensive and coordinated administration of local social and economic affairs. In China, regional government also performs the dual economic functions of implementing the special supply system and regulating economic activities.

(a) The Supply System In the transition period, when the expected return of certain institutional arrangements is higher than the cost of change, and institutional demand is greater than supply, regional government is bound to promote and ensure the completion of institutional change. It covers two aspects: one is the supply policy. Regional government can formulate macro-level regulative policies suitable for the region and supporting its leading industries and superiority industries in terms of industrial policies and its overall layout on the basis of geographical location, transportation conditions, natural resources, human resources, etc. Regional governments can take advantage of the fiscal hierarchical administrative system and local financial organizations to create favorable policy environment for fundraising and capital accumulation. In addition, regional government can also make relevant policies for regional market, science and technology, investment, talent attraction, etc. The other is the supply regulation. The orderly socio-economic operation requires laws and regulations, without which government behavior cannot be standardized and market operation will be in a state of disorder. Regional government can rely on local people's congress and judicial authorities in areas of legislation, law enforcement and supervision and employ administrative measures to formulate rules and regulations and standardize government behavior and market.

(b) Regulation of Economic Activities. In cases where market is immature or slow, market system is imperfect, and market cannot effectively allocate resources, regional government can adopt investment and taxation policies to improve resource allocation functions of market. For example, regional government can use investment to support innovative technology research and development, establish investment companies under the jurisdiction of regional government, regulative funds and foundation organizations to adjust regional market, guide business behavior, and organize the investment and construction of local infrastructure and public projects so as to accelerate the growth of regional industries, their structural upgrading, and the coordinated development of society and economy.

2.4.3 Regional government competition and foresighted leading

2.4.3.1 Competition of first mover advantages

Due to the path dependence, chain effect and time delay of institutional changes, differences between regions have for long existed, and whoever takes the lead in institutional changes is bound to gain first mover advantages.

According to the principles of new institutional economics, on the assumption of increasing marginal returns, the economic system can generate a kind of local positive feedback and self-reinforcing mechanism, and this self-reinforcing mechanism will lead to what is called "lock-in effect", which means that once contingency factors enable the system to adopt certain aspects, the mechanism of increasing returns will protect it from being interfered by external factors or being replaced by other schemes, and small events and the result of the accident situation may lead to a specific path once they turn possible solutions into advantages. Structural changes of institutions in any region may be affected by "path dependence" and will eventually form a long-term, stable system structure. Without the effects of certain power, structural differences of institutions in different regions will exist for a long time under the influence of "path dependence" of institutions.

The "chain effect", when applied to the process of institutional change, means that the system structure of a country or a region is made up of numerous formal and informal institutional arrangements, which are interrelated within the system. The operational efficiency of a system arrangement is closely related to the efficiency of other arrangements within the system. Once certain system structure is formed in the initial stage of regional development, possibilities and space will be opened up for other institutional changes to take place if one part of the initial institution structure changes. The whole-scale institutional transformation will be unlikely to take place without the impetus of external forces, and impossibility and difficulty will increase for institutional changes and innovation without the simultaneous and coordinated changes of other institutional parts of the system structure so that institutional changes will be difficult to push forward and may even stop midway. The "chain effect" of institutional changes add greatly to their costs.

A long time interval and process exists from the recognition of institutional imbalance, the discovery of potential profits the actual institutional changes, which is the time delay in institutional changes. The existence of time delay in institutional changes means that a country or a region's institutional changes can only take place gradually and slowly. The long-term existence of structural differences in system structure between regions enables regional government to gain institutional monopolistic benefits over a certain period of time through institutional innovation, so regional government has strong motivations for institutional innovation.

2.4.3.2 The interest goals of regional government and businesses and innovation motivation

The interest goals of both regional government and businesses generate their innovative motivation and momentum. Regional government has its own interests and preferences, i.e. maximizing disposable fiscal revenues to provide more local public products. It has to seek both support from local people and compliments from central government. The increase of local fiscal revenues comes from two sources: the development of local economy and the remaining proportion of fiscal revenues regional government controls after sharing with central government. After the tax system reform which identified the tax authorities of local government from those of central government and their respective scopes, the fiscal revenues of regional government have been more intimately related to regional economic development.

As a result, regional government pays special attention to economic development and tries every means to protect institutional innovation within the region. It will give active support and cooperation when micro-level economic entities raise demands for institutional changes that are conducive to regional economic development and will start bargain with central government in the capacity of "the first action group" and remove barriers to institutional breakthroughs. As Yang Ruilong (1998) remarked, "With the change of behavior modes, regional government is strongly motivated in institutional innovation in order to pursue rapid economic growth and benefiting opportunities. In the capacity of the first-level administrative agent, regional government can make use of its political power to actively pursue local economic benefit maximization and possesses stronger capability to organize collective action and institutional innovation than microeconomic entities."

On the other hand, the microeconomic entities that benefit from benefit maximization deeply understand that technological changes, including production technology and management technology, etc. are important means of improving efficiency and increasing interests. However, they understand better that in the period of system transformation, institutional changes mean more to profit growth. The reason that the great majority of state-owned enterprises in China have conducted fewer technological changes and more institutional changes is that they recognize the primary importance of the latter to their survival and development.

Comparing technological and institutional change, businesses realize that they have the initiatives for technological innovation but are faced with great risks of success, such as difficult market prediction and project selection, etc. The case is quite different with institutional change. It requires certain costs to achieve breakthroughs out of barriers government sets up for entry into institutional innovation, but there is relatively smaller risks. Businesses will require regional government to give support to their institutional innovation especially when they realize that regional government is in a good position to haggle with central government and hope that institutional innovation will contribute to the development of local economy. Although regional government and businesses differ in interest goals, with the former focusing on the maximization fiscal revenues and the latter on profit maximization, they share the same goal in institutional innovation.

Yang Ruilong (1998) pointed out the possibility of cooperation between businesses and regional government, as "this kind of cooperation is in essence for businesses to seek potential institutional benefits by breaking out barriers with the help of regional government, so that regional government shares the benefits." Regional government hopes that long-term institutional advantages can be formed through institutional innovation so that it can reap monopolistic benefits from inter-governmental competition between regions. Whether regional government can perform their functions well in this process determines regional economic development. Judging from the actual situation, ranging from central government to regional government at all levels and from coastal regions to mainland regions, imbalance can be detected between the performance of regional government functions and the development of regional economy.

Those who have broad visions, great audacity, and foresighted thinking are courageous enough to break through the shackles of the old system and make great headway in institutional innovation so that the development of regional economy is led and strongly facilitated. In the forefront regions of China's reform and opening up, regional government has been moving faster toward functional transformation. Government in these regions, starting from the internal requirement of market economy, took one step ahead in exploring and practicing the role of government in market economic development, won in the time lag of reform, and seized the initiatives of development so that its socio-economic development took the lead in China. Guangdong Province is a typical case in this regard. On the contrary, in areas where ways of thinking needs to be further changed and market economy is still poorly understood, the transformation of regional government functions is faltering so that the development of regional economy is affected to varying degrees. A retrospect of China's reform over the past three decades demonstrates that the progress of regional reform largely depends on the audacity of reform and foresighted thinking on the part of government officials.

2.4.3.3 The advantages of regional government in institutional innovation

Regional government, as an important component of national government administration system, plays similar roles and perform similar functions in promoting institutional innovation. In particular, regional government, as the grassroots level of administrative units, is strongly motivated and empowered to promote local socio-economic development and to pursue the maximization of their own interests. Relative to microeconomic entities, regional government has stronger capabilities to organize collective action and conduct institutional innovation. Regional government has obvious advantages in terms of institutional innovation: regional government has a better understanding of the demand for institutional innovation and expected returns; regional government acts as the intermediary mediator between its induced institutional change and the forced institutional change of central government; and regional government's institutional innovation has the features of testing, partiality and demonstration, so institutional changes promoted by regional government has the advantages of low costs, small risks and less resistance.

In the gaming between central government and regional government, central government stands in the position of the principal, while regional government stands in the position of the agent and therefore has relative information superiority. Regional government has information advantages because: (a) it is closer to information source while the information required by central government is usually the information concerning regional government behavior; (b) it has a natural monopoly on its business operations and can make use of its monopolistic status to blockade information regarding some public goods and services and their relevant resources and costs; (c) some departments of central government, such as statistics, auditing, public finance, mass media, etc., are engaged in information collection, processing and categorization, but the information they require is largely is provided by regional government or by the units under their jurisdiction, and regional government can control the amount of information provided and the degree of its authenticity.

Regional government has direct contacts with local individuals and groups and can, in a timely manner, know about spontaneous innovation intentions from individuals and groups and the expected returns of new systems. It can grant legitimacy to new system arrangements in certain local areas so as to protect the initiatives of innovation before they obtain full legitimacy. Regional government, as the contact intermediary between central government and local individuals and groups, can serve as the transformational bridge between induced institutional change and mandatory institutional change from central government. A classic example is China's land contracting system innovation. The household contract responsibility system is a major historic revolution in China's rural land system. In its initial stage, the household contract responsibility system was spontaneously practiced by farmers themselves in the form of nonstandard induced institutional innovation, and its subsequent practice became gradually standardized under the influence of regional government.

Regional government's institutional innovation is usually characterized by trials and testing and thus has the advantages of great benefits and small risks. Effective system arrangements in one society may not be effective in the other. Likewise, an effective system arrangement in one region does not necessarily work well in the other, which is particularly prominent in China. In such a vast country like China, with such great differences between regions, new institutional arrangements will be difficult to put in place, ineffective and highly risky, if they are pushed at the outset by central government. Just as Thrainn Eggertsson said, one of the costs of institutional change is the uncertainty concerning what products the new system will bring forth.

As far as this is concerned, all system innovation will have to take risks. The best way to reduce risks is trial and testing in local areas. One of the important reasons that China's reform and opening up have achieved remarkable success at low costs and with almost no serious risks is that many new institutional arrangements, which were first put forward by regional government, underwent gradual trial and testing in different regions. Only when practice proves that the new system arrangements will bring greater benefits than the old and that it is feasible and has universal application will central government use its coercive power to grant legal status and promote new institutional arrangements in the form of legislation. It has turned out that there is extremely rich referential implication in China's strategy of "going from point to surface and from regional government innovation to national innovation through gradual promotion".

However, it cannot be denied that problems of adverse selection and moral hazard may occur in the benefit gaming between regional government and central government under conditions of asymmetrical information owing to the fact that regional government has its own relatively independent economic interests. At the same time, adverse selection and moral hazard on the part of regional government can also lead to the formation of vested interest groups.

In China, in addition to businesses, regional government is also the entity of market economic competition. China's development is the result of competition between businesses and between regional governments. These two levels of competition are the double engines for China's rapid and sustainable economic development. Although inter-governmental competition between regions promotes innovation and can exercise foresighted leading in economy, the role government can play in economic development varies considerably, due to the selfishness of government and government officials and the limitation of government capabilities (e.g. knowledge, institution, system, etc.). Some may become development-oriented government that can promote economic development, and the others may become plunder-type government that will hinder economic development. Therefore, there are certain prerequisites and constraint conditions for determining whether regional government can exercise foresighted leading and to what extent it can do so, which will be addressed in the next chapter.

3　The practice of government foresighted leading

Theory is the generalization of practice, and GFL is the practical crystallization of global regional economic development. From a global perspective, China has spent more than 30 years in reform and opening up and has reached such a level of development that took the Western world almost a century, and Singapore has become one of the most developed countries in the world in less than 50 years, in spite of its extreme scarcity of resources.

Behind the historical experiences of Singapore and China's rapid economic progress over the past decades, there is one common thread going through them— the effects of GFL in such areas as industrial policies, talents strategy and environment construction. It is those government officials with broad visions, great courage, and admirable insights and sophisticated thinking abilities who have broken through the constraints of old systems to make continuous progress in institutional innovation, which has been promoting and leading the development of regional economy. The agglomeration of the Pearl River Delta cities in Guangdong Province, China, is a good case in point.

3.1　The practice of institutional foresighted leading

Institutional foresighted leading means giving full play to the role of government, particularly regional government, in institutional innovation so as to improve the efficiency of resource allocation and realize sustainable social development and reform as well as economic growth through creating more innovative incentive systems and normative regulations. Its core resides in innovations of political, economic and administrative systems, which dominates the changes of the rules of human behavior and mutual relationship and the alteration of relations of organizations to their external environments. It inspires human creativity and initiatives to continuously create new knowledge, rationally allocate resources, generate social wealth and eventually promote social advancement. Innovative systems can only be formed by innovative governments that can adequately exercise foresighted leading.

Institutional innovation and GFL prove to be of greater importance for those countries and regions with incomplete market economic system. As there exist path dependence, chain effects and time lag in institutional innovation, the regional differences in institution do exist and for a long term, and, consequently, the first mover advantage can be acquired by governments that initiate the earliest innovation. System innovation and foresighted leading enable local governments to gain first mover advantages of systems. As a result, local governments have strong motivations for institutional foresighted leading. Regional governments with great insights, sagacity and audacity that have implemented induced system innovation before others have also brought the growth of regional development ahead of others, which is amply demonstrated by the competition of regional governments in China's economic reform and opening up.

Institutional foresighted leading should be exercised not only on the regional government level but on the national government as well. China's social and economic progress is ascribable to the institutional foresighted leading of the central government, which implements reform and opening-up policies and introduces market economic system so that market plays a fundamental role in resources allocation and regional government can act as the principal of development. It is these institutional innovations and the foresighted leading of government in these areas that have enabled China to overtake the former Soviet Union and east European countries that were also conducting reforms.

3.1.1 The practice of industrial transformation in Singapore

GFL is practiced in China and in other countries and regions of the world as well.

Singapore, one of the Four Asian Tigers, was originally a small country of more than only 400 square kilometers (over 700 square kilometers after land reclamation) and with a small population of only a little over 5 million. When it gained independence in 1965, over 90% of its citizens thought that international tourism was their only choice to incur wealth, due to its extremely scarce resources (only coastlines), backward industrial foundation, and high unemployment rate. However, the Singapore government, headed by Lee Kuan Yew, held different views. Despite unfavorable conditions, he put forward the policy of opening up to the outside world to attract investment and accelerate industrial construction. After nearly half a century's rapid expansion and five successful economic transformations, Singapore has gradually got onto the right track of development towards industrialization and pluralistic economic structure, which leads to the unique Singaporean model. Singapore's GDP went up from 0.974 billion dollars in 1965 to 295.75 billion dollars in 2013, an increase of 300 times within a period of nearly 50 years, and its per capita GDP rose by 106 times from 516 dollars in 1965 to 54,776 dollars in 2013, ranking first in Asia and marking it as a developed country. Meanwhile, it enjoys great prestige and high reputation for its clean environment and civilized citizens. It has become a role model for other countries to follow.

What has turned Singapore into a developed country? The answer lies in the innovative power and the foresightedness of its leadership in decision making, in other words the effects of GFL. In the whole course of rapid economic growth of Singapore, its government has always played the leading and decisive role, which is manifested by timely industrial policy guidance, continuous and rational reform and transition of industrial structure, rational guarantee system of industrial policies and accurate assessment of the world situation.

3.1.1.1 The evolution of industrial structural transformation in Singapore

A comprehensive survey of Singapore's development over the past five decades shows that its economic miracle has been closely related to its industrial structural transformation. Economic transformation occurs every ten years in Singapore, from labor-intensive industry in the 1960s, to technology-intensive industry in the 1970s, capital-intensive industry in the 1980s, science-and-technology-intensive industry in the 1990s, and finally to knowledge-intensive industry in the past decade.

(a) Labor-intensive industries in the 1960s

Singapore's distinctive geographical location and long-term colonial status resulted in the malformed development of its industrial structure in this period, demonstrated by its transit trade, coupled with agriculture, fishery, mining, manufacturing and construction industry. The development of direct importing and exporting trade in other Southeast Asian countries during this period drastically reduced the volume of its transit trade and dealt a serious blow to its economy. Its unemployment rate rose to 13.2% in 1959. Under these circumstances, the Singaporean government put forward the economic development strategy for its industrialization, focusing on import substitution industries so as to lessen its dependence on transit trade. Due to the backwardness of its industrial foundations, there were few options for investment promotion. Just like coastal cities of China in the early stage of reform and opening up, Singapore had no choice but to attract labor-intensive enterprises. The economy of Western developed countries, however, was entering into the stage of continuous development so that they were eager to transfer their labor-intensive industries to those developing countries. Singapore took advantage of this international opportunity to prioritize its pillar industries, such as shipbuilding, electronics and oil refining. Rapid economic development was achieved and the problem of high unemployment was solved by introducing a large number of labor-intensive industries with favorable conditions. In the mid-1960s and 1970s, the average annual growth rate remained over 10%. Singapore soon became a manufacturing base by completing the first stage of industrial transformation through rapid industrialization and through the construction of industrial parks.

(b) Technology-intensive industries in the 1970s

Since the late 1970s, the pay-rising wave had been sweeping through Singapore, and the growth rate of wages outgrew that of its productivity. Severe unemployment problems had been gradually replaced by the lack of labor, and problems had occurred in local labor market as most people were unwilling to work in Singapore for low wages, which was similar to the situation in the coastal cities of China, where inland labor force was reluctant to come for low-wage work. Therefore, its labor-intensive export industries lost comparative advantage as the export-oriented economy was strongly impacted by those labor-intensive industries in other Southeast Asian countries and influenced by trade protectionism of Western developed countries. The government of Singapore also worried that over-reliance upon cheap foreign labor and low-value-added products would hinder the promotion of its productivity and its long-term economic growth. As a result, the Singaporean government implemented the strategy of "second industrial revolution" in economy in 1979, which focused on restructuring economic structure, vigorously introducing high technology, capital and technology-intensive industries, transforming its manufacturing towards export industries with high added value, high intensive capital and technology, and gradually phasing out labor-intensive industries.

(c)   Capital-intensive industries in the 1980s

Through the analysis of the difficult situation of domestic economy in the previous stage, the Singaporean government put forward the strategic adjustment of its economic development and countermeasures for economic difficulties, which officially recognized the manufacturing and service industry as the double engines for its national economy, prioritizing the service industries with high growth potentials (mainly including logistic industry, financial industry, etc.) while developing capital and knowledge-intensive industries, so as to make Singapore the regional service center of Southeast Asia and the Asia-Pacific region.

(a)   The dual development of science-and-technology-intensive industries and service industries in the 1990s

In this stage, the service industry was identified as the second driving force of Singapore's economic growth. Singapore turned into a diversified economy with manufacturing and service industries as its two pillars of economic development after 50 years of efforts. Meanwhile, Singapore also embarked upon many newly emerging industries, such as environmental science and technology, clean energy, and so on.

(b)   Industrial restructuring based on knowledge economy since 1997

Singapore's economy suffered again from the unstable world economic environment upon its entry into the twentieth century. Its economic growth rate was 9.9% in 2000, down to -2% in 2001, and increased to 1.1% in 2003. To cope with the recession and the changing world economic environment, Singapore began to conduct comprehensive structural transformation, emphasizing on service and information industries, accelerating economic internationalization and liberalization, high-tech development, active innovation, and formulating and implementing the strategic plan of transforming traditional economy to knowledge economy. The government of Singapore started to promote research and development in 2010, aiming to take its research and development expenditure accounts for 3.5% of GDP in five years. The statistics released by Singapore's Agency for Science, Technology and Research reveals that the annual average composite growth ratio of its total expenditure over the past 10 years in R & D was 7.8%.

Through five stages of industrial transformation, Singapore had developed from its original single line of transit trade industry into an economy of diversified industrial structure, incorporating into it knowledge, technology and innovation. As a result of its timely continuous industrial restructuring, Singapore quickly got over the plight of economic recession and achieved the fast and sustainable growth of its national economy and international competitiveness.

3.1.1.2 Singapore's experience reference of industrial transformation – continuous institutional foresighted leading

In the course of Singapore's industrial transformation and economic boom, its government's institutional foresighted leading played a dominating and decisive role. The success of its economic transition was attributable to the fact that the government, in the light of its accurate orientation of national conditions, pioneering macro thinking, and pragmatic microcosmic measures, put forward new economic development strategies in a timely manner and formulated sophisticated systems, which led to every successful economic transition and eventually pushed its economy onto new levels and new tracks of benign and sustainable development.

The Singaporean government adopted active industrial policies and development guidance, transforming import substitution into export orientation in its industrial development strategy, which evolved from the single mode of industrial structure to diversified modes. Concomitant with that evolution, the nation's leading industry also gradually changed from the construction of logistics parks, high and new technology industrial parks (including electronics and precision engineering, information industry, fine chemical and biopharmacy) and financial industry to the present service industries.

When the severe financial crisis tortured the globe, Singapore's economy also suffered a heavy blow. However, it did not take a long time before it got out of the trough and accomplished the miracle of its high economic growth, which made the world look at it with new eyes. All this is ascribable to the efforts of its government in the correct assessment of the situation and the timely adjustment of its economic strategy.

To cope with the international financial crisis and ensure the sustainable development of Singapore's economy, the Singaporean government set up a national economic strategy committee in June 2009, which consisted of eight teams to propose economic strategies and ensure its continuous and stable development.

Prime Minister Lee Hsien Long spoke highly of the committee's economic strategies tailored to Singapore's economic development in the following decade as significant contributions to the development direction of its national economy.

In addition to foresighted leading in macroscopic development strategies, the Singaporean government established a series of microscopic policies conducive to the development of enterprises based on their practices to improve their operational conditions and promote business development. For example, Singapore has always attached great importance to the liveable environment and favorable scientific research facilities, which provides high-end scientific manpower with commendable R&D environment. For another example, Singapore is one of the countries worldwide with the lowest corporate tax rates. In terms of personal income tax, the upper limit of the top marginal tax rate is 20%. If someone earns an annual salary of $100, 000 and has two family members, he only needs to pay 9% in Singapore, which plays a crucial role in attracting high-end talents into it.

In terms of industrial transformation, Singapore's Bureau of Economic Development has played a vital role, which was a manifestation of not only institutional foresighted leading but organizational foresighted leading as well.

The Bureau of Economic Development was founded in 1961 as the main government agency for planning and implementing economic strategies, currently with a total of 23 overseas branch offices and considers and solves problems mainly from the business perspective. For example, in the early stage of economic development, the government would provide appropriate timely support for businesses that needed rapid plant construction and tax incentives, launch various education and training programs to meet enterprises' requirements for high-caliber talents. In addition, in economic transition, the demand of enterprises for high-end talents appeared particularly urgent, as those talents could accelerate industrial transformation, and the government acted as go-between for enterprises. In biopharmaceutical industry, the government helped to introduce high-end experts from Europe and the United States and invited them to stay longer in Singapore to lead research and development. In clean energy, the government also introduced German high-end experts to help enterprises to conduct R&D and innovation.

Singapore's government has been following the changing trends of international competition patterns and proposing foresighted development strategies, which have been implemented through strong, effective, detailed and comprehensive system innovation at both macro and micro-levels and have enabled the country to continue industrial structural upgrading and scientific and sustainable economic growth. All that is the embodiment of the foresighted-leading function of its government systems.

3.1.2 The practice of government foresighted leading in Foshan, China

The City of Foshan is located in the hinterland of the Pearl River Delta, which has neither mineral resources nor sea resources nor policy advantages of China's special economic zones. Its resources endowment is ordinary and regional advantages are not obvious, though its population amounts to more than 7.3 million over an area of 3 800 square kilometers (2013). However, within just a short span of 30 years, Foshan has completed its industrial upgrading from agriculture-dominating industry to manufacturing-dominating industry, from domestically-oriented economy to externally-oriented economy, and from low-end to high-end industry. It has achieved the total GDP volume of more than 700 billion yuan, with per capita GDP nearing 16 000 U.S. dollars. When the international financial crisis struck the city, it aptly turned the crisis into opportunities, took the lead among the Pearl River Delta cities, realized industrial transformation and pushed its economy to a higher level. Similar to the Singaporean case, one important reason behind the above achievements is that the Foshan government has been continuously playing its foresighted-leading role, especially its foresighted leading in systems and institutions.

3.1.2.1 The institutional foresighted leading in Shunde

Shunde, a city under the jurisdiction of Foshan, enjoys demonstrative experiences of economic development in Foshan. Before reform and opening up, Shunde was simply an agricultural county with a few traditional projects focusing on silk reeling and with unstable and unsustainable agricultural development. From the 1980s, it became a pioneer in reform and put forward the strategic goal of "strengthening the county through agriculture". After 30 years of development, it ranked among China's top counties, with its GDP exceeding 250 billion yuan (2013). It has developed itself into the world's home appliances manufacturing center and is recognized as one of "Guangdong's Four Tigers", along with Dongguan, Nanhai and Zhongshan. "Made in Shunde" becomes synonymous with China's electrical appliances industry. The "Shunde phenomenon" has drawn considerable attention from the economic world as a hot topic of China's reform and opening up.

(a) Shunde's industrialization through Three-Key Strategy

Before China's reform and opening up, it was rather difficult for the traditional agricultural economy to accommodate Shunde's development. From the 1980s, it started to transform from a typically traditional agricultural county to an industrialized county by unequivocally putting forward the industrializing strategy and emphasizing the importance of strengthening the county through industry and leading Shunde's development via industry. The Shunde County Party Committee proposed the "Three-Key Strategy", with collective economy, industrialization and backbone enterprises as the three keys of its economy, which was then a significant example. Every village, town, and village was encouraged to set up their own collective enterprises (collective economy), which highlighted the importance of its industry that was represented by those large-scale backbone enterprises. The "Three-Key Strategy" laid a solid industrial foundation for Shunde to nurture a large number of backbone enterprises.

The figures from the statistics department shows that Shunde's gross output value of industry and agriculture in 1978 was less than 1.6 billion yuan according to the 1990 constant prices. However, it doubled by 1985 and approached 9 billion yuan in 1990. By then, Shunde had already become one of "Guangdong's Four Tigers", and five township enterprises in Shunde appeared on the list of China's top ten township enterprises. Hereafter, its home appliances swept all over China and took a large part of China's home appliances market share. The Shunde-made home appliances, like refrigerators, air conditioners, microwave ovens, electric fans, rice cookers, electronic disinfection cabinets, water heaters, together with dozens of other electrical appliances products, all ranked on top in terms of production quantity and sales. Its gross output value of household electrical appliance industry accounted for about 15% nationwide. Five famous Chinese enterprises, i.e. Kelon, Rongsheng, Midea, Macro and Galanz, line along the 10-km-long Shunde Road from south to north, assuring Shunde's position as the home appliance manufacturing center in China and the world.

In addition to electrical appliances, furniture manufacturing and horticulture are also Shunde's strong industries. Lecong Town is widely recognized as the furniture center of the world and is one of China's largest furniture distribution centers. Longjiang Town is named as "the first town of Chinese furniture" and collects two-thirds of Shunde's furniture factories, with a total number of more than 1,200. Shunde is also China's largest flower production base, with a cultivating area of 45,000 mu, nearly half of which is located in Chencun Town. Although the planting area of flowers accounts for only 20% of Shunde's total area of the planting industry, the sales value of flowers accounts for 60% of Shunde's planting industry. Horticulture has now become one of the leading agricultural projects in Shunde.

(b)   The pioneering reform of property rights

From the early 1990s to the early twenty-first century, Shunde had been exerting strenuous efforts to achieve breakthroughs in various reforms that guided development. The "Three-Key Strategy" brought forth strong industrial economy for Shunde, but the single development pattern of collective economy had unsustainably hidden troubles. The Shunde government was determined to conduct reforms, transform development modes and change enterprise ownership, converting collectively-owned property rights into private ownership, which signified the critical breakthrough time of the reform. The reform was highly controversial and even risky, as it was not the best time for such reforms, because there was still no clarification of public ownership, private ownership, socialism and capitalism. The government regulators with courage and foresighted-leading thoughts unswervingly promoted reforms, including government withdrawal of shares, private ownership of shares, implementation of "small government and big market" policy, vacating the greatest space for enterprises to upgrade and enlarge their scales so as to compete in the global market. Eventually, giant enterprises such as Midea, Galanz and others, with total assets of ten billion yuan each, have appeared one after another, giving rise to such new industrial groups as coating, machinery, electronics, biopharmacy, etc.

(c) The "Triple-Three Strategy" for industrial development has been leading Shunde's economy

Shunde has been taking the lead in China's county economy. Smooth progress has been made in the three industries and in urbanization, but will Shunde be able to maintain its advantages of continuously leading county economy in the face of fierce international industrial upgrading and competition?

An investigation of Japan's industrial structure gave the Shunde government officials deeply-shocking impressions and inspirations during their investment promotions in Japan. Japan's industrial structure consists of three to five pillar industries, with each supported by three to five leading enterprises, Integral chains have been forged surrounding pillar industries and leading enterprises. Take Toyota motors for example. There are more than three hundred first-level accessories firms, more than four hundred secondary accessories firms, and more than four hundred third-level accessories firms. This industrial structural pattern set the Shunde government officials thinking. At that time, Shunde's total output value was over 60 billion, and more than 70% was generated from household electrical appliances industry in which more than 70% of the products were turned out by Midea, Galanz, and Kelon. If these household electrical appliances enterprises met with problems in domestic or international market that make it difficult for them to further develop, that would leave tremendous impacts upon Shunde's economy.

Therefore, in the light of foreign experience and practical thinking, the Shunde government proposed the "triple-three strategy" for industrial development, which integrates and coordinates the development of the three principal industries. The first "three" of the strategy refers to the coordinated development of the three principal industries, the second the selection of three key lines of each principal industry, and the third the development of three leading enterprises in each key line. This foresighted leading took into consideration the overall coordinated development of industries, key lines of industry and enterprises, which has proved to be of vital importance.

One case can be cited here to illustrate how government can lead the development of enterprises and exercise foresighted leading in industrial transformation. In the course of transforming from "domestically-oriented economy" to "externally-oriented economy", it is necessary for enterprises to attend all kinds of promotional exhibition both at home and abroad in order to continuously expand overseas and domestic markets. However, most private enterprises were contented with what they had achieved due to narrow visions and poor awareness of their necessity and were lacking in enthusiasm for outward expansion. To cope with this, the Shunde government implemented the subsidiary policy for exhibition attendance. The expenses involved in business trips to and participation in promotional exhibitions were subsidized by the government, no matter whether they were held in

Beijing or in other parts of the world, like in Cologne, Germany for household electrical appliances exhibitions.

In February 2004, the Shunde government provided 10 million yuan for a delegation of 52 home appliance enterprises to attend a household electrical appliances exhibition in Cologne, Germany to promote products "Made in Shunde", which demonstrated to the Western world for the first time the complete image of Shunde's home electrical appliances and its industries and brought back an intentional transaction volume of $450 million and a contractual transaction volume of $130 million. That simple institutional innovation greatly aroused the enthusiasm of Shunde's entrepreneurs, built up their confidence and interest, and substantially improved the market influence and market share of its household electrical appliances at home and abroad

The Shunde government released the "Triple-Three Strategy" in 2005 and proposed to build a new "economic Shunde" in five years. Shunde's GDP exceeded 100 billion yuan in 2006. It amounted to 158.2 billion yuan in 2008 and 193.6 billion yuan by 2010. The goal of building a new "economic Shunde" was accomplished in only four years, which amply showed the effectiveness of GFL.

3.1.2.2 The transformation of "three outmodes" in Foshan

(a)   The background for the transformation of "three outmodes"

Over 30 years of accelerated industrialization and urbanization, it took Foshan only three times the construction land to achieve 30 times the economic growth than before. The amount of land already used for construction in Foshan accounted for 33% of the total area of its administrative division, which is far higher than that of Hong Kong, and over twice that of Japan's three metropolis satellite rings. The development intensity of land in Foshan reached the limits of ecological environment protection. There was an industrial boom for a certain period in Shunde, where "every family and village set up their factories" and village industrial zones mushroomed all over the county. That development mode cultivated the foundation of its private economy, but it resulted in the inefficient use of land and unsustainable development. According to the second survey of land use in Shunde, the total amount of construction land has accounted for 47.9% of its land area of 806 square kilometers. Its development intensity of land has surpassed that of Shenzhen, Dongguan and other surrounding areas, which has led to land unavailability in some towns and has approached the limits of environmental and resources capacities.

Meanwhile, there were 253 000 mu of old towns, factory sites and countryside residences, which is equivalent to the new addition of construction land within the whole city over the past 20 years. Serious problems existed in land use, like low rates of land utilization and disordered structural layouts, which turned Shunde a gathering place for enterprises of "high consumption of energy, high pollution and low productivity". Inadequate infrastructure support in old parts of the county and urban villages seriously affected the residents' quality of life.

The world development experiences have shown that Foshan could no longer follow the old track of exchanging economic growth with great amount of newly added construction land, and its development should depend on solving the conflicts between the limited supply of newly added construction land and the strong demand for land caused by social and economic development. The transformation of the "three outmodes" (i.e. outmoded towns, factories and villages) and the revitalization of land stock not only solves the problem of shortage of land for development, optimize the structure of land utilization and improves the efficiency of land use but also helps to achieve the goals of upgrading industrial structure, transforming city functions, improving urban and rural environment and integrating urban and rural development.

In June 2007, the Foshan government issued "The Provisions Regarding the Acceleration of Reforms of Old Towns, Factory Sites and Countryside Residences" so as to promote and fully implement the transformation of "three outmodes". By the end of February 2011, more than 960 "three outmodes" transformation projects were put into action, with an area of about 80,000 mu, a newly added construction area of 40 million square meters and a capital investment of 114 billion yuan.

(b)   The mode of "three outmodes" transformation

In transforming the "three outmodes", the Foshan government played a foresighted-leading role and fully mobilized participation of all sectors of the society by means of market mechanism. The government started by launching a series of government documents, such as The Provisions Regarding the Acceleration of Reforms of Old Towns, Factory Sites and Countryside Residences and three supporting documents guiding the transformation of "three outmodes". While providing necessary guidance, strengthening supervision and standardizing processes, the Foshan government vigorously promoted the mode of marketization reform focusing on "government laying down policies, owners' (users') providing land and investors raising funds" and followed the principle of "whoever invests will reap benefits" in the construction of specific projects, which aroused, to the greatest extent, the enthusiasm of all sectors of the society in the transformation of the "three outmodes". This mode created an all-win situation and deftly solved the problem of financial shortage. By February 2011, in addition to an investment of 18.16 billion yuan by governments of various levels, a social capital of 96 billion was introduced into the "three outmodes" transformation, which means that one yuan of government funding generated four times that of social capital, another successful case of GFL. Moreover, the municipal government encouraged county governments to take bold action to try new practices and create new modes of distinctive features and operational advantages.

For example, in the reconstruction of the old town, the biggest project – the reconstruction project of the Ancestor Temple – Donghuali area, which was funded by Hong Kong investors, adopted a model characterized by "government leading, unified planning and market operation", an innovative model of government-led harmonious demolition and whole land leasing that completely overcame the drawbacks of the old town reconstruction mode typified by individual building restoration and partial repairs and renovations.

In the reconstruction of old countryside residences, the model for the Southwest Sanshui Renovation Project can be cited as an example, which focused on environmental reconstruction and regulation and built an iconic urban ecological landscape zone. Another example, the Xiaxi Village Renovation Project, was financed by the village collective and the profits gained from that project became the income of the villagers. That model opened up a new path that led rural collective economy onto the new track of developing urbanized economy. A third model, the stone village project, which attracted joint development through land property sharing, has not only realized the goal of "demolishing the old residences and building a new community" but also ensured long-term stable income of farmers. One more model, the BOT project of Phoenix Village, which attracted reconstruction capital by exchanging land for the right of lease management for five years by developers, has created a win-win mechanism of "borrowing water to sail the boat" for mutual benefits.

In terms of transforming old factory sites, four models have been set up. The model of "Foshan Creative Industrial Park" has been introduced to transform and renovate the old factories by retaining their former appearance, increasing public supporting facilities and open space and bringing in newly emerging industries. This model has endowed old factories with new industrial modes and "saved one cage for more birds". The self-reconstructing and independently operating model, The Lanshi Metal Trading Market, transformed those old real estates of small scale, low end and low efficiency into a large stainless steel trading market, which has brought about huge economic and social benefits by "breaking the old cage, driving away the old birds and constructing a large new cage". The model of Tianfulai Industrial City adopted a new mode of government claiming land first and then raising social capital, which has transformed the single village industrial base into a new industry-dominated urban area with complete residential and public service supporting facilities with the effect of "emptying the cage for new birds", i.e. creating a harmonious and coordinated development pattern of promoting commerce through industrialization and stimulating industrialization through commerce. One last model, the Nanhai Jiaobiao Joint Inventory Project, integrated the land of ten economic entities through joint efforts of several villages and set an example of agglomerated land development.

(c)   The effects of transforming "three outmodes"

For any government, land is the most important resource and the toughest problem as well, as it is likely to trigger off social conflicts if land problems are not properly handled. Although the system for permanent rural residence registration was abolished in Foshan in 2004, complicated problems persisted in the reutilization of collective land and the renovation of old factory sites and villages due to the remaining dual rural-urban structure. Foshan, on the basis of the market-oriented principle, led governments of all levels and other social forces to employ various measures and individual wisdom and solve the problem – breaking through the bottleneck of land development, revitalizing rural collective land and protecting the interests of villagers. All that has directly brought about social stability, promoted industrial upgrading, urban transformation and environmental reengineering, and further released the creativity and flexibility of pioneering reformers.

Foshan has achieved rapid agglomerated industrial development through transforming inefficient "old three's", weeding out enterprises of small-scale, low-efficiency and high-energy consumption, implementing land consolidation to make room for large high quality projects, high-tech industries and cultural creative industries and converting industrial transformation towards low energy consumption, low pollution and high added values. Among the renovation projects, 205 focused on readjusting industrial structure from the secondary industry to the tertiary industry, and 12 of them were in high-tech industry, 21 in cultural creative industry. According to the statistics, there was an added value of 336 million yuan for per square kilometer of construction land in the secondary and tertiary industry in 2008, a 20.7% increase over 2007, an added value of 369 million yuan for per square kilometer of construction land in the secondary and tertiary industry in 2009, an increase of 10% over 2008. Meanwhile, more than 240 industrial relocation projects had been completed in combination with energy conservation and emissions reduction, 84 projects were launched by 44 enterprises among the world's top 500 enterprises, with an investment of about $3.47 billion, and 149 projects by 87 enterprises among China's top 500 enterprises. Consequently, the strategy of "emptying the cage for new birds" achieved substantial results, optimized industrial structure and replenished energy for further development.

The transformation of "three outmodes" has also promoted the economical and intensive utilization of land. According to the 2010 statistics, prior to the transformation, 960 projects which was completed or under reconstruction occupied about 80 000 mu of land, with an average plot ratio being 0.8 and the average building density being about 60%. After the transformation, the average plot ratio increased to about 2.0 and the average building density decreased to about 35%. The GDP output per square kilometer of land for construction in the city increased from 284 million yuan in 2007 to 376 million yuan in 2009, an increase of 32.3%. The land consumption of GDP per hundred million yuan was reduced by 8.6 hectares in 2009, a decrease of 24.4%, compared with that in 2007. Through unified planning and integration of discretely inefficient use of land, the efficiency of land use was greatly improved, and the pressure of land use had been lessened to a great extent. For example, the project of Coastal Imperial Garden in Chancheng District in downtown Foshan occupies a construction area of 326 000 square meters, which was reclaimed from land transformation and reconstruction and was 5.6 times that of the old area of 58 000 square meters. For another example, in the industrial city of Tianfulai, Shunde, the plot ratio of its new factory site was 5.65 times that of the old site, the construction area was increased from the original 400 000 square meters to 2.26 million square meters, and the output value rose from the original 1 billion yuan to 15 billion yuan.

More importantly, the transformation of "three outmodes" added considerably to the income of urban and rural residents, rather than diminishing the interest of the original land owners, improved urban and rural environment, drove forward the development of the tertiary industry, and increased the market value of land and property. The collective income of villages and the employment rate have increased annually by 200% on average, which has brought to the village residents substantial benefits. For example, the project of Violet Gold City in Xiaxi Village of Nanhai District has incurred an annual rental income of 3.6 million yuan, with a progressive increase of around 20% for five consecutive years and an increase of around 20% for the village collective economy. For another example, the project of Foshan International Furniture Exposition, provides the village collective economy with an annual land rent of over 40 million yuan, five times higher than that before land transformation. Moreover, the associated industrial clusters of hotels, tourism, trade, exhibitions, entertainment, catering and other upstream and downstream service industrial projects also bring huge economic benefits to the village and villagers.

The transformation of the "three outmodes" in Foshan attaches great importance to both development and stability and has been recognized as a role model for other cities to follow. Chancheng District alone, for example, received 1 075 delegations inside and outside Guangdong who came to learn the practices and experiences of "three outmodes" transformation in less than 3 years. In 2008, Foshan was identified as "pilot demonstrative city for "three outmodes" transformation in Guangdong Province". On December 15, 2009, Premier Li Keqiang inspected Foshan and spoke highly of the transformation programs and the integrated urban and rural development. On July 11, 2010, the program of "Focus Interview" of China Central Television made an exclusive report about Foshan's innovative ways of breaking through the bottleneck of land shortage through land transformation. Wang Shiyuan, the vice minister of National Land Resources, paid an inspectional visit to land transformation in Foshan in the mid-May 2011 and commented that land transformation in Foshan has created a triple-win situation, which has delighted the general community, businesses and governments.

The transformation of "three outmodes" in Foshan fully displays the role of foresighted leading on the part of government, especially regional government. The Foshan government has formed a favorable system of government guidance and social participation through market-oriented reform and innovation. It has integrated the "three outmodes" transformation into the overall planning of the city's economic and social development, rather than the traditional renovation of old towns and cities. The transformation has become intertwined with the adjustment of industrial structure, promotion of urban functions, improvement of living conditions and urban-rural integrated development. The government has also paid special attention to adjusting and balancing the interest relations, properly handling the relationship between the state, the collective, the land owner and the related obligees, investors and the public interests, and in particular, encouraging farmers to employ their land in the urbanization process and fully enjoy land revenues and benefits so as to achieve benefit sharing, all-win, and the most important, benefiting the people first. It is just due to these foresighted institutional arrangements of the government of Foshan that have enabled the "three outmodes" transformation to contribute to the improvement of allocation efficiency of social resources and to promote the sustainable growth of its economy.

3.2 The practice of technological foresighted leading

As mentioned in the previous chapter, technological foresighted leading refers to giving full play to the government role in collecting social resources, involving the government in direct or indirect technological invention, promoting technological progress and enhancing technological innovation capabilities for enterprises. It covers two aspects: the first is to create favorable external environment for enterprises to improve their technological innovation capabilities, such as strengthening the construction of patent system, etc., and the second to adopt a series of incentive measures and policies to directly stimulate technological innovation of enterprises by economic means, such as the funding schemes in research and development of key technology, the establishment of technological funds, or the introduction of leading personnel, etc. In addition to direct government involvement in technological innovation and technological development guidance, technological foresighted leading of government, in most cases, is associated with its foresighted leading of systems and organizations, such as protecting innovation by establishing patent laws, and promoting technological innovation for enterprises or individuals by setting up research and development funds or technological funds, etc.

The second chapter of this book has indicated that the government can reduce costs of technological innovation through government subsidies, or guarantee profit levels of producers approximating to that of average social levels, such as the subsidiary policy for new energy in Germany. The government can also subsidize individual research and development activities through public spending to improve the marginal benefit of private capital and promote technological innovation. It can invest directly in research and development through public spending to enhance technological innovation. It has also been mentioned in the same chapter that technological foresighted leading can achieve its desired effects only when a nation or a region can comprehensively consider the long-term trend of the world economy and science and technology on the basis of its own resources endowment and economic situation, and through options of public expenditure policies, promote its highly demanded or efficient technological innovation.

Nowadays, technological innovation has been upgraded to the dimension of national strategy, and the governments of Western developed countries have played a more and more important role in ensuring and encouraging technological innovation. Government organizations in Europe and the United States have been strongly supporting cutting-edge technology research to ensure that their innovation can be transformed into commercial products in a timely manner. American professor Matthew Keller went so far as to conclude that innovation in science and technology after 1970 in America has mainly originated from the promotion of the United States government. Thus, GFL in technology has both universal and significant implications.

3.2.1 *The practices of developed countries*

3.2.1.1 *Singapore's research and development through government investment in R&D infrastructure*

In the initial stage of launching R&D projects, the Singaporean government invested to build R&D facilities to attract talents and create scientific research atmosphere. It went on to invite private capital injection to form large-scale R&D economic entities. Today, private enterprises of Singapore have come to consider their investment in research and development as their driving power for business development. The proportion of R&D spending accounted for 71.8% of its total, compared with the proportion of 66.8% in 2007, which has been the highest in recent years. In other words, one dollar of R&D funding in 2008 could bring forth 2.5 dollars from the private sector, while the ratio was only 1:1.5 in 2000. This statistics has fully proved the Singaporean government's foresighted leading role in technological innovation.

As suggested in The Singapore National Scientific Research Survey in 2009, intellectual capital will be the key to its economic development in the next phase of Singapore. The Prime Minister of Singapore, Lee Hsien Loong promised on behalf of the government that the government will invest 1% of its GDP, which is equivalent to $16.1 billion Singaporean dollar in research, innovation and creation between 2011 and 2015. Consequently, Singapore will achieve the goal of heightening its total scientific research input in 2015 to the level of 3.5% of its GDP and turning Singapore into the center of international scientific research and Asian innovation.

3.2.1.2 *America's organizational and individual research and development through government promotion*

Innovation in science and technology has been the main reason why the United States can maintain its leading position in the world. According to a report released by an organization of America's future of scientific innovation, at least half of America's economic growth has directly resulted from its scientific innovation over the past half a century or so. The United States has been inputting its utmost in scientific and technological innovation. In 2000, the R&D investment in the United States amounted to $264 billion, accounting for 45% of the world's total R&D investment. The following may explain why the United States has become the world's most successful country in scientific and technological innovation.

(a) The effective macro-level regulation and leading of the government

Due to the ideology of neo-liberalism and bi-partisan opposition in American politics, the federal government has been vigorously promoting technical innovation and commercialization of new technology in private enterprises, often through financial support. On the surface, the U.S. government does not seem to be closely associated with science and technology, and it is the enterprises and universities that shoulder the responsibility for scientific and technological innovation, which is certainly not the case. The U.S. government has formed a set of administration mechanisms for science and technology commensurate with its tripartite political system. Although no specific institution in the federal government has been set up for the organization, coordination and planning of national activities of science and technology, the administrative, legislative and judicial systems have been involved, to varying degrees, in the formulation of national policies for science and technology and the administration of science and technology. Through effective regulation and monitoring, the federal government promotes the continuous innovation in science and technology.

On November 17, 1944, President Roosevelt proposed to conduct researches concerning the application of the experiences of national scientific research and development in the Second World War to the peace times. On July 19, 1945, Vannevar Bush, director of the Office of Scientific Research and Development, submitted a report to the president—"Science – the Endless Frontier", which proposed that national policies for science be formulated, national science foundation be established, and the spirit of freedom in scientific exploration be guaranteed. The invention of the steam engine, motors, and aircraft mainly stemmed from individual efforts or efforts of enterprises. However, since the Second World War, the development of nuclear weapons and nuclear technology, the implementation of the Apollo moon landing project, the development of space technology and the birth and widespread use of the computer have mainly originated from the integration of strengthened macro-level regulation and guidance of government in combination with the innovative spirit of scientists and enterprises.

Among the three systems, the administrative system has been involved to the greatest extent. The most notable performance is the launch of key projects of science and technology that are carefully selected and organized by the federal government. The famous "Manhattan Project" for the development of atomic bombs during the Second World War, the Apollo moon landing project, the Star Wars Project, the long-term research on information technology and the National Nano-technological Initiative have all been masterpieces of the federal government. The federal government has recognized as its key areas for scientific and technological investment basic research that businesses have tended to overlook. The federal R&D input has been maintained at a fairly high level for years, far higher than those of other countries. The funds have been invested in federal laboratories and in well-known research universities, like Harvard University, Yale University and the University of Pennsylvania. Multinational companies may also apply to the federal government for research funds. In addition, the federal government has been actively guiding and encouraging enterprises to develop and apply high and new technology through high-tech products procurement.

The legislation is committed to guaranteeing the development of science and technology through its legislative power for national science and technology, the authority of allocating funds to large scientific research projects, and the examination and approval authority for scientific research funds of government departments. The science and technology committees of the U.S. House and Senate have the right to entrust the relevant scientific research departments to constitute "special advisory groups" for inquiry, evaluation, and authentication of research projects. In order to encourage technological innovation, the Congress has enacted a series of relevant laws and regulations, including the federal law of technological innovation, the law of technological diffusion, and the patent law, etc.

(b) Great importance being attached to scientific and technological personnel and their care to create favorable innovation environment

The United States offers substantial support and care to scientific and technological personnel. Academic staff in the Ivy League universities are the major forces of scientific and technological innovation. Many of them get an annual income of around $200 000, and some exceptional members may get $800 000 annually, more than their presidents. Such high income is enough for professors to live a decent and comfortable life so that they will concentrate on teaching and research without having to worry about livelihood. In addition, universities are under the governance of academics who have the right to make decisions concerning teaching and research. The system of tenured professors endows scientific and technological talents with a greater sense of professional security and greater audacity of achieving breakthroughs in scientific research, which is undoubtedly beneficial to the development of innovative thinking.

(c) The tolerance towards innovation and crisis consciousness

Innovation may bring risks, which means there are bound to be "losers" in scientific and technological undertakings. For those who have been long conducting serious research without any achievements, the government will not abandon them. Instead, they are treated with the greatest tolerance and care. For example, the federal government invests huge amount of funds in cancer research every year, though only slow progress is made so far. The government continues its strong and regular support rather than striking off appropriations from the budget simply because of its slow progress. The government will pay close and immediate attention and provide adequate support to any innovative ideas and proposal researchers put forward in the field of cancer research. All this satisfies the curiosity of scientists to the greatest extent possible and helps to nurture more innovative followers.

The United States rarely loses itself in its achievements and always has a sense of urgency and even crisis. On March 11, 1999, the U.S. Council on Competitiveness for non-profit organizations published a report titled "The Challenge to America's Prosperity", which points out that if America's current national policies and investment options remained as they are, it would lose its position as a leading innovative country. On January 27, 2000, President Bill Clinton made his final state of the union address in his term of office, which again stressed the importance of innovation in science and technology. He emphasized the importance of sketching a revolution in the United States for the twenty-first century from that day onwards so as to make it a new country and raised the strategy and policy for the development of information technology, biotechnology and nanotechnology.

(d) To promote scientific and technological innovation and achievements transformation – the innovative research programs of small businesses

The research and development of innovative and high technology has the high risk and challenging characteristics, especially at the initial stage of the project. Considering it is necessary to support science and technology innovation of many small businesses which have been acting as hotbeds for technological innovation, the government of the United States officially launched the innovative research program for small business (SBIR) in 1982, boosting private scientific and technological innovation by the government funding and the industrialization of scientific and technological achievements.

It is the responsibility for relevant ministries of the federal government to implement the SBIR program specifically, and each of them should offer 2.5% of the annual research and development expenditure to support innovative research of small businesses. 10 federal government departments participating the SBIR have offered $2 billion to the project so far. The Congress has instructed the Small Business Administration to take full charge of supervising SBIR in case of fragmented implementation and being incapable of realizing the integration of resources, which makes the management process more simple and orderly. The annual report of the S.B.A. is submitted to the Congress and it would evaluate the progress and effects of the SBIR project accordingly.

Every ministry undertakes public bidding at least once a year and the most urgent research tasks are included in the invitation for bid. The small businesses applying SBIR must meet the following conditions: independent and profit-seeking enterprises operated by American citizens, appointing their own employees as lead researchers, with no more than 500 employees for each of them. After receiving the project bidding documents, every ministry SBIR office would distribute them to the five most authoritative experts in their research fields to evaluate, and the evaluative criteria are listed as quality, innovation, technology content and market potential of every bidding enterprise.

The three stages of capital injection program would be implemented after the completion of the evaluation:

The first stage: the funding of $25,000 to $100,000, with the deadline for six months, aims to develop technological connotation and complete the feasible research mainly;

The second stage: the funding of $20,000 to the maximum of $750,000 in 2 years for every different ministry, which is eligible to the enterprises which have obtained the fund of the first stage;

The third stage: no more fund for the selected enterprises by the Small Business Administration and attaching most importance to risk investment and other private sources.

SBIR projects have played an irreplaceable role in the process of the transformation of scientific and technological achievements and development of science and technology in the United States. During the 20 years of implementing SBI program, 400,000 innovative research projects had been selected, 65,000 projects were funded and $13 billion were invested, which have made great contribution to the transformation of scientific and technological achievements. Among the 100 winners selected annually by the R&D magazine, about 25% of them were the enterprises previously and presently funded by SBIR program, which have strongly proved that the program had greatly promoted the scientific and technological innovation.

It is worth of learning that the SBIR program was based on market and the transformation of scientific and technological achievements, not for filling the blank of the science and technology to reward scientific and technological innovation, but for solving the practical problems in reality and transforming scientific and technological achievements into productivity. The SBIR program has provided a new channel of financing for the small businesses with potential for science and technology innovation, and promoted the large-scale transformation of scientific and technological achievements by the mode of driving private capital of science and technology by national R&D capital.

The experiences of managing SBIR program deserve to be used for reference. First of all, it is respectively managed by the SBIR office of each ministry, which has the most understanding of its own requirement for scientific and technological innovation, and could put forward the feasible research topic. Second, various ministries of the government have actively promoted innovation and achievements transformation of science and technology, which had improved the former condition of only being participated in by the science and technology department to promote the comprehensive development of science and technology. In the process of appraisement and selection of the SBIR program, the impersonality could be guaranteed as no economic interests are involved in the selection process by the evaluation experts who are top national experts and scholars.

To sum up, the U.S. government has promoted the foresighted leading in technology through a series of institutional, organizational and notional innovation in capital, talent and infrastructure and so on. It is just because of the appropriate policy of science and technology, abundant scientific research conditions and enormous human resources as well as state innovation system constructed by the unique innovative spirit that the United States has maintained the pioneering advantages of global science and technology in more than half a century.

3.2.2 The practices of government foresighted leading in technology in Shunde, China

The above discussion has illustrated the effect of government foresighted leading in technology on the state level. In fact, it is not only the national government that could apply the strategy of foresighted leading to technology innovation, but also the regional governments could play an important role in the foresighted leading in technology.

Since the reform and opening up, the electrical appliances industry of Shunde has experienced the economic development history from the imitation and manufacturing to creating, and becomes the largest production base of air conditioner, refrigerator, water heater, disinfection cupboard currently in China, as well as the world's largest supply base of electric fans, rice cookers and microwave ovens, reputed as the "kingdom of household appliances" and the "capita of home appliances". Household appliance industry has become the pillar industry of Shunde economy, with its output value accounting for more than 40% of the industrial output of Shunde, which has formed a complete industry cluster of modern household appliance industries.

These splendid achievements are closed associated with the positive and effective macroeconomic regulation and control of the Shunde government and foresighted-leading measures and reflect the foresighted-leading effect in technology for regional governments sufficiently.

Because the research and development involve great risk and enormous investment, the small and medium-sized enterprises are generally reluctant to conduct technology research and development spontaneously. In order to promote the upgrading of home appliance industry, the Shunde government adopted the pattern of cooperating with enterprises and scientific research institutions to forge the public service platform of home appliance industries and research and development platform through a series of system and organization innovation to solve the bottleneck of technology development and technology upgrading for small and medium-sized enterprises.

(a)   To build a perfect public service platform

Shunde government centered around consulting activities of academician of Chinese academy of engineering (Shunde), with the hi-tech industry incubator, the productivity promotion center, the information center, the chamber of home appliance, the patent association of Shunde as the main body, to integrate household electrical appliances industry such as the existing international exposition of home appliances of Shunde, raw materials of household electrical appliances, the spare parts procurement fair and other public service resources, and construct the public service system of home appliance industry by providing services such as consulting, training and guidance for the existing traditional home appliance enterprises to promote their technical progress, technology improvement, upgrading ad updating of products. Through the implementation of manufacturing informationalization and construction of "digital city" strategic projects, the management and service of the electrical appliances enterprise have been informationized and intelligentized, promoting industrial upgrading and optimization. The positive policy of talent introduction had been implemented to introduce the first-class domestic and foreign technology and management talents enhancing personnel training and management, to provide the guarantee of human resources for scientific and technological innovation and industry upgrading.

(b) The cooperation of science and technology between institutions and the Shunde city for building public research and development platform

The Shunde government had united Department of Science and Technology of Guangdong Province to establish the research institute of home appliances of south China in Shunde, relying on the two local colleges as well as the famous domestic and foreign universities and research institutes to jointly research and develop the core technology, core components, and generic technology of home appliance industries and provide the research and development services for home appliance enterprises. The research institute of home appliances of south China is a non-profit regional industrial technology innovation platform based on the home appliance industry, facing and serving the home appliance industries of south China, which is guided and supported by the government and market-oriented operation of enterprises to adopt its own research and development platform and braches of research institute of enterprises, colleges and universities and scientific research institutions. The institute integrates all resources for home appliance enterprises to provide services such as the technical research, technical development, technical training, technical consulting, detection, industrial standard setting, and etc. as well as for establishing the shared platform aggregating information, facilities and personnel, which had formed the public research and development facilitating agency to improve the abilities of technological research and development for electrical appliances manufacturing enterprises and related industries.

With the guarantee of the government investment, research institute could conduct the research and development of the core industrial technology which most enterprises are unwilling or unable to develop independently, through the integration of resources and inputting human resources, funds, and equipment to exploit the technologies of home appliances industries to improve the price of industrial products and the competitiveness of performances, getting rid of the passive situation of relying on foreign technology of home appliance for us. Moreover, it had also carried out the study on regional development strategy of home appliance industries and industrial policy research, to guide the enterprises to implement the macroscopic development strategy and goals.

Besides of the research institute of home appliances of south China, the government has promoted the establishment of various forms of industry – study-research cooperation entities including characteristic research and development center and intermediary service agencies, to promote the research and development of new and high technology and transformation of achievements tremendously.

(c) Using the experiences of Singapore industrial park for reference, making industrial park of home appliance, and promoting the upgrading of industrial clusters and industry

In the process of industrial development and transformation of Singapore, all kinds of industrial parks dominated by the Singapore government have played important roles in industry agglomeration, leading the industry upgrading of Singapore. The Shunde government has actively learned from international experiences, on the basis of the existing home appliances industry, forging the development park of household electrical appliance industry in Shunde to cultivate industrial cluster and stimulate the industrial upgrading.

The industrial park is located in the south of the city centre of the Shunde District in Foshan City, with an area of 40 square kilometres, which was listed in the national torch plan, and classified as five separate zones according to the current development trend of new home appliance industry: the zone of intelligent information appliances industry, the zone of energy-conservation appliances industry, the zone of environmental protection appliances industry, the zone of healthy home appliances industry and the zone of appliances industry in new material, which has formed a complete cluster of home appliance industry initially.

The Foshan government has established the leading and coordinating group of constructing household electrical appliance industry base in Shunde, consisting of the leading subgroup of Shunde to provide strong organizational guarantee for smoothly promoting the construction of the industry development park. In addition, the government also has invested a special fund of 50 million – 100 million yuan annually since 2004 for public construction of the base.

(d)   Adopting favorable and supportive policies to lead scientific and technological innovation

The Shunde government has adopted a series of preferential policies to lead scientific and technological innovation and promote industrial upgrading. It has been stipulated in the policies first that all enterprises in home appliance industry base could enjoy provincial, city and district preferential policies for high-tech enterprises; second that "the special funds of development of science and technology", " the special fund of industry-university-research" and "the special fund of manufacturing informatization" should be established by various levels of finance, to support the research and development of high-tech projects and achievements transformation in priority; third that the backbone technicians of enterprises should be rewarded regarding to the contribution; fourth that the special funds should be invested by various financial levels to establish business incubators and the information service platform to provide enterprises with information, technology, training and patent services; fifth that the center of the risk investment in new household appliances industry should be organized in 2005 to provide financing services to small and medium-sized enterprises.

The inherent development of an enterprise can be divided into five stages, including lay a solid foundation, creating brand, registering patents, setting standards and outputting of the brands. In order to lead the enterprises to conduct scientific and technological innovation and establish brands, the Shunde government has been guiding and support through financial funds. The annual fund of around billion yuan from various levels of finance of Shunde is rewarded only to the enterprises which have been rated as the national well-known trademarks and brands, or have acquired the patent (especially the patent for invention), or their standards have become industry standards, national standards, and even international standards. In 2008, the private capital of more than 22 billion yuan for independent innovation has been brought in the private enterprises by the government finance capital of 1 billion yuan, which had reached the growth rate of 47%; in 2009, the incurred private capital amounted to 30.8 billion yuan, with the growth rate of 39%; in 2010, the incurred private capital still exceeded 34.5 billion yuan.

Driven by all leading measures of the government, the science and technology innovative platform has been established basically in three levels of the districts, towns and enterprises of Shunde to support the science and technology innovation and industry upgrading objectively. By 2010, 18 provincial research and development centers of engineering technology, six municipal engineering centers, and 52 district-level engineering centers had been set up in Shunde, among which the high and new technology industry output value accounts for 42% of gross industrial output value. Shunde's high-tech industrial output value reached 63 billion yuan, with a year-on-year growth rate of 34% and the contribution rate of science and technology to the economy reaching 60.2%, which set up a unique example for county-level regions in China. By 2012, Shunde's high-tech industrial output value rose to 220 billion yuan, and its proportion in total industrial output increased from 38.6% in 2011 to 41%, with an increase of the number of high-tech industrial enterprises from 104 in 2008 to 220.

It is not only the government of Shunde but also the government of Foshan to plays the positive roles in the foresighted leading in technology. The Foshan government has launched bold innovation to cooperate fully with the Chinese Academy of Sciences. In July 2009, it concluded and signed "the co-building agreement of the Foshan industrial technology innovation and incubation center of the Chinese Academy of Sciences", which had adopted the "1 + N" mode of government guiding and market domination to build professional center and innovation platform covering areas such as energy, environmental protection, information technology, medicine, and etc. and fill the gaps of the innovation platform for those professional fields. The significant achievements have been made in the cooperation with only one and a half years by the project. Seven professional centers and eight innovation platforms had been established, with nearly 400 college cooperative projects, among which nearly 200 belong to the projects of strategic emerging industries, accounting for about 50% of the whole; the large-scale butt joint of scientific research institutes and enterprises had been held for more than 70 times, forming nearly 44 pilot-test products, realizing the industrialization of 12 projects, and driving the output value of nearly 9.1 billion yuan.

Moreover, the Foshan government invested 100 million yuan in 2010 to establish the "fund of science and technology incubation of Foshan", which has contributed no less than 20 million yuan to subsidize cooperative centers, platforms and projects in universities and the City of Foshan. The special fund devoted to constructing Guangdong's new highland from the Chinese Academy of Sciences was also tilted to help Foshan in such endeavours. Within only a year and a half, the Chinese Academy of Sciences and governments at both provincial and municipal levels jointly invested 112 million yuan in cooperative projects, and the Foshan government alone invested over 70 million yuan, which solicited nearly 1 billion yuan of enterprise and social investments. In 2012, 12 high-tech enterprises in Shunde received 7.75 million yuan from the State Innovation Fund, 7 received 1.6 million yuan from the Provincial Innovation Fund and 53 received altogether 10 million yuan from the District/County Innovation Fund.

3.3 The practices of organizational foresighted leading

The organizational foresighted leading refers to the innovative activities of organ-ization structure, organization form and organizational systems by the govern-ment, especially the regional government, and aims to improve the organizational foundation of economic and industrial development so as to promote the eco-nomic development and social progress. Generally speaking, the connotation and purpose of organizational innovation are institutional innovation and technologi-cal innovation in essence.

3.3.1 Japan's Trinitarian system of "government-manufacturer-university" for scientific research

After the Second World War, Japan had realized the economic recovery and growth and created the "Japanese miracle" carrying out national construction by exclusively relying on processing trade as the basic state policy. However, in the 1970 s, great changes had taken place in the world economic situation, which the needs of the development of Japanese economy could not be met by carrying out national construction by exclusively relying on processing trade. Consequently, Japan established the strategy of "developing a nation via science and technol-ogy" in the 1980s, and put it as a basic state policy to promote the development of Japanese economy in the new period.

After establishing the strategy of "developing a nation via science and tech-nology", it took only a decade or so for Japan to make obvious achievements in technology and become a veritable technology power, which had caught up with and surpassed Europe and the United States in technology. Japan's remarkable accomplishments in science and technology had much to do with its implement-ing the strategy of "developing a nation via science and technology" and its policy of "government-manufacturer-university" integrated scientific research system, which largely reflects the Japanese government's foresighted leading role.

As a late-developing country and a country with an economy that was catching up, Japan took the path of "technological introduction, assimilation and innova-tion" in the early phase. The cost of technical research and development had been saved and less detours had been spared through introducing the advanced tech-nology of developed countries largely. In addition, the Japanese adopted the eco-nomic policy of attaching to the United States after the Second World War to gain sufficient benefits in the international market, by virtue of the "umbrella" from the United States. In the entire boom after the war, Japan's manufacturing had not only expanded the U.S. market quickly but also unceasingly nibbled the world market share of U.S. manufacturers, realizing the export-led economic growth at a high speed. In 1968, Japan's GDP had become the second major economy secondary the United States.

After entering the 1970 s, with the change of the situation at home and abroad, two pillars of the policy of "carrying out national construction by exclusively relying on processing trade" – resource imports and exports encountered unprecedented difficulties.

First, the bottleneck of resources was encountered especially after the oil crisis broke out, which had completed the era of importing a large amount of the petroleum as cheap as plain boiled water in Japan. Up to this point, the Japanese high economic growth had been concluded, and the foundation of carrying out national construction by exclusively relying on processing trade began to shake.

Second, after the oil crisis, Western economy entered into the period of "stagflation", the exuberant global market demand tended to shrink. Meanwhile, the developed countries became more and more vigilant to the Japanese products to adopt trade protectionism and improve the protection of domestic industries and to reinforce the import restrictions against Japanese products.

Furthermore, the export businesses of Japanese companies also faced many dilemmas. Besides of the energy crisis, the subtle changes of economic relationship with the United States and the higher yen quotation had both impacted the export businesses of Japanese enterprises.

Therefore, the Japanese government began to seek a new outlet and attach great importance to technological innovation, and established the strategy of "developing a nation via science and technology" in the early 1980s.

In 1980, Japan's MITI proposed formally the strategic slogan "developing a nation via science and technology" in the "vision of MITI policies for the 1980s" and "developing a nation via science and technology" as the its objective of the struggle to conduct creative technology development with effective use of brain resources to improve the economic capability and economic strength, which was the only way to the development of Japan.

At that time, all kinds of scientific research institutions of Japan carried out scientific research activities autonomously based on their respective research funds, which lacked of cooperation among research institutions and had become the serious contradiction in the process of promoting the progress of science and technology.

In the 1980s, the development of science and technology increasingly tended to be more advanced, complicated, large-scaled and integrated, among which many major emerging problems in science and technology were difficult to conquer by a certain scientific research institution. In order to adapt to the new situation of new technology revolution, Japan's MITI industrial technology institute established the "seminar of the long-term plan for developing industrial technology" in 1977, which proposed a report titled "for new research and development" after four years of investigation.

This report proposes to establish and strengthen the consortium of officer (national research institutions), production research institutes of (private enterprises) and study (the scientific research institutions of universities). On October 1, 1980, Japan's ministries and agencies held a joint meeting to formally propose to establish a new cooperative system of scientific research of "the trinity of officer, production and study".

The scientific research system of "the trinity of officer, production and study" refers to the system centering on the scientific research task, funded by Japan science and technology department to sign with the researchers affiliated units the lease contract of personnel use and research facilities while retaining their original personnel relations in work units, and unite both existing national and foreign talents of public and private enterprises and university researchers in scientific research institutions to constitute joint research project research teams. After the completion of the research topic, the research team would be dissolved and the researchers go back to their original unit, and the research results, such as patents would be shared by the Japanese science and technology department, or the inventor's unit could also inherit the inventors" rights.

In the scientific research system of "the trinity of officer, production and study", the trinity gave full play to their advantages of science and technology by fostering strengths and circumventing weaknesses. Japan's national research institutions mainly undertake scientific research projects which are significant for national economy and people's livelihood and long time consuming as well as the risky and leading in tip, and are engaged in the study of applied research and development, and play a guiding role in the consortium; national universities, public universities and private universities delivery personnel for the national scientific research institutions and scientific research institutions of private enterprises, mainly engaging in fundamental research and providing basic scientific research as much as possible; Japan's private enterprises have the advantages of the human power (accounting for 57.3% of Japan's national research strength), financial resources (with scientific research funds input accounting for about 80% of the total input of the country), material and other advantages, thus are mainly engaged in R&D in the consortium. The role of scientific research system of Japanese government in "the trinity of officer, production and study" is to formulate policies and guidelines and at the same time, organize and coordinate with the relations among "officer, production and study". The Japanese government also supports private enterprises from the aspect of tax revenue and finance to carry out the scientific and technological research, promotes the transfer of technology both at home and abroad, protects and evaluates the invention of science and technology, as well as carries out the international academic exchange and cooperation, etc.

It has now become a new kind of strategic decisions in organizing the working of science and technology to establish "the trinity of officer, production and study" as the liquid scientific research system, which the Japanese government has adopted since the 1980s. In January 1981, the former Japanese Prime Minister Suzuki presented in his administrative speech "our country had been in the leading position in electronics, industrial robots and other technologies, and we must try our best in the universe sciences, life sciences and new material technology such as core technology in future. Based on this understanding, industrial circles, academia and the government should cooperate closely and concentrate all our strength to promote and create the science and technology of the new era to heighten the industrial structure supererogation and make national life better off as well as contributing to the development of the international community."

To achieve the new strategic target of scientific and technological development, the Japanese government not only developed the new policy of science and technology but also increased the input of the scientific research expenditure. In 1991, the total collaborative research spending of the affiliated national universities, the national research institutions and private enterprises had reached 4.51 billion yen, which had been increased 6.6 times of that of 1983. Meanwhile, the number of institutions of higher learning had been increased, cutting-edge universities and graduate schools of science and technology were founded to cultivate creative high-tech personnel. According to statistics, the total number of researchers in the natural sciences in Japan has been on the rise, with 172 000 in 1970, 302,000 in 1980, and 484,000 in 1990 (314,000 research staff on "corporate level", 36,300 researchers in government research institutions, 134,000 university researchers), with an annual increase of over 10,000 people, which exceeds that of other developed countries except for America. Out of 10,000 people, Japanese researchers account for the ratio of 45.3, which takes the first place in the world.

After the implement of scientific research system "the trinity of officer, production and study", remarkable results had been achieved only within more than ten years the strategy established. From 1981 to 1992, Japanese high-tech industries accounted for 31% of the manufacturing output value, an obvious rise of 17% from that in 1981; in the output value of high and new technological industries of all member countries in the OECD, the Japanese proportion had risen from 22% to 28% (Feng 1998). According to another statistic of "industrial white paper" in 1989, there were 36 kinds of high-tech products which Japan had forereached the United States out of 40 commercialized products.

To take the example of semiconductor chip production representing the high and new technology, according to the American government in the early 1989, it was estimated that its existing 14 production technologies of semiconductor chip out of 26 had fallen behind Japan. In 1988, Japan had accounted for 91% of the world market in production of 1M chips, compared to only 6% of the United States. In 1990, Japan had mass produced4M chips and pilot produced16M chips. Japan had mastered the production technology of 1,000M chips at that time, which was bemoaned for its inadequacy in the face of the cutting-edge high-tech by Western European countries and even the United States.

As mentioned in the article "The U.S. recedes its place to Japan and Western Europe in science and technology" carried on *Reference News* on August 16, 1989, 48% of 77,825 patents registered in the United States in 1988 belong to foreigners who are mostly Japanese (21%), Japanese companies had actively pushed aside U.S. companies in areas such as home appliances, cameras and automotive production. In terms of perfecting the internal combustion engine in 1987, 41% of patents in the United States belong to the Japanese, and only 30% belong to

Americans. Japan's great achievements in science and technology are obviously an outcome of its government's establishing dynamic scientific research systems of "government-manufacturer-university", which played a significant role.

Japanese ministries and agencies had different relevant provisions and practices of the liquid scientific research system of "the trinity of officer, production and study", but had all concentrated the scientific research personnel, material and financial resources as well as science and technology information of the trinity through the form of contracts to organize into temporary technological teams to tackle hard-nut problems to conduct cooperative research for some important research projects. In 1991, 1,139 collaborative research projects of the national universities of the MEXT, national research institutions and private businesses were implemented just in 1991, about 20 times of that in 1983, when the collaborative research system was just established.

In order to make the collaborative research projects of "the trinity of officer, production and study" implement more effectively, the related Japanese departments and experts analyzed and summarized various kinds of past research plans to set up a batch of collaborative research institutions to push the trinity of officer, production and study, which mainly included the JSPS, RIKEN, the institute of semiconductors, the collaborative research institute of electronic projects, the international research center of superconducting industrial technology, the research center of cutting-edge science and technology of the University of Tokyo, the technological development institutions of new generation of electronic computers and Kanagawa scientific and technological park, etc.

In 1981, Japanese science and technology agency and MITI had, respectively, founded "the creative propulsion system of technology", and "the research and development system of industrial base technologies in the next generation" and put them as the specific measures of the strategy of "developing a nation via science and technology". In 1986, the Japanese government formulated "the promotion law of research exchanges", and the following year the Japanese Congress passed the decision on "the basic principles of promoting the cooperation of the industry-university-research and applying the related systems of overseas study and exchanges"; in early 1992, the Japanese government had again revised the relevant research results of the clauses of "the promotion law of research exchanges". In addition, Japanese science and technology agency had formulated the collaborative cutting-edge research systems of the "trinity of officer, production and study" in 1986, 1988 and 1986 successively, as well as the inter-provincial fundamental research and regional flow systems etc.

The "cutting-edge research system" was designed to boost the systems of pilot fundamental research in the unknown areas, aiming to obtain the brand-new knowledge for becoming the foundation of technical revolution in the twenty-first century. The implementation of the system is based on the union of "officer, production and study", widely absorbing multidisciplinary research strength both at home and abroad, to conduct the basic research of long-term (up to maximum five years), flowing, internationalism and leading edge. The objectives of later two systems lie in breaking the departmental and regional boundaries to concentrate the research force of the "officer, production and study" and overseas, to give full play to the advantages of regions or departments to conduct the fundamental and pioneering research.

In recent years, Japan had selected scientific research task in major field of science and technology, to organize researchers of three aspects "officer, production and study" to break through the difficulties of science and technology, which had promoted the progress of science and technology and the development of the Japanese economy, enhancing the Japanese national power. This had not only embodied the foresighted leading of the Japanese government on the technology, but also the important foresighted leading in organization.

3.3.2 *The credit guarantee of small and medium-sized enterprise in Shunde, China*

Whether in the Western developed countries or China, small and medium-sized enterprises are important sources of social innovation. However, it is very difficult for them to obtain loans of financial institutions as they lack strong economic foundation; whether in the Western developed countries or in China, the financing problem of small and medium-sized enterprises seems to be very prominent, particularly in China.

Faced with this problem, the government of Shunde creatively established in 2001 the credit guarantee fund for small and medium-sized enterprises, in the light of advanced international experiences and the actual development of Shunde's small and medium-sized enterprises, so as to assist in their growth. The Shunde government arranged the special fund of 50 million yuan, joining hands with professional guarantee institutions and commercial banks to provide guaranteed loan for the growth-type small and medium-sized enterprises which were unable to obtain loans from the bank due to lack of enough collateral capital.

3.3.2.1 *Specific practices*

The credit guarantee fund for small and medium-sized enterprises was established in 2006 by the fiscal appropriation of the district of Shunde, with the total of 50 million yuan and the an expiration period of five years, which started from July 1, 2006, and ended on June 30, 2011. The guarantee fund was put in place in line with the principle of "governments' guidance, marketized operation and risk-sharing", entrusting the professional operation of guarantee institutions and banks and undertaking the risk of loan losses with clients in proportion. According to leveraged amplification effect of guaranteed loans, guarantee funds could provide the total loan commitment of 500 million yuan for small and medium-sized enterprises in Shunde District. The cooperative guarantee institutions of guarantee funds and cooperative banks preferentially conduct the approval process of guaranteed loan for the eligible small and medium-sized enterprises in favorable conditions. The operation of guarantee funds was supervised by the supervision and management committee of credit guarantee fund for small and medium-sized enterprises in Shunde, and its member units include the government office, bureau of trade and economic cooperation, bureau of finance, auditing bureau and the people's bank of China. In order to meet the financing demands of more small and medium-sized enterprises, the Shunde government added 5 million yuan respectively in 2009 and 2010 to increase the total fund to 150 million yuan and cover the planned credit loan of 2 billion yuan and extend the expiration from June 30, 2011, to 2013.

3.3.2.2 Features of mechanism

(1) The government grasped the use of funds with the banks and guarantee institutions participating in the operation. The credit guarantee fund of small and medium-sized enterprises in Shunde was established by the financial allocation of the government, in which the funds were deposited in the cooperative bank as the cash deposit of guaranteed loans of the enterprises and the risk loss reserve funds. When the loan transaction guaranteed by funds occurs, 10% of the loan value from the special accounts of the funds would be served as the cash deposit which should be returned after returning the loan.

(2) The government policies guide the direction of use of guarantee funds. The small and medium-sized enterprises which have acquired guarantee funding loans must comply with the government's industry-oriented policy and apply to the relevant government departments. Eligible enterprises would be brought into the support list of the guarantee fund to be recommended to cooperative guarantee institutions and cooperative banks, which would examine and approve corporate loans within the scope of the recommended list and issue loans to those approved enterprises.

(3) The financing cost reduction of small and medium-sized enterprises. For those enterprises obtaining the loans of guarantee funds, no higher than 2% of the guarantee fees would be charged by the guarantee institutions of cooperative funds, and cooperative banks would issue loans referring to the simultaneous benchmark interest rate of the people's bank of China, with the rising range of interest rates generally no higher than 10%. The guarantee funds advance the bank cash deposits for enterprises, 10% of the loan value, and the government introduced the mating "The administrative methods of credit guaranteed loans with discounted interests for small and medium-sized enterprises in Shunde" meanwhile, rendering the subsidies 20% of the interest rates.

(4) Risk sharing. Guarantee funds undertake 30% of project risk loss of guaranteed loan projects of credit guarantee funds for small and medium-sized enterprises, compensating for the risk loss of the cooperative guaranteed institution, which have initially formed the risk-sharing mechanism between governments and the credit guaranteed institutions to enhance the guaranteed capacities of the guarantees institutions.

3.3.2.3 Implementation effects

Although the government's total input into the fund amounted to 150 million yuan, the leveraged amplification effect of guaranteed loans had brought into full play by virtue of the government's credit, which enabled 2 billion yuan of loans to be granted to small and medium-sized enterprises, about 14 times of the original amount, and helped small and medium-sized enterprises out of their immediate financial difficulties. Moreover, due to the introduction of government credit, the financing cost of the small and medium-sized enterprises has been reduced greatly to promote the development of small and medium-sized enterprises.

Except for solving the problem of corporate financing, the effective operation of the guarantee fund also contributed to the scientific administration and regulated development of small and medium-sized enterprises in Shunde. Many small and medium-sized enterprises of Shunde developed rapidly, but they lacked proper corporate governance and standardized financial management procedures and systems, which caused commercial banks to balk at granting loans. Financing problems eventually hindered their growth. Since the guarantee funds came into operation, the functional departments of governments had united banks and guarantee companies to interview enterprises applying for guaranteed loans, assist them in standardizing the financial control system and guide enterprises in their gradual establishment of modern enterprise systems so as to win approval of commercial banks and prompt their eventual growth.

The small and medium-sized enterprises supported by the credit guarantee fund must be those listed as the priority industries of Shunde characterized by high growth. The flow of guarantee funds was directed by the government to lead bank capital to invest in small and medium-sized enterprises conforming to the industrial policies of Shunde and to facilitate their fast growth, which played their role in accelerating the upgrading of industrial structure of Shunde.

According to the statistics, by September 30, 2011, the guarantee fund in Shunde had accumulated to an actual amount of 4.208 billion yuan, with 1.901 billion of guaranteed residues. The 480 enterprises benefited from the guarantee fund by 1.66 million yuan of interest subsidies for enterprises and over 10 million from guarantee organizations. Shunde's success promoted the development of credit guarantee funds for small and medium-sized enterprises in other parts of Foshan as well. By the end of 2012, the credit guarantee fund contributed by financial departments of various districts in Foshan for small and medium-sized enterprises had totaled to 410 million yuan (30 million yuan from Zencheng District, 180 million from Nanhai District, 150 million from Shunde, 30 million from Gaoming District and 20 million from Sanshui District), which provided a total guarantee fund of 17.96 billion yuan to 4,746 small and medium-sized enterprises in Foshan, covering industry, agriculture, commerce and trade, science and technology, etc.

It is worth mentioning that in the operation of the guarantee funds, the government of Foshan did not adopt the traditional contracted practices of the governments, but introduced the market mechanism sufficiently in accordance with the principle of "government guidance, marketized operation and risk-sharing", to entrust the professional operation of guarantee institutions and banks financed by the fiscal appropriation of each district and assume the risk of loan losses in proportion with clients. The practices of respecting and conforming to the market rules have optimized allocation of resources to a large extent and played the true function of the foresighted leading.

3.4 The practice of notional foresighted leading

Notional foresighted leading refers to the prospective rational analysis of and theoretical thinking, in the course of exercising authorities and power, on constantly emerging situations and problems, the new revelation and foresight of economic and social phenomena and the new rational sublimation of historical and practical experiences so as to guide innovation and advancement in economic systems and institutional structuring. In the new phase of economic development, only by continuously transforming and upgrading government notions, such as notions of civilian community, notions of restrained government, notions of open government, notions of government efficiency, can government innovate administrative systems, behavior, methodology and technology and provide right value guidance and boundless innovative incentives.

The government's governing concepts can be understood as the guiding ideology for administration, the main part of which is its value orientation. Proper government conduct results from right concepts and ideology. Government will formulate foresighted administrative concepts and will be able to guide the innovation and development of economic systems and their organizational forms so as to exercise notional foresighted leading if government can promote new rational sublimation of historical and practical experiences. The significant progress that has been made since China's reform and opening up shows that significant innovations of governing concepts and ideology often predate major institutional economic reforms, which means that institutional foresighted leading has often been driven and enhanced by innovations in leading concepts and ideology.

3.4.1 The notion of "practice is the sole criterion for testing the truth" and China's reform and opening up

China's reform and opening up was germinated from the Third Plenary Session of the Eleventh CPC Central Committee held on December 18, 1978. That plenary session discontinued the slogans and theories of "taking class struggle as the key link" in a timely and resolute manner and transferred the focal points and attention of CPC work to socialist modernization and the implementation of reform and opening up, signifying an end to "the era of class struggle" that continued for several decades. The session also determined the future work guidelines: "Emancipating Our Minds, Working Our Brains, Seeking Truth from Facts, and Looking Forward with Monolithic Solidarity". It fundamentally broke the long-term ideological shackles of "leftism" and ushered in a new and vigorously constructive age of practicality and realism. Subsequent to that session, the household contract responsibility system, the special economic zones and the policies of introducing foreign capital were put into operation in close succession. All that symbolized the official ring of China's reform bell.

In actual fact, debates concerning ideological innovation had started well before the Chinese government made the historic decision to conduct institutional reform. Ideological innovation laid a theoretical basis for the implementation of China's reform and opening up policy and cleared away ideological obstructions, which was ideological foresighted leading in every sense. Before the Third Plenary Session, China had been for long following the thought of "two whatever's". Deng Xiaoping challenged this thought from the practical perspective of China's economic and social reality. On May 11, 1978, an article by "special commentator" was published under the title of "The Practice Is Sole Criterion for Verifying Truth" in the *Guangming Daily*. On the same day, the Xinhua News Agency also released the article. The following day, the *People's Daily* and the *People's Liberation Army Daily* printed it. That article caused a great stir and serious debates and triggered off nationwide discussions concerning the issue of criteria for truth verification. It made possible the emancipation of minds and the opening up of the new historic period of reform and opening up in China.

The greatest ideological shackle for the Chinese community was the so-called two whatever's. The discussion of criteria for truth verification was directed at the "two whatever's" and enlightened the general Chinese public that the judging criterion for truth is practice rather than the "two whatever's". This ideological liberation movement prepared China for its new period of reform and opening up. As Deng Xiaoping once commented, the significance of debating whether "the practice is the sole criterion for verifying the truth" could never be belittled, and it had huge implications. That debate turned out to be a major breakthrough in the subsequent reform and opening up, and the proposition of "the practice is the sole criterion for verifying the truth" became the loudest and most frequently quoted philosophical slogan since the launch of reform and opening up.

It followed from that philosophical proposition that class struggle could no longer be reckoned as the key link and should be discontinued, as it would lead to enlarged gaps between China and developed countries in economy and in science and technology. That was why the Third Plenary Session of the Eleventh CPC Committee decided to abolish the doctrine of "taking class struggle as the key link", shifted the focus of party work to socialist modernization and economic construction, and made the great decision of reform and opening up to the outside world. Practice shows that China's modernization would be on the right track that conformed to objective economic laws only by reforming traditional management systems that constrained the enthusiasm and initiative of the masses in implementing reform and opening up and introducing foreign capital, advanced technology and management experiences.

Largely due to that great debate regarding criteria for truth verification, Deng Xiaoping's ensuing speech of "Emancipating Our Minds, Seeking Truth from Facts, and Looking Forward with Monolithic Solidarity" made at the central work conference on December 13, 1978, received wide recognition and positive responses, and the subsequent Third Plenary Session could smoothly shift the focus of national work to economic construction and reform and opening up. All that became possible owing to notional foresighted leading.

3.4.2 The notion of "development is an unyielding principle" and China's establishment of market economic system

It was proposed in 1992 that China establish the goal of socialist market economic system, start to build modern enterprise system and market economic system and allocate resources on the basis of market. A series of reforms were put into effect to bring China's economy out of its previous downturn and back into an accelerated development.

Since reform and opening up in 1978, the principal axis of China's development shifted to economic development, but new economic phenomena kept popping up, and people tended to assess and criticize them by ideological standards. In case of macroeconomic volatility, the voices of criticism and accusation would come up and develop into the largest ideological barrier possible to the sustained economic growth in China. Even before proposing the establishment of socialist market economic system, there had been a great deal of wavering and argument regarding the issue of "socialism" and "capitalism" in China. Ideological confusion caused the standstill of reform and opening up, and coupled with unfavorable external factors from the former Soviet Union and Eastern Europe, China's national economic development experienced a huge landslide, with only 4.1% and 3.8% of GDP growth rate in 1989 and 1990, respectively, which was the lowest point since reform and opening up.

It was against this background that Deng Xiaoping made a down-south inspection between January 18, 1992, and February 23 from Wuchang to Shenzhen, Zhuhai, Shanghai and other places and made a series of important talks that unequivocally clarified his famous doctrine of "development is an unyielding principle". As Deng Xiaoping pointed out, "Our reform and opening up cannot make great strides. The root cause is the fear that our economy contains too much of capitalism and is taking the capitalist road. The crux of the issue is whether our economy is "socialist" or "capitalist". The standard for such judgment is to see whether it is favorable to the development of socialist productive forces, whether it is conducive to enhancing the overall strength of socialist countries, and whether it is beneficial to improving people's livelihood." During his visit to The Pearl River Refrigerator Factory (currently Shunde Kelon Electrical Holdings Co. Ltd.), he said joyfully, "Nations are bound to develop, poor development would incur bullies, development is an unyielding principle," when he learned that the production volume of that small factory, which was originally only a township business, had increased 16 times in seven years and ranked first in China in terms of refrigerator manufacturing, with its products being exported to southeast Asia.

"Development is an unyielding principle", "Three Favorables" and other important ideas had broken through the long-term ideological forbidden zones for people, removed the difficult problems in reform that kept puzzling the Chinese community for years and indicated the path for another round of emancipation of thoughts. After Deng Xiaoping's down-south inspection talks, China changed the previous proposition of establishing planned commodity economy to an official proclamation of establishing and developing the socialist market economy, which raised a new round of upsurge of reform. It is no exaggeration that Deng Xiaoping's ideas of "Development is an unyielding principle" and "Three Favorables" are important ideological innovations in China, which had pivotally promoted China's economic reform and social progress in the 1990s, and are another manifestation of notional foresighted leading on the part of the Chinese government.

3.4.3 The concept of "service-oriented government" and the reform of administrative systems

In March 2005, the former Premier Wen Jiabao clearly proposed the requirement of service-oriented government in his government work report, which was another innovation of government administrative ideology. In the phase of taking economic construction as the central task of government, government was omnipotent and play a multi-fold role of producers, supervisors and regulators, and its function of public service for the society and the public was desalted.

With the development of market economy, especially the strategic adjustment of the layout of state-owned economy and the reform of state-owned property management systems, the government function of public administration was gradually identified from the function of contributors of national assets, and the aliasing of the role of government and that of state-owned enterprises in market was diminished. The development of non-public economy forced government to transform its mode of economic management. The establishment of modern property right system also changed the situation of non-identification between government administration and business management, between government and social communities and between government role and social affairs. However, government of different levels still adopted administrative means for economic activities and social affairs, playing the roles of producers and supervisors, which led to the non-differentiation of government and businesses and government role and social affairs, and the serious distortion of the fundamental role of market in resources allocation.

The perfection of market economy requires government to relegate economic activities of microscopic entities to market regulation. Under market economy, the government is endowed with a series of responsibilities, including remedying market failures, offsetting market defects, providing the society with public products and services that market is unable to supply in an effective way, formulating fair rules of market and rules of supervision, creating favorable development environment, establishing good public service systems and concentrating government function on macro-control, market supervision, public administration and public services. It has been proven by the facts that governments in some regions, under the guidance of this notion, started their efforts in reforming administrative systems and creating service-oriented government and achieved good effects.

On September 16, 2009, Shunde District, Foshan officially launched the restructuring of administrative system reform, which merged the original 41 party and government institutions into 16 and streamlined the administrative range by nearly two-thirds, turning Shunde into the most compact county in terms of institutionalization in China's party and government organizations. The intensity of institutional reform and innovation shocked the whole nation. It has been four years since the restructuring reform that has gained commendable effects. It has turned out to be of great significance to the scientific transformation of economic and social development in Guangdong and even in China, the institutional reform of county-level government and to the construction of public service government.

3.4.3.1 Reform and functional overlapping and service awareness

Shunde has established the distinct inter-departmental administrative system after the reform and has formed the work pattern that integrates and coordinates planning, economy, construction, culture, guarantee and supervision. This system and pattern have solved the previous problems of department redundancy, functional overlapping, endless haggling that resulted from the system of small departments. The provincial and municipal vertical administrative departments ranging from industry and commerce to taxation, quality controlling, drug supervision, public security, land, planning and social security have all been incorporated into the scope of institutional integration to make government functions more complete, which is conducive to removing the existing administrative barriers between higher and lower levels and between different departments and regions so as to provide "seamless" public services for enterprises and the general public.

3.4.3.2 Reform and government administrative efficiency

Reform has considerably increased decision-making efficiency through the execution of decisions at one go by 16 departments, because it has shortened administrative chains and reduced the number of administrative levels. For example, the purchase of H1N1 flu vaccine would take at least two weeks before the reform as the purchasing application would have to go through hierarchical levels of government to solicit instructional approval, and now three days suffice to complete all the formalities after the reform. The inter-departmental restructuring reform has greatly strengthened the executive force of government departments, solved the problem of diverse administration and "ball-kicking" between departments and made application approval easier for enterprises and citizens. Take pig slaughtering for another example. Previously, the procedures would have to go through departments of agriculture, public health, economy and trade, industry and commerce, etc. and now all the procedures can be handled in a single department —— Market Safety Supervision Bureau and at one go. It is obvious that the reform has effectively improved the administrative efficiency of government and reduced administrative costs.

3.4.3.3 Reform and administrative responsibilities

Previously, the problem of too many departments led to diversified administrative functions and policy making and ambiguous responsibilities, which went against the implementation of the accountability system. Under the present administrative system, responsibility goes with power, and the same thing can be handled in one single department. In the above-mentioned case, if some problem occurs with pork, the Market Safety Supervision Bureau will have to shoulder direct responsibilities. All this has reinforced the leadership responsibility system and helped to put the administrative accountability system into actual operation and to build up responsible government.

Shunde's inter-departmental reform has demonstrated exemplar effects of "first trial and first move". During his inspection of Shunde on October 16, 2009, Wang Yang, vice premier of the State Council and the former party secretary of Guangdong Provincial Committee of CPC, said, "Shunde has the strongest capability of cracking nuts in social and economic development and exercised the most extensive influence upon scientific development". He reiterated, "The inter-departmental administrative restructuring in Shunde is representative of county-level cities, while that in Shenzhen larger cities. Their reforms will have provincial and national implications if they eventually succeed."

Facts have proved that Shunde's bold and groundbreaking explorations have gained beneficial effects in promoting administrative system reform at the county level in Guangdong and even in China, in enhancing scientific development and in building up service-oriented governments.

4   The conditions for bringing government foresighted leading into full play

The GFL theory has been adopted to explain the causes of economic development in China and other regions of the world. Then what conditions are necessary for government to perform foresighted leading? This chapter addresses this question.

The prerequisite for government to perform foresighted leading is the creation of perfect market mechanisms and legal environment. Market economy is not only the foundation for government to perform foresighted leading but the foundation and driving force for government to better allocate resources. Second, government must be endowed with economic authorities and competitive forces. In terms of global economy favorable environment must be created for development and competition, and in terms of national economy, regions or cities must be encouraged to conduct orderly competition so as to promote development. Third, information disclosure must be in place so as to consolidate the public trust in government and guard against corruption. Finally, excellent selective mechanisms must be created to select personnel of high caliber and put them into government administration.

4.1   Good market mechanism and legal environment and government foresighted leading

It must be emphasized that the foundation of market economy is prerequisite to GFL. Without it, GFL will make no sense, and GFL must resort to market mechanisms, market measures and forces and eventually create a better market. Market economy is legal economy. Legal environment is not only the guarantee of GFL but also the goal that government must strive to achieve in the course of foresighted leading.

4.1.1   The degree of marketization and the effects of government foresighted leading

4.1.1.1   The establishment and amelioration of market mechanism and government foresighted leading

Take China for example. Since the reform and opening up in 1978, China has been transforming from its planned economy to market economy and its focus has been on the establishment of market as the sole allocator of resources. Three phases can be identified for this process: between 1978 and 1991 – the transition from planned economy to market economy, between 1992 and 1997 – the initial establishment of market economy, and from 1998 onwards – the development of market economy and the completion of China's entry into WTO. It becomes obvious from the changes in these three phases that GFL gets gradually strengthened with the establishment and amelioration of market mechanisms. In the initial stage of market economy, GFL is mainly manifested in changes of notions, systems and organizations and gets shifted to institutional and technological innovation when market economic system has taken shape.

(a)   Between 1978 and 1991 – the transition from planned economy to market economy

Between the founding of the People's Republic of China in 1949 and 1978, China practiced planned economy, a highly centralized economic system. All social resources were allocated according to unified national planning. Market was basically taken out of economic activities. The function of the central government was boundlessly expanded to replace almost all the economic policy making and almost everything was included within its power, under which case local government became the transfer point that performed the only function of passing information from the central government down to grass-root units, and businesses became production units of government. Production, supply, marketing, human resources, resources and all that were related to production must be done according to government policies. Government went even so far as to take charge of employment and daily consumption. The basic components of market played no part and did not seem to exist. The central government was responsible for investment, pricing, taxation, legislation and all other administrative instruments. Regional government could by no means enhance the efficiency of resource allocation through organization, systems and technological innovation or play its part in economic guidance, regulation and predictive warning. Under such an economic system there is no room for government, especially regional government, to exercise foresighted leading.

After 1978, China shifted its focus from political movement to economic construction and introduced commodity economic system. The central government delegated part of its authority to regional government. The land contract system implemented in the countryside greatly increased farmers' production enthusiasm and invigorated rural economy. Business production was also liberalized from government plans, which considerably promoted the enthusiasm and initiatives of workers. Meanwhile, the central government took gradual steps to delegate the power of collecting and expending fiscal revenues so that local government assumed a certain degree of administrative independence and responsibility. All this contributed to local government becoming the main body that enjoyed some autonomy in conducting economic activities. What is particularly noteworthy in this period of focal shift is that in order to gain the advantage of prior development and secure a good place in competition, local government of all levels were encouraged to carry out incentive innovations in systems and policies for the purpose of regulating economic activities on all levels in the region.

The Chinese economy was chiefly characterized by government planning prior to 1992, but the planned transition towards commodity economy took place between 1978 and 1991. Whether judging from the ability and knowledge of government administrators or from the means of government's allocating resources, central planning still typically featured the Chinese economy. As blindness was inevitable in macroeconomic regulation, there were great ups and downs in economic development.

To address the problem of economic overheating around 1979, the central government took a series of regulative measures, tightened investment and consumption and decreased the rate of economic growth from 11.7% in 1978 to 5.2% in 1981, thus causing the "great ups and downs" of economic development. This feature became even more apparent between 1985 and 1990s. Close to the end of 1984, the rate of economic growth jumped to 15.2% owing to the government's excessive supply of currency, the excessive supply of bank credit, and other factors. Consequently, the central government implemented the "double-contraction" policy of fiscal tightening and reduction of currency supply and exercised macro-level regulation with credit balancing and inflation reduction as its main objectives. The economic overheating was diminished to certain extent, but the problems such as economic imbalance and strong price increasing still persisted.

From 1986, the central government tried to improve macro-level regulation and adopted the "soft landing" strategy to solve the problem of aggregate demand surpassing aggregate supply. Between 1986 and 1988, the central government adopted the policy of "double relaxation", which led to the failure of "soft landing" in 1986 and the more rapid increase of aggregate demand and eventually strengthened the contradiction between aggregate demand and aggregate supply. The rate of economic growth reached 11.6% and 11.3% in the respective years of 1987 and 1988. In 1988, CPI got to the new height of 18.5%. The excessive increase of currency supply, bank credit, and investment of fixed assets and the expansion of both aggregate demand and aggregate supply were responsible for the economic overheating.

In the fourth quarter of 1988, the central government decided to implement the macro-level regulative policy of "forced hard landing", took the administrative measure of "improving economic environment and readjusting economic order", tightened fiscal expenditures and bank credit, and exercised overall strong tightening of investment and consumption, which led to the "economic overcooling". By 1990, the rate of economic growth dropped to 3.8%, resulting in large amount of overstock products, the poor cash flow and increased unemployment.

Over this period, a new type of financial system was taking shape, with the central bank as its main body, supplemented by various commercial banks and financial institutions. Financial instruments, such as commercial papers, securities and business bonds, came into use. The measures of macro-level regulation began to be diversified. The central bank set up and consolidated the system of deposit reserves. Indirect regulatory measures, such as interest rate, currency exchange and rediscount rate, were also put into operation. However, owing to the unreliability of economic foundations, macro-level regulation in this period was still mainly exercised by administrative means, and the effect of GFL was offset to a great extent, as government did not understand the basic rules of market economy and could not act accordingly.

(a) Between 1992 and 1997 – the initial establishment of market economy

Since Deng Xiaoping delivered his talks during his inspection to South China in 1992 and the Fourteenth National Congress of the Communist Party of China, tremendous changes have taken place in the ideology of the Chinese people and the development of China's economy. The market economic system has been set in place, and macro-level regulation, in the sense of market economy, gradually appeared on the historical scene.

From 1992 to the first half of 1993, the Chinese economy became overheated as a result of overexpansion of both investment and consumption demands and the surpassing of aggregate demand over aggregate supply. The rate of economic growth in 1992 got to 14.2%, and the national commodity retail price index reached 13.2% in 1993 and 21.7% in 1994, which was a clear indication of serious inflation. The central government learned the lesson of "indecisive action and ineffective implementation" in previous regulations and responded with resolution to this inflation.

In June 1993, the central government implemented contractual macro-level regulation, which focused on readjusting financial order and considered it a primary task to put inflation under control. This macro-level regulation took various administrative means to overcome the chaotic financial order in the initial stage, but in the late stage more financial means were employed, such as the tightened control of currency supply, interest rate, tightened fiscal policies, and reforms in financial and taxation systems, to achieve the goal of putting aggregate demand under control. Although measures were taken to tighten controls over investment and consumption, the strategy of "moderate control" was adopted, which lowered the growth rate of GDP from 14.2% in 1992 to 8.8% in 1997 and the increase rate of CPI from 24.1% in 1994 to 2.8% in 1997, which showed a successful "soft landing" of the Chinese economy.

It is apparent from the national level that the macro-level regulation in this period changed the previous practices of purely relying on administrative means. Its objective was clear, and its regulative measures were gradually ameliorated and perfected. Moreover, not only were economic and legal measures were adopted, but necessary administrative means as well, which displayed obvious characteristics of rational intervention.

The situation in Guangdong Province, China shows that the more developed economically, the more obvious the separation of government from business. For instance, during that time, a number of township governments in the Pearl River Delta region set up economic development corporations with the status of a legal entity to represent the ownership of township assets. Township governments managed the corporations chiefly from three aspects — the appointment and employment of the corporation manager, the examination of annual plans, and the rate of profit to be handed over to township governments, and the remaining power all lay within the corporation.

The corporation had many branches and affiliations. The interest relations between the corporation and its branches or affiliations were clarified through the commonly practiced "director/manager responsible system" and "system of profit contract and responsibility". The corporation could not transfer the assets or interest of its branches or affiliations. The separation of ownership and managerial authority in today's enterprises was taking shape. In subsequent years, a great number of township enterprises, influenced and led by businesses in Shunde, underwent property rights reforms, which brought forth modern enterprise system, characterized by the withdrawal of state-owned enterprises and the appearance of privately owned enterprises, which turned, by and large, township enterprises into large-scale modern businesses and further emancipated productive forces.

The establishment of these systems and the structuring of organizations and institutions gave strong impetus to Guangdong's economic development and guaranteed rapid and sustainable growth.

(b) From 1998 onwards – the development of market economy and the completion of China's entry into WTO

Owing to the impacts of the Asian financial crisis, China was confronted with the first deflation from the time of its implementation of reform and opening up in 1978, as its economy began to slow down and prices began to drop. In order to offset the effects of deflation the central government conducted macro-level regulation by means of expansionary fiscal policies and moderate monetary policies, coupled with necessary administrative measures. That regulation lasted until 2002, which pushed the growth rate of GDP from 7.8% in 1998 up to 9.1% in 2002 and propelled a new cycle of China's economic growth.

In the second half of 2003, there was overheated investment in some industries. The central government took the actual situation into serious consideration, identified and differentiated between lines of industry, and laid down the guidelines of "being resolute and decisive, moderate at good timing, differentiation and effectiveness" for macro-level regulation with a view to preventing "great ups" of economic development and relaxing pressures of price increase. The economic policy that integrated promoting and controlling regarding different lines of industry gradually took effect.

In 2004, the central government increased the intensity of macro-level regulation. The regulative measures were put into immediate and effective operation. The overheated investment and the tendency towards blind expansion were under control, and China's economy entered into a new period of high growth and low inflation. China's economy was going at moderate rates in the following years, but there still persisted the problems of high pressure of fixed capital investment and inflation, the overheated real estate investment, and macroeconomic restructuring, and regional problems. In order to offset their negative effects the central government adopted a combination of regulative measures that enabled China's economy to develop at a relatively high rate within moderate limits.

In order to deal with partial overheating that started in 2006, macro-level regulation in 2007 became moderately tightened in terms of monetary policies, and only micro-level regulation was implemented, which turned out to be effective in preventing economic growth turning from somewhat fast to overheated and prices from structural increase to inflation. In 2008, America's sub-prime crisis put China's economy under low-rate development and under risks of deflation. Under these circumstances, the central government implemented expansionary fiscal and monetary policies, which curbed the downturn of China's economic development.

Over this period, Chinese government's regulative policies displayed striking features of being predictive, clear aim and flexibility, with right manipulation of direction, rhyme and strength of macro-level regulation coupled with various regulative measures and means. In the meantime, great transformation also took place in ways that China's local government-led economic development, and there appeared in close succession new government administrative notions, such as operating cities, service-type government, and so on.

Before 1992, local government in China was in direct charge of business management and set limits for the development of private enterprises. After 2000, local government released its hold upon the power of setting up enterprises. Instead it began to strongly encourage businessmen to set up their own enterprises with policy incentives. Its focus of power was laid on the control of regional factors of production, i.e. those factors pf production that are needed for making private or public products in a region but cannot be transferred to other regions, such as land, supply facilities for water and electricity, roads, ports, investment environment, etc.

Around 1995, local government-initiated reforms of state-owned enterprises and the privatization of enterprises. Instead of managing family businesses one by one, it began to get them unified and administer the region as one big enterprise. One of the most important motivations for this was that domestic market liberalization and the intensification of market competition resulted in local government propelling the privatization of public businesses, which originated from the central government propelling market reform (Zhang Weiyin, Li Shuhe, 1998).

Local government in China diminished their control over enterprises, but some scholars believe that their transfer of power from the control of enterprises to the development of land and their administration of the region as one enterprise were adverse to market reform. Some even thought that apart from land planning, environment protection, construction of soft environment for investment and some others, which should be under government administration, all the rest of those items that were still in the charge of local government should be open to the public. For example, the supply and development of land on the primary market, the construction and management of industrial zones and so on should be generally open to public operation. However, these were still under the control of local government.

There is some justification for the above arguments, but they fail to explain the reasons that local government behaved in such ways and whether such government behavior was conducive to economic development. These questions are to be addressed in Chapter 5. What needs to be mentioned here is that over that period, active efforts were also made on the part of local government in some regions to reform administrative systems and transform from omnipotent government to service-type government.

The administrative restructuring reform in Shenzhen and Shunde, for example, reduced the number of government departments and cross-department functions and enhanced government service. That reform considerably increased the administrative efficiency, reduced administrative costs, clarified leadership responsibilities, and landed government administration on solid ground. It is of great illuminating significance to the scientific transformation of socio-economic development in Guangdong and the rest of China, the further reform of government administrative systems and the build-up of service-type government.

4.1.1.2 Better marketization and government foresighted leading

As discussed previously, why has Malaysia, which enjoys the same geographical location as Singapore and more superior natural resources than it, not achieved similar economic miracle? Why does there exist imbalance between regions though they are all involved in reforms and opening up in China? Why have some regions become so outstanding in comparison with some others though they have similar geographical locations and natural resources?

It must be admitted that one region's economic development is determined by a combination of factors, such as historical conditions, cultural background, internal and external environment, and policies and systems. However, one important factor that can never be overlooked is the leading role that regional government plays in economic development, i.e. the effect of foresighted leading. The exercise of foresighted leading is intimately related to the degree of marketization. The greater degree regional marketization, the better the effects of foresighted leading, and the lesser degree, the poorer the effects. The economic reform and opening up in Guangdong Province in the 1980s went hand in hand with the delegation of government administrative authorities and the nurturing of market economy. The cultivation of market economy enabled local government to develop regional economy.

After obtaining a certain degree of autonomy, local government is bound to set up enterprises. Only by so doing can it reap its benefits. Under market economy, China's local government has to turn to market for resources. In the 1980s, local government in Guangdong had to turn to market and actively opened up new channels for resources. For instance, many villages and township governments in the Pearl River Delta region, thanks to the development of market economy, applied for bank loans by using their business credit and then granted them to township and village enterprises at low rates, or borrowed money from foreign companies, or solicited funds from the public by issuing bonds and securities. Obviously, it would be extremely difficult and even impossible to find resources or open new channels for resources without the development of market economy.

It must be mentioned that China's reform and opening up was catalytic to Guangdong's rapid development of market economy. Hong Kong and Macao have had a long history of market economic development and intimate international exchanges. They know how to act economically in accordance with international practices and have established their good legal systems. China's inland reform and opening to the outside world have built an economic bridge between Guangdong and its neighboring Hong Kong and Macao. In the 1980s, contradictions appeared between them due to inconsistency between the highly centralized economic system in the inland regions and the market economic systems in Hong Kong and Macao. These contradictions sped up the steps of the adaptation of Guangdong's economic operation mechanisms to international market. The more open the regions, the more sharp contradictions between the two systems, the greater the need to settle them by quick means. The more contradictions settled, the more rapid the development of market economy, and the better effects GFL has achieved.

Certainly, market mechanism and GFL are mutually dependent and interacting. More effective GFL will help to promote the formation and perfection of market mechanism, which will in turn improve government's leading role, thus forming an ever-moving positive incentive cycle. In order to ensure the increase of local fiscal revenues, China's local government is bound to try every means to help enterprises open up new markets, gain access to new resources, introduce new technology and expand new varieties. Only by so doing can local government form a collective power with enterprises to cope with market changes and accelerate their growth in market economic activities. The most obvious example in Guangdong Province is the growth of its township enterprises, which have been of great vitality and played an important role in market economy, thanks to township government's vigorous support.

In Guangdong Province, all levels of local government have been trying to integrate government's leading role and market mechanism, taking advantage of its adjacency to Hong Kong and Macao and good market foundation, and further opening to the outside world, which have combined to enable Guangdong's economy to develop ahead of other regions in China.

4.1.2 The market-oriented resources allocation and government foresighted leading

There is a two-fold implication to the concept of market-oriented resources allocation: first, there should be the basic environment of market economy, and second, government should respect the basic rules of market economy. In order for local government to play its leading role in economy, it must integrate its leading role into market mechanism. Let's again take China for example.

*4.1.2.1 The basic environment of market economy and government
foresighted leading*

From the perspective of China's system reform, there have been two major rounds of system adjustment. The first round took place at the end of the 1950s, when China's economic administration system underwent adjustment from centralization to decentralization, which enabled local government to obtain a certain degree of autonomy but still to manage economic operations in the administrative way. It therefore failed to separate government administration from business administration, and enterprises, as market entities, were still in bad need of vitality. In essence, that was the repetition of disadvantages of centralized mode in decentralization.

The second round took place in the mid- and late 1980s, when China was practicing the fiscal responsibility system, which led to serious trade protection on the part of local government and isolated local economies though it vitalized local economy. The lessons that can be learned from those two rounds of adjustment show that the root cause does not lie in whether it should delegate authorities but in the lack of effective market environment.

In the age of planned economy, the first round of system reform failed to resolve the fundamental problem of underpowered development in the old system due to its leaving resource allocation mechanisms out of account. Due to the highly centralized planned economic system, all social resources were planned and allocated as a whole, and market was largely excluded from economic activities. The functions of government, especially those of central government were unprecedentedly expanded to replace almost all the opportunities for economic decisions and choices on the part of economic entities. Under such circumstances, the role of local government role in economic activities was mainly an intermediary agency that transmitted central command to enterprises and institutions, playing merely the part of the transfer station. It had no independent economic interests and responsibilities and therefore was by no means a real economic entity, to say nothing of the role of foresighted leading.

The second round of system reform hindered the formation of a unified market for lack of effective market rules though it initiated the transition from planned economy to market economy. In short, it was all because of inadequate development of market economy, but it demonstrated that it is just not enough only to transfer power between different levels of government and that there should also be an effective operation mechanism of power to develop economy, i.e. the market mechanism. Without market economy, there is no likelihood of forming an orderly economic operation system, and any way of separating powers will be to no avail.

*4.1.2.2 The basic rules of market economy and government
foresighted leading*

As mentioned earlier, the rapid development of Guangdong's economy is the result of both the leading role of local government and its good construction of market economic mechanisms.

In the early 1980s, while promoting the fiscal responsibility system and the decentralization system, Guangdong provincial government also actively and steadily spurred the construction of market system, including market mechanism, market system and market rules. It implemented the pricing reform policy of "regulation-decentralization combination" and "giving priority to decentralization", which started from the gradual marketization of product prices, first most of agricultural and sideline product prices, followed by prices of most of the means of production, such as grain, oil, coal and other key product prices.

In the process of price marketization, Guangdong Province also implemented the policy of "opening city gates and keeping all markets open", which broke the traditional unified underwriting system, reduced the number of intermediate links in commodities circulation and increased circulation channels. Price marketization pushed prices in Guangdong to a relatively higher level than neighboring regions, and that attracted more products and resources into Guangdong Province, and in this way, prices in Guangdong Province have maintained a steady and moderate level. These policies helped to nurture commodity market and vitalized urban and rural markets in Guangdong.

With the gradual formation of market mechanisms, it became increasingly necessary to perfect the market system, i.e. the system of economic activities that is market oriented, including market trade, industrial goods, means of production market, capital market, foreign exchange swap market, labor market, technology market, real estate market, market information, etc. Among them all, the financial market is the core of market system, and capital market is the lifeblood of economic activities. So, the development of capital market represents the maturity of the market system. Since 1984, Guangdong Province began to employ social fundraising to construct new transportation systems and opened an innovative channel of "using roads and bridges for roads and bridges" by collecting tolls. The mid- and late 1980s witnessed the positive development of bond and stock markets, which absorbed social idle funds for economic development. The development of financial markets led to the development and maturity of other markets, including real estate market, labor market, technology market, information market, etc.

In nurturing market mechanism and market system, Guangdong provincial government has also been actively formulating market rules, the laws and regulations that are formulated in accordance with the laws of market operations and that all entities of market activities, such government, businesses, social groups, and individuals, must abide by. In the early 1980s, Guangdong provincial government took necessary measures and formulated regulations concerning urban traffic, public health and urban appearance management while making decisions to allow farmers to do business in cities. In addition, the government also formulated a series of laws and regulations regarding social security, labor safety and health standards, environmental protection, and other aspects so as to change the situations like conflicting policies from different departments and government policies being liable to change under the old system and meet the need for the development of market mechanism and system.

While stressing the leading role of government in economy, one tendency must be guarded against, i.e. the one-sided exaggeration of the role of government and the ensuing unlimited expansion of government functions. Government inaction on economy will affect the long-term stable development of economy, but the emphasis on government role does not mean it must take charge of everything. Inappropriate government intervention might interfere with the normal development of market, leading to more government intervention. On the other hand, moderate government intervention is beneficial not only to the realization of social goals but also to the maturing of market. A certain balance must be struck and a certain degree of moderation must be maintained in the relation between government and market. As Arthur Lewis indicated, the failure of government may be either due to its doing too little or due to its doing too much.

So the question is, what is the appropriate way of government leading? What kind of measurement is needed to maintain the proper balance between government and market? The following three principles should be generally followed: operative resources (private products) should follow market principles and be handled by market; non-operative resources (pure public products) should be provided by government; and for quasi-operative resources (quasi-public products), the principle of government promotion, enterprise participation and market operation should be adopted, depending upon government financial strength and the economic situation of the private sector, through a variety of organizational forms and by allocating resources via market and employing the operational and technological advantages of the private sector.

The public good and private good are only relatively defined, and the difference between them is whether a good is exclusive and competitive. If a good can be consumed non-competitively and non-exclusively, it is no doubt a pure public good and can be clearly distinguished from private good. However, these two features are not simultaneously present in many cases. If this happens, the good can be termed quasi-public good or quasi-private good.

The non-competitive feature of public goods shows that although the exclusiveness of some public goods can be easily identified, this identification is not necessarily efficient. Take the set-up of a toll station at the end of a bridge for example. According to the conditions of efficiency, the general pricing principle the vendor should follow is that the price should approximate to marginal costs, and if the bridge is provided by the private sector, they will ask for a price equal to marginal costs. Since the marginal cost the vendor spends on each car is close to zero, then the vendor's price should be equal to zero, so it is unlikely for the private sector to supply these products. This nature of public goods deprives the private market of motivation and makes it ineffective to provide public goods and services.

The mechanism of government running differs from that of the market in that the government finances public good mainly by collecting taxes. Taxes can be quantitatively measured, but the consumption of public good can hardly be quantitatively gauged. Besides, the public good is non-exclusive and non-competitive, so the need for it and the consumption of it are public or collective. That is to say, the consumers will have similar access to the public good, whether or not they pay for it. Their rational choice is thus to wait for others to pay for it rather than paying themselves. This is the "free-rider" effect in the literature of economics.

It can be derived from the above analysis that the market is effective in providing the private good but ineffective in providing the public good, which usually turns out to be the duty of the government. The public good can be then classified into pure public good and quasi-public good. Generally, the former can only be provided by the government, but the latter is either provided by the government or supplied privately with government subsidies.

As shown in Figure 4.1, the pure public good is not suitable for private production as its marginal production cost and marginal congestion cost are both zero. The DD line stands for the demand curve, and MC, the marginal cost curve (also the x-axis. The two curves determine the optimal quantity of public good Q^*, in which the cost of providing the good is unlikely to be sufficiently paid back and thus the provider will suffer a loss. If the provider is permitted to charge a fee, say P_0, he will choose to supply the public good of the equilibrium amount Q_0, which is smaller than the optimal amount Q^*, leading to a net loss of social welfare ($\Delta Q_0 E_0 Q^*$). So the pure public good should be provided free of charge by the government and financed by collecting taxes to pay for the fixed cost.

As shown in Figure 4.2, the quasi-public good has the marginal cost of production that is zero but its marginal congestion cost is not always zero. The DD stands for the demand curve, and the MC stands for the marginal cost curve. The congestion cost is zero before congestion occurs, but it will rise after congestion. If the public good is free, say, the price is zero, the equilibrium consumption of public good is Q_1, resulting in a loss of social welfare associated with the congestion

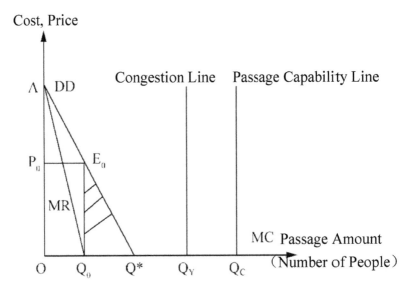

Figure 4.1 The relation between supply and demand of pure public goods

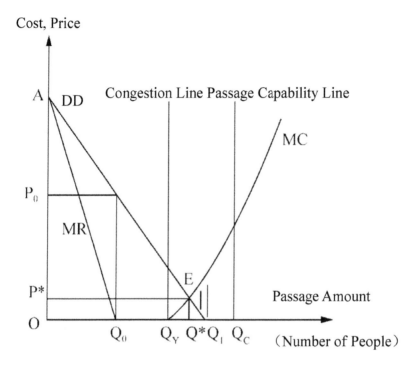

Figure 4.2 The relation between supply and demand of quasi-public goods

effect. If a fee is charged, the equilibrium E (P*, Q*) will maximize social welfare by avoiding congestion. As a result, this kind of quasi-public product can be charged fees, which should not be higher than the necessary level that helps to avoid over-congestion.

The quasi-public good is a kind of public good that can be charged fees and the fees should not be too high, so it can be provided in two ways. One of them is that the government directly supplies the good and collects some fees, like roads and bridges. The other is that it is supplied through the market and subsidized by the government, such as theaters and sports facilities. It must be noted that there is no simple way of providing the quasi-public good, and that depends on actual situations, the fiscal capability of government, and the economic strength of the private sector. In order to take advantages of the efficiency of market in resource allocation as well as the skills of the private sector in management and technology, the principles of government promotion, enterprise participation and market operation should be followed.

The quasi-public good can be directly provided by the government if the government has enough fiscal resources that are well operated. Otherwise, the mode of BOT (build-operate-transfer) can be adopted if the private sector has strong financial capabilities and higher operation efficiency. The government can grant franchising contracts to private enterprises (including foreign enterprises), permitting them to build and operate infrastructures. They are then authorized to charge fees to pay off loans and costs and retain reasonable profits during a period. Upon the expiration of franchising, the infrastructure should be transferred to the government gratuitously. This mode has been employed for many domestic projects like highways, sewage facilities, etc., for it helps to gather social capital and speed up the supply of public good.

4.1.3 Sound legal system and government foresighted leading

Market economy must resort to legislation to solve the problem of the order of economic activities. Only when sound laws are in place can market perform the function of efficiently allocating resources. Market economy is law-governing economy, emphasizing the use of legal means to resolve the problems of market economic development, adjust economic relations, regulate economic behavior, guide economic operations and maintain economic order. The rule of law is the cornerstone for the establishment of modern market economic system. Without the safeguard of laws, property rights are insecure, businesses cannot be truly independent, market competition environment cannot be created, the efficient operation of market cannot be guaranteed, and there will not be sustainable development of economy.

First, the continuous establishment and perfection of the legal system for market economy not only provides important legal conditions for the cultivation and development of market economy but also provides more effective and comprehensive institutional guarantee for the protection of public and private property rights and the orderly market competition.

Second, it is of primary importance to establish government of law, comprehensively promote administration according to law, strengthen administrative consciousness and capability of administration according to law, improve the quality of system construction and standardize the operation of administrative power so as to improve government credibility and executive capabilities and achieve the goal of building up a government of law.

Finally, the favorable legal environment to business must be created, such as strengthening the protection of intellectual property rights, innovating government management service modes, establishing legal, scientific, streamlined administrative examination and approval systems and eliminating improper intervention by administrative means in microeconomic activities. Measures must also be taken to strengthen public participation in administrative decision making and to enhance the transparency of administrative power.

In terms of the construction of orderly market competition environment, the goal is to revitalize market entities, promote honest and trustworthy transactions on the part of market entities and enhance the fair and efficient distribution of factors of production so as to effectively lower the threshold of market access and operating costs. In terms of the construction of market supervision systems, innovation must be made in market supervision mechanism and regulating manners so as to gradually form a unified, open, competitive and orderly market environment, establish a new pattern comprising government responsibility, department coordination, industrial standardization, and public participation, perfect quality supervision system, strengthen quality and technical standards, quality inspection, testing, early warning and risk prevention, reinforce supervision of market behaviors that are in violation of market competition order, such as monopoly and unfair competition, establish and perfect a comprehensive supervising and monitoring mechanism through abolishing, controlling, preventing, and regulating market disorder, create a long-term and standardized supervising and monitoring system, strengthen industrial self-discipline, and promote the transfer of those administrative functions from government to industrial organizations, and give industrial groups in making industrial self-disciplinary norms and establishing industrial entry and exit mechanisms.

4.2 Economic functions and motivating power for competition and government foresighted leading

The reason that government can exercise foresighted leading is that it performs the dual function of quasi-state and quasi-business. On the one hand, regional government represents the central government in carrying out macro-level administration and regulation of its economy and thus plays the role of quasi-state in leading and regulating regional development. On the other hand, regional government also represents non-government organizations in the region and thus plays the role of quasi-business in allocating resources, soliciting central government support, and competing with other regional governments through system, institutional, and technological innovation so as to maximize its economic benefits.

In China, for example, regional government must have the following attributes to exercise foresighted leading:

(a) Regional government has relatively independent administrative and fiscal power

Before 1980, when China was under planned economy system, the central government had highly centralized power in such aspects as political, administrative, economic and fiscal areas, and national interests were equivalent to regional interests. The central government was the organizer and administrator of the economic development of the whole society. It unified the whole nation's economy through plans, which meant integrating the central government, local government and all businesses and institutions into an entity. Local government performed the simple function of managing and operating its affiliated enterprises and institutions well and fulfilled the national plan. Governments at all levels were only different in size but not in behavior or in interests. They shared common goals.

Zhou Yean (2003), professor of the Remin University of China, believed that in the period of planned economy, the central government mainly adopted planning measures to regulate and control local resources, and the competition between local governments was one kind of between brothers but not between economic entities. From 1980, the central government introduced and abandoned four different income distribution systems and fine-tuned the incentive mechanisms to local governments. In 1988, the financial responsibility system was put into operation, followed by the tax distribution reform in 1994, which was derived from the original supply system for governments. Under the tax distribution system, proportion of local government revenues decreased, but both the supply system and the tax distribution system, compared with planned economy system, gave local governments a high degree of autonomy and strengthened their power as economic entities for economic competition.

In order to ensure the continuous increase of local fiscal revenues, local governments were bound to try every means to help enterprises to open up new markets, gain access to new resources, employ new technology and increase new varieties of products. By so doing, local governments and their affiliated businesses could form joint forces in response to market changes and accelerate the growth of market entities in economic activities, which made it possible to play a leading role in economic development.

After decentralization and granting benefits to local governments, more decision-making power was delegated to local governments and production units, which endowed local governments with relatively independent benefits and strengthened administrative functions of economy. Local governments became not only the controlled object in regional balance of the aggregate national economy but also the controlling subject with autonomous power in regional economic activities that can exercise direct regulation of regional economy on different levels.

(b)   Better market mechanisms are put into operation

Economic development shows that it is not enough to only change the distribution of power within the administrative system from the centralized to decentralized type. In the administrative adjustment of China's economic management system in the late 1950s, for example, centralization was changed to decentralization, but local government that obtained a certain degree of autonomy still conducted economic management in the administrative way, with entangled government-business relations and lack of vitality in enterprises. Although devolution produced many interest entities with local government standing at the core, there was no change in resource allocation mechanisms. After gaining power, local governments still issued administrative orders to allocate resources, and the lack of vitality in production units remained a serious problem. More seriously, local governments began to struggle for more investment and construction projects in chaos, which shows that under planned economy, the simple devolution failed to solve the fundamental problems of underpowered development in the old system because it did not change resources allocation mechanisms.

As mentioned earlier, in another adjustment in the mid- and late 1980s, the fiscal responsibility system was widely implemented, which led to serious trade protection on the part of local administrative institutions and the rise of local economic regimes though it infused vitality into local economy, for lack of effective market rules, and prevented the formation of a unified market. That shows that without market economy, there is no likelihood for orderly economic operation. Under such circumstances, all forms of devolution would be to no avail. Without the introduction of market mechanisms, government decentralization would not produce the effects of foresighted leading. Rather, it would be likely to produce the negative effects, such as abuse of power.

Practices show that the higher degree of openness, the faster development of market economy, and the better role government played in foresighted leading. The combination of administrative decentralization and market economy can avoid not only random resource allocations under administrative imperatives but also the problem of simply pushing forward the construction of market economy while overlooking the inadequate development of economic entities. Governments of all levels in Guangdong Province have been able to take the lead in national economy because they have had a good combination of GFL and market mechanisms, capitalized on its adjacency to Hong Kong and Macao and its sound market foundation and implemented further opening to the outside world.

(c)   Motivations for competition between local governments

Over the past 30 years or so, China has maintained an average of about 10% of economic growth rate, and academics have come to conclude that China's regional governments have played a vital role in promoting local economic development. So what has inspired the fierce competition between local governments? A lot of serious explorations have been made about this question. Qian Yinyi (2002), for example, focuses on the incentive motivation of the separation of power and the fiscal responsibility system to regional government officials, and some other scholars emphasize the incentive of promotion to local officials. Zhou Lian (2007) points out two key factors, i.e. the promotion of local officials and the retained proportion of central government to local governments in the fiscal responsibility contractual system, that have effectively motivated local officials to promote regional economic growth.

China conducted its fiscal reform in the 1980s, which determined the respective fiscal revenue allocation proportion between central government and local governments through the fiscal responsibility system. In 1994, the tax distribution reform was undertaken so that the retained proportion for local governments was decided on the basis of their total economic volume and tax collections. After the reform of "decentralization and benefits awarding", part of the financial authorities and the power to handle local issues were devolved to local governments. Local governments have relatively independent interest of their own, because the faster their economic growth, the higher their tax revenues, and the greater their retained proportion of tax collections. Local government revenues do not belong to government officials, but property rights do not just mean property rights. They cover the use of property rights. Therefore, as long as local governments have independent fiscal authorities and power to handle local issues, they will certainly mean incentives to local economic growth.

In addition, central government is directly responsible for the promotion of local government officials at the provincial level, and the provincial government is in charge of the promotion of municipal government officials. As a result, whoever perform best in their government positions at the same level will be rewarded with the greatest opportunity for promotion, which will then enable them to have greater authorities to control property rights and their use.

It is this inter-province, inter-city and inter-county competition that has really become the fundamental driving force for China's regional economic development and given regional government a better position to exercise foresighted leading in economic activities.

4.3 Information transparency and reduction of government malfunction

Every organization has its own interest, and government is no exception. As a public interest group, such negative phenomena as power peddling and corruption will occur in government if information is not transparent, and that may lead to government failure. Sunlight is the best preservative. Transparent information can not only prevent corruption in government but also help citizens participate in government administration, enhance citizens' trust in government and form national and regional cohesive force.

4.3.1 Lack of information transparency and supervisory mechanisms and the inefficiency of government foresighted leading

As mentioned above, not only will there occur market malfunction but government malfunction as well. It is often the limitations of government behavior and other objective factors that cause defects and failures to make social resource allocation efficiency achieve the best scenario, and thus occurs what Samuelson called government malfunction. Government malfunction covers:

(a) Low efficiency of government policies

The low efficiency of government policies implies public decision-making errors. Relative to market in terms of decision making, public decision making is an extremely complicated process, with considerable uncertainty, various difficulties, obstacles, or restrictions, which make it hard for government to formulate and implement good or reasonable public policies, thus public decision-making errors, such as supply shortage or surplus. If government intervenes in such ways as to fix prices above the non-equilibrium level, then production shortage or excess will take place, and when the price is fixed below the equilibrium level, production shortage will take place, and production excess if it is the opposite case. The main reasons for public policy making are generally as follows: (1) lack of information. Government may not know all the costs and benefits of their policies, nor is it clear about the consequences of their policies, so it is difficult for them to evaluate their policies; (2) lack of market incentives. Government intervention eliminates the force of the market or offsets part of market effects, which may eliminate some beneficial inspirations at the same time.

(b) Low efficiency of government bureaucracies

Government bureaucracies tend to be inefficient, especially in developing countries, which is generally ascribed to the following reasons: (1) Lack of competitive pressure. On the one hand, government bureaucracies monopolize public goods supply, without competitors. That may lead to excessive investment on the part of government departments and production of more public goods than needed. On the other hand, with the protection of lifetime employment regulations, government personnel do not have enough pressure and motivation to improve their working efficiency. (2) No incentive mechanism for cost reduction and administrative resources tend to be wasted. Government officials spend taxpayers' money. Because there is no property right constraints, they do not have to worry about costs no matter what they do. Moreover, government officials have a monopoly of their power and there is an endless possibility of overdraft. (3) Incomplete supervision information. In reality, social supervision over government may lose effectiveness due to incomplete supervision information. Coupled with the previously mentioned government monopoly, supervisors may be manipulated by those who are supervised.

(c) Government rent-seeking

According to Buchanan's definition (1989), rent-seeking is such that voters, especially interest groups, attempt through various efforts, legal or illegal, such as lobbying and bribery, to push government to help them build monopolistic positions in order to gain higher monopolistic profits. It follows that the profits power peddlers gain are a redistribution of existing production results rather than the result of production. Rent-seeking is therefore characterized by non-productivity. Meanwhile, the premise of rent-seeking is the intervention of government power in market trading activities, and the intervention of government power causes the inefficient allocation of resources and the distortion of distribution patterns and produces a lot of social costs, such as the waste of resources caused by rent-seeking activities, the waste of resources caused by political rent-seeking that arises from economic rent-seeking, and the loss of social efficiency resulting from rent-seeking success. In addition, rent-seeking can allure government officials into struggle for power and benefits and eventually harm government reputation and increase the costs of anticorruption.

According to the public choice theory, rent-seeking can be mainly classified into three categories: (1) rent-seeking through government control and regulation; (2) rent-seeking through tariffs and import and export quotas; (3) rent-seeking in government procurement.

(d) Government expansion

Government expansion includes the expansion of government department personnel and the increase government spending. Scholars, like Buchanan, tried to explain government expansion from the following five aspects: (1) the role of government as a provider of public goods and an eliminator of external effects, (2) the role of government as the redistributor of income and wealth, (3) the existence of interest groups, (4) the existence of bureaucracies, (5) fiscal illusions.

Government can perform the role of foresighted leading, but the causes for government failures may weaken the government foresighted leading role. Accordingly, GFL will not work properly without the proper functioning of government.

The above section has elaborated upon the fierce competition between regional governments, which can lessen the seriousness of government failures to certain extent. However, government malfunction, such as rent-seeking and low efficiency, can still take place, without open and transparent information disclosure and supervision mechanisms.

4.3.2 *Information transparency and the competency and effectiveness of government administration*

The cooperation and interaction between government and folk organizations and between the public and private sector can maximize the effectiveness of public administration to the greatest extent possible. Government as executor of state power should attach great importance to public interest and the role of social media as well. Government credibility will be seriously undermined if attempts are made to block information within government and expose it only under the strong pressure of public opinion. The openness and transparency of government information will enhance the basic guarantee of citizens' right to know and to participate, help to improve the degree of citizen's political participation, which is advantageous to the democratization and rationalization of government decision making, help to strengthen social supervision, prevent the abuse of public power, and help to improve government administrative capability and administrative efficiency.

The United States boasts a comparatively perfect government budget information disclosure system. The government (including federal, state and local governments) budget information can be obtained from related websites and publications. Budgets of all levels are open to the Congress, the Parliament as well as the general public. Through the extensive disclosure of budget and related financial information, taxpayers can get a detailed understanding of government tax policies, expenditure policies and the usage of financial capital. They can get information concerning government assets and liabilities, operating costs and performance of government, government's cash flow, budget implementation, and so on.

The U.S. budget information disclosure practice began in the early twentieth century as a result of the budget exposition organized by New York Municipal Research Office. In 1908, the New York Municipal Government formulated the first modern budget in American history. On October 15, 1908, New York Municipal Research Office, in collaboration with The Greater New York Taxpayers Consultation, initiated and organized the exposition. One of the most impressive items at the exposition is a 6-cent peg, with illustrations of $ 0.65 per peg, plus $2.22 for fixing them at the right positions. Seventy thousand citizens visited the exhibition, and more than one million read the news about the exhibition from the press. That exposition ignited the enthusiasm of the American public for a better understanding of government through budgets.

During the reform of information disclosure in the United States, a series of laws and regulations were formulated and put into effect and provided strong guarantee for the openness and transparency of budget information. In 1921, the U.S. Congress passed the Budget and Accounting Act. In 1946, laws were revised in preparation for the formulation of the Freedom of Information Act. In 1966, the Freedom of Information Act was implemented in its revised version to promote the publicity of government information. It greatly expanded the disclosure scope of government information. It is one of the most comprehensive laws concerning government information disclosure and has become a role model for other countries to follow. In 1974, the Federal Privacy Act was passed to stipulate rules for the public disclosure and confidentiality of meetings, documents and matters related to information. In 1976, the Government in the Sunshine Act was enforced that requires government to expose public fiscal spending and government financial information so as to facilitate the supervision of mass media, public opinion and the public.

Moreover, the Electronic Freedom of Information Amendments, which was enacted in 1996, along with the Government in the Sunshine Act and the Public Records Act issued by the state government and below, also acts as the important basis for the disclosure of government budget information. All these laws enable the United States to expose to the public the budgeting information along with each of its components and at all levels. Every year, the U.S. government exposes to the general public, through the Internet, mass media, publications and other channels, all the budgeting information and financial reports of the federal government, including all the official documents relating to the federal budgeting, no matter whether they are intended for submission to the president or the Congress.

The budgeting document the federal government exposes to the public consists of five parts: the first part is the budget, which mainly shows the budgeting arrangements according to 20 or so functions; the second part is the appendix, which mainly shows the budgets of over 20 departments and other independent agencies; The third part is overview and analytical perspectives, including the analysis of various factors in the budget and forecasts; the fourth part is the budget system and concepts; and the last part is historical statements and data. The budget document generally includes budgeting guidelines, functional classification, economic analyses, the classified documents of various departments, etc. Among them, the attachments to department budgets provide such details as to display the spending of each specific item. The president of the United States' budget is no exception. The president's budget of 2007, for example, consists of the president's union address, budget overview, economic operation analysis, the national fiscal outlook, effect controlling, etc., in addition to the budgets of 21 departments and other institutions.

In addition to payment information, the U.S. government budget information also includes assets, liabilities, owners' equity and other financial information and statistics. Information about government balance sheets can be obtained in *The Comprehensive Financial Report* at the end of the fiscal year. The contents of the financial report are determined and specified by The Accounting Principle Board. The government must disclose all the information concerning government assets and liabilities rather than merely the information concerning major government departments, including balance sheets information of those entities affiliated to government departments and of those entities that were originally established by government departments with financially independent business accounting to provide public service (e.g. profit-making government entities).

The U.S. budget information disclosure system has its distinctive features. First, legislation goes first. The American budget information disclosure is based on a series of legal norms. The American constitution requires that the reports and accounts respecting the receipts and expenditures of all public money should be open to the public. Along with the constitutional requirement, the relevant stipulations laid down by the Congress and the United States.

Government Accountability Office in the Budget and Accounting Act, the Federal Financial Integration Management Act, the Freedom of Information Act, the Government in the Sunshine Act, *The Federal Agency Policies and Procedures Manual*, and other legal documents constitute a legally standardized system of budget information disclosure.

Second, complete and specific disclosure is assured. The U.S. government budget information disclosure is required throughout the whole budgeting process, from its preparation, examination, approval, execution to auditing. The budget report consists of income and spending reports. The income report contains information concerning fee collections, assets sale, social donations, and other income sources, as well as all kinds of tax revenues. The spending report is so specific and detailed as to reveal the expenditures of each project and each department and the specific spending amount is given down to two decimal places. All government spending is specified in the budget and the budget-related documents, and there is no government spending outside of government budgeting.

Third, budget information is disclosed in advance and in a timely and continuous fashion. America's fiscal year starts from October 1 and ends on September 30 of the following year, and budget preparation starts 18 months ahead of the beginning of the fiscal year. All congressional committees shall submit budget review reports to the budget committee before February 25 of the same fiscal year, and the budget committee shall hold hearings concerning draft budgets. After the passage of the budget resolution by the Congress, the approval and funding shall be completed before the budget year starts, and then the resolution shall be sent for the president to sign and announced to the public. In every stage of budget spending, the government shall make timely and detailed releases of relevant information, with the exception of those documents exempted by laws and regulations. Since the implementation of budget information disclosure policies, significant achievements have been made in government spending reduction, and government efficiency has improved to a considerable extent, especially during the Clinton administration when massive fiscal deficits turned into surpluses.

4.4 High-caliber government personnel and good selection mechanisms and government foresighted leading

4.4.1 The importance of selecting high-caliber personnel for government and creating healthy market environment

Just as Schumpeter remarked in *Business cycles: a theoretical, historical, and statistical analysis of the capitalist process*(1939), without innovation there would be no entrepreneurs, and without their accomplishments capitalism would not work. In Schumpeter's view, the motivation for capitalist development resides in entrepreneurs' innovative spirit, and therefore, the government role in economic life is a good manager of cycles, which requires highly qualified civil servants and professionals, because only truly wise persons, when performing economic regulatory functions, can use their meticulous hand to adjust the engine of capitalism so as not to stifle entrepreneurship. A good government is basically a good administrator of cycles, and it shall perform more functions than just what Adam Smith cited, such as the protection of property rights and the supervision of contractual responsibilities.

Schumpeter disagrees with the traditional idea of economics, namely the pursuit of benefit maximization as the sole purpose of capitalists for production. He believes that the innovative spirit, e.g. the preference for changes in order to change and adventures, is the more fundamental force that drives them to engage in economic activities. He regards those capitalists with such spirit as entrepreneurs.

Schumpeter expects market regulators to have a profound understanding of the nature of capitalism, to know how to adjust economic cycles deftly and discreetly, to maintain the entrepreneurial spirit of innovation and to further maintain the capitalist economic system, rather than the other way round. He believes that in a country where the basic principles of economics are disregarded, government intervention, which is simple and brutal, cannot exercise regulatory effects upon economy and will only continue to oppress the innovative spirit of entrepreneurs, which will eventually break down the foundations of economy.

History has shown that the laissez-faire market economy free from supervision and devoid of guidance will inevitably invite economic crises and market volatility. However, improper economic intervention will kill the entrepreneur spirit of innovation. For Schumpeter, that is a dilemma.

"In making a wheel, if I proceed gently, that is pleasant enough, but the workmanship is not strong; if I proceed violently, that is toilsome and the joinings do not fit. If the movements of my hand are neither too gentle nor too violent, the idea in my mind is realized. But I cannot tell (how to do this) by word of mouth; there is a knack in it." These remarks of Lun Bian's in *Chuang Tzu* can apply metaphorically to the role of government in economic life. Here "knack" can be interpreted as professional knowledge, i.e. the expertise that those wise government officials Schumpeter believes in should have.

Therefore, GFL must involve professional scholars of economics and let them lead the process, rather than letting amateurs act like "the blind feeling the elephant" or "crossing the stream by feeling the stones". According to Schumpeter, the starting point of GFL is the selection of wise government officials, the creation of healthy market economic environment and continuously lead and inspire the innovative spirit of entrepreneurs.

It is clear from the profiles of the following four senior officials of the four U.S. government officials that the U.S. government has been selecting its officials in the light of Schumpeter's standards: Timothy Franz Geithner, who served as the 75th United States Secretary of the Treasury, under President Barack Obama, from 2009 to 2013 and was previously the president of the Federal Reserve Bank of New York from 2003 to 2009 and vice chairman of the Federal Open Market Committee; Robert Edward Rubin, who, an American economist and banking executive, served as the 70th United States Secretary of the Treasury during both the first and second Clinton administrations; Lawrence Henry "Larry" Summers, who, also an American economist, served as the 27th president of Harvard University from 2001 to 2006 following the end of Clinton's term and was awarded John Bates Clark Medal for his remarkable achievements in macroeconomics; Henry Merritt "Hank" Paulson Jr., who, an American banker, served as the 74th United States Secretary of the Treasury and the Chairman and Chief Executive Officer of Goldman Sachs.

Developed countries have been trying to attract specialized talents from all parts of the world, while China is still in its initial stage of socialist construction and the selection mechanisms for talents need improving and upgrading. There still remain problems like talent selection according to seniority, no differentiation of ages, and some degree of hatred for capable persons. Government administrators who are involved in economic work are not armed with necessary expertise in economics, and there are even fewer people who are also expert at business management. Some regional government does not respect the laws of market economy, and in some extreme cases, serious mistakes are made, such as misleading the direction of economic development, and bring about grave economic losses. All this seriously hinders the process of government exercising foresighted leading.

According to the 2005 statistics of the Development Research Center of the State Council, CBD is under construction in over 40 of China's inland cities, like Beijing, Shanghai, Chongqing, Wuhan, Shenyang, Tianjin, Shenzhen, Guangzhou, Nanjing, Zhenzhou, Ningbo, Qingdao and Dalian. Among them some are only medium-sized or even small cities. Judging from the perspective of economic laws, the construction of CBD in the majority of the cities above is beyond their own capability of development and does not fit in with the requirements of their economic development. The prospects for such giant planning with such large scales are really far from promising. It takes about 20 to 30 years for developed countries to naturally form a CBD area and CBD becomes tactic planning for urban development after its introduction into China.

The construction of CBD requires a huge economic volume, but many of the cities that have planned for CBD construction are far from that. The construction of CBD needs a solid industrial foundation, in particular that of modern service industry, and judging from the industrial perspective, many of the cities still depend on traditional manufacturing, though they have acquired a large economic volume. The construction of CBD is contingent upon the position of the city in regional economy or in global economy and its capability of radiating to neighboring areas. The great majority of China's cities are still in the transitional stage from manufacturing industry to service industry. Modern high-end service industry is still underdeveloped. CBD, which is established under such circumstances, will be susceptible to functional imbalance. Currently in China, conditions are ripe for the construction of CBD only in those large cities, like Shanghai, Beijing, Shenzhen and Guangzhou.

In the eyes of municipal administrators, CBD is conducive to urban development but they overlook the economic foundation for CBD construction and take it for granted that CBD is bound to promote economic development, which is obviously wrong. Lessons can learned from this case: a leader from a small inland city in China's Western region paid a visit to Shanghai and found that an office building of Grade A could create tens of thousands of jobs and produce several billion economic output. He thought it a good idea to build a landmark office building in his city. However, the construction of the building had to stop for lack of funds, and it was hard to lease even after its completion. The municipal government had to issue its administrative order that all banks in the city move into the building.

Another motivation for the construction of CBD in China was that municipal administrators were keen on urban image projects in order to win their promotions. Local government needs to be responsible only to higher-level government, and their work performance has to be recognized by higher-ranking officials if they want to be promoted. CBD, as the urban card, is the most direct instrument for reflecting their work performance, and it takes time for higher-ranking officials to know whether the income of urban residents has risen, whether their health condition has been improved, and whether their education has been enhanced. It turns out to be much more difficult to achieve all that than just CBD planning and construction.

In the construction of CBD, there existed serious powerpeddling and rent-seeking, which is another important reason behind it. The construction of CBD needs a large amount of land and a huge amount of urban construction. Government officials may have opportunities for power peddling and rent-seeking to earn benefits for themselves if the construction procedures are not standardized, regulated or supervised properly. The above case demonstrates that selection mechanisms and standards for government administrators need improvement and standardization.

4.4.2 The significance of good selection mechanisms to molding leading-type government

Just as Schumpeter believes that the main body of innovation rests with entrepreneurs and entrepreneurs are the scarcest resource of market economy, so excellent government administrators are scarce resources and are of vital importance if GFL is to exercised.

Some people claim that what is needed in China is not talents but selection mechanisms for talents. China's government administration personnel selection is to a great extent based on seniority and the "age" principle of "one size fits all". What problems will the wrong selection mechanism bring? Here, a model created by Zhou Lian can be cited to illustrate this.

Zhou Lian, according to the principal-agent theory, assumes that the participants are the central government and the N number of provinces, the central government is in the position of the principal, the provincial government in a position of the agent. In this model, if government performance at the provincial level is the best, then the top government official at the provincial level will be promoted.

There will be a reaction function for provincial government officials, who will act according to the proportion permitted in the central government's fiscal responsibility system. If the central government adopts the age principle of "one size fits all" to provincial officials, it is evident from his model that, if provincial officials are younger, they will be in office many years after their promotion and have the opportunity for further promotion, they will work harder, and the benefits they earn from their efforts will be greater, but if they are rather advanced in age, they will have to retire soon, even if their performance is excellent, so the benefits earned from their efforts will be relatively small, and their efforts will not be optimized as much as those of younger officials. Therefore, even if their professional ability and experience are better than younger officials, the selection system and mechanisms will not encourage them to make greater achievements, which considerably reduces government foresighted-leading role.

Judging from the current situation in China, there does exist the tendency of selecting younger officials. Over the years, emphasis has been laid on younger officials, and talent and experience have been overlooked. For example, county officials who reach the age of 50 will feel their promotion hopeless, but officials of this age actually are the most mature at the county level.

After investigations of economic development and social welfare in different countries and different regions, we come to the conclusion that the most fundamental factor is talent selection mechanisms, in addition to resources endowment, systems, technological factors. Where there is good development and fast economic growth, there must be excellent government administrations teams who play a crucial role. In the frontier regions of China's reform and opening to the outside world, such as Shunde, owing to its adjacency to Hong Kong and Macao and other favorable market factors, their foundation of market economy is good, government leadership has broad visions and foresighted thinking. They are apt to seize the opportunities of reform and development initiatives so that they have achieved remarkable economic success. On the contrary, in some regions where government administrators lack foresighted leading and thinking, the foundation of market economy is weak, and government function transformation falters, it is hard for government to play a leading role so that regional economic development is relatively slow.

The example of Singapore also obviously shows the vital importance of high-caliber government administration talents to regional development. Singapore has always attached great importance to attracting talented people and involving them in government management. The ruling party vigorously promotes statecraft and elite selection to the country's most important leadership positions and ensures the high efficiency of government administration. Lee Kuan Yew even argues that as long as there are five national leaders who are really keen on work, it takes only a decade to build a new nation and that if Singapore is controlled by ordinary people and opportunists, there will be a heavy price to pay.

An old Chinese saying goes like this: The splendid steed can be found some-where, but Bo Le, the person who can recognize the steed, cannot be found often. Bo Le counts more than the splendid steed. And today's Bo Le is a good talent selection mechanism. A good talent selection mechanism, first of all, depends on fair competition in talent selection and meritocracy, and second on the principle of "putting the right people in the right positions" so that their positions fit their capabilities, and finally the dynamic management so that capable government officials continue and poor officials quit. GFL can work to the most satisfactory extent, as long as talents are respected and are given opportunities to give full play to their capabilities.

5   Government foresighted leading and mezzoeconomics

The GFL theory stems not only from thinking about China's economic miracle over 30 years' reform and opening up but also from the introspection of the theoretical systems of modern economics. Economists have generally concluded that the current mainstream economics cannot provide full explanation for China' rapid economic growth over the past decades. Mainstream economic theories have presented fundamental flaws in analyzing economic issues concerning transformation and development, such as failures to provide reasonable explanations for the effects of China's reform of the double-track system and for China's sustained high rate of economic growth. Some well-known economists in the mainstream economics have even made misdiagnoses and forecasts about China's economic transition. Why have there been misjudgments and erroneous explanations about the phenomena in China's reform and opening up? It is mainly due to the flaws of existing economic theories, which call for theoretical innovation.

Within the theoretical framework of GFL, there exists an additional level — mezzoeconomics represented by "regions" in between microeconomics represented by "enterprises" and macroeconomics represented by "state". This theory has not only provided a theoretical explanation of the cause for China's economic miracle but also enriched and ameliorated economic theorization. Just as the theory of market economy lays the foundation for microeconomics and Keynesianism identifies macroeconomics from microeconomics, so the GFL theory divides economics into macroeconomics, mezzoeconomics, and microeconomics, which not only fills up the gap in the theoretical system of economics to lead the major direction of economic system reform but also incorporates regional economics and regional governments into economic systems to create a multi-layered market system and enhance the stability of national economy.

5.1 The philosophical logic of mezzoeconomics

Economics studies the productive relations that are determined by productive forces and adapt to the development of productive forces, namely the economic structure. The nature of economic base will bring about its corresponding superstructure, and the economic base determines the substance and nature of superstructure. It follows that economic theories are also determined by the economic base, which means the kind of economic base will bring about the corresponding type of economic theories. Productive relations must adapt to productivity, and superstructure must adapt to the economic base, which forms the philosophical foundation of mezzoeconomics.

5.1.1 The microeconomic theories of classical economics and laissez-faire capitalism

The historical origins of microeconomics can be traced back to Adam Smith's *The Wealth of Nations* and Alfred Marshall's (1842–1924)*The Principles of Economics*. After the 1930s, Joan Violet Robinson (1903–1983), a post-Keynesian British economist, and Edward Hastings Chamberlin (1899–1967), an American economist, proposed the manufacturers equilibrium theory on the basis of Marshall's equilibrium price theory, which marked the ultimate establishment of microeconomic system. It mainly covers equilibrium price theory, economics of consumption, economics of productivity, manufacturers equilibrium theory, welfare economics, etc.

The development of microeconomics has so far experienced four stages: the first stage — from the mid-seventeenth century to the mid-nineteenth century, which is the early phase of microeconomics or the infancy of microeconomics; the second stage — from the late nineteenth century to the early twentieth century, which marks the birth of neoclassical economics and the foundation of microeconomics; the third stage – from the 1930s to the 1960s, which is the formation stage of microeconomics, and the fourth stage – from the 1960s up to present, which marks the further development, expansion and evolution of microeconomics. It is clear that the emergence and development of microeconomics are in full accordance to the basic law of social development that production relations must adapt to productivity and that superstructure must adapt to the economic base.

The great geographical discovery at the end of the fifteenth century and the beginning of the sixteenth century demonstrated the necessity of world market expansion to commodities production development and foreshowed the new era of capitalism. Handicraft workshops, which were based on the division of labor and appeared in a special form of capitalist production, had occupied the dominant position in Europe from the mid-sixteenth century to the end of the eighteenth century.

With the outburst and flourishing of the Industrial Revolution in Britain in the mid-eighteenth century, machinery replaced manual labor, and large-scale industrialized production substituted individual manual workshops, which signified that capitalistic production had completed the transition from handicraft workshops to machine industry and the important transformation from traditional agricultural society to modern industrial society. As a result, social productivity had been considerably emancipated and improved, and the mercantilist policy that restricted the freedom of economy and trade was not congruous to the social and economic development in the new era. Under that context, mercantilism was replaced by the liberal economic theory, and Adam Smith came into the economic scene. He emphasized that wealth growth should be studied from the angle of production and advocated laissez-faire economy, which marked the first radical change in the history of Western economics and is termed "classical revolution" by Western economists. Eventually, scholars in the West were able to establish the first theoretical system of Western economics, namely classical economics. As a token, Adam Smith's "*The Wealth of Nations*" (1776) signified the shaping of the first relatively integrated theoretical system of modern political economy – microeconomics.

During this phase, the expansion of world markets had immensely increased the market capacity and the contradiction of overproduction was less prominent, as technological progress and the changes of production mode had tremendously promoted productivity. Therefore, the focus of economic theories was on individual economic units, such as family workshops, individual vendors, etc. with a view to exploring answers to questions of resources allocation, namely what to produce, how to produce and for whom to produce, and maximizing individual benefits. As remarked by J. Vernon Henderson, the American economist, the optimized behaviors of individual units like households and manufactures laid the foundation for microeconomics.

In such an unprecedented phase of laissez-faire capitalism, when productivity developed at an unparalleled rate and social and economic progress was going on at an accelerating speed, productive relations were in proportion to the development of productive forces, and no oppositions or contradictions occurred between the two. Under such circumstances, the basic theories of microeconomics were taken for granted, on the fundamental assumptions of market clearing, entire rationalization and sufficient information, that the optimization of production could be realized by "the invisible hand" freely allocating and regulating resources.

5.1.2 Macroeconomics and world economic crises

The term "macroeconomics" was first put forward in 1933 by the Norwegian economist Ragnar Anton Kittil Frisch (1895–1973). The explorations in macroeconomic phenomena can be traced back to the classical school. The *Tableau Economique* (1758) written by François Quesnay (1694–1774), the founder of the Physiocratic School of Economics, is the earliest economic literature that analyzes the total process of capitalistic production. However, the analyses of microeconomic phenomena were not identified from those of macroeconomic phenomena in the works of classical economists and their subsequent vulgar economists. Especially from the so-called marginalist revolution, economists basically obliterated the possibility of economic crises and overlooked the contradictions and conflicts in the total process of national economy, while focusing merely on microeconomic analyses so that the analyses of macroeconomic phenomena were nearly submerged in the common economics works.

Following the decline of traditional classical economics under question owing to the economic crisis in the 1930s and the publication of Keynes' *The General*

Theory of Employment, Interest, and Money, the macroeconomic analyses had gradually developed into an independent system of modern economics on the basis of Keynesian theories of income and employment. After the publication of *The General Theory of Employment, Interest, and Money*, many Western economists abandoned the traditional ideas and began to follow Keynes' theory by annotating, supplementing and developing his principles of effective demand, which contributed to a complete theoretical system of macroeconomics. The Keynesian economic theories and policy views exerted profound influence upon the capitalist countries after the First World War. That is why some Western economists called the 20 years or so after the First World War the "Keynesian era".

Economics studies productive relations that are determined by and must adapt to productive forces. It follows that the emergence and development of economics should go hand in hand with the development of productive forces and productive relations.

In Adam Smith's age, though the Industrial Revolution brought about the emancipation of productive forces, rapid social development and fast economic growth, the economic aggregate was still limited. According to the economic data in *The World Economy- A Millennial Perspective* by Angus Maddison (1926–2010), a British economist and a world scholar on quantitative macroeconomic history, British GDP in 1700 reached about $25 billion (in 1990 international dollars), with the GDP per capita of $1 250 international dollars (1990). In 1800, American GDP was only about $400 million at the same year's prices (about $8 billion at the prices of 2008). In addition, the national economic aggregate was relatively low over that period, the industrial structure of the society was relatively simple, mainly the primary industry and commerce and international trade with relatively limited state revenues. The domestic economy was handed over to the private sector, and the state undertook the functions of "night watchman", namely necessary internal public affairs, such as military actions, diplomacy, administration and national security. Under such backgrounds of productivity and productive relations, economics focused more on questions of what to produce, how to produce and for whom to produce through the allocation of resources so as to maximize individual benefits of the residents and manufacturers. That is where the philosophical foundation for microeconomics stands.

In the Keynesian era, the world economy achieved rapid development, with American GDP amounting to about $100 billion in 1929 (calculated at the same year's prices, about $1000 billion at the 2008 price), a 125 times increase over 1,800. More importantly, significant changes took place in the economic structure, with more diversified economic entities and the rise of many large multinational corporations and other forms of monopoly, such as cartel and trust. As a result of advances in science and technology and the further development of productive forces, large quantities of surplus existed in production, and the world economy was faced with serious crises, which made economists realize that market was not omnipotent, occasionally with market failures. Monopoly would occur in free market competition and come to influence market efficiency, cause huge fluctuations of economic cycles, result in serious imbalance between wealth and income distribution and eventually give rise to intense conflicts of social contradictions. Under such backgrounds of productivity and productive relations, the most essential issue of economics was how to determine the level of national income.

Consequently, modern macroeconomics came into being, which regarded the allocation of resources as the vested premise and studied resource utilization within the scope of social domains in order to maximize social welfare. Macroeconomics studies economy in its entirety, such as inflation, unemployment and economic growth, and explains why the economy experiences recession and growing unemployment and why some economies grow much faster than other economies in the long term. It stresses the imperfection of market mechanism and the capability of government to regulate economy and remedy the defects of market mechanism through "the visible hand".

Almost simultaneously, another economic theory was put forth to cope with market failure, namely the theory of socialist planned economy. While the Western capitalist world was fighting against economic crises, the Soviet Union, which represented the socialist camp in the oriental world, was boasting its economic prosperity. The Soviet Union implemented the planned economic system and planned the deployment and management of its social and economic resources as a whole. It implemented the first-five-year construction program in 1928, which completed its industrialization in the short run and turned from an agricultural country to an industrial country, with rapid economic growth and social stability and prosperity. It is evident that the theory of socialist planned economy was generated from the background of the relatively backward semi-feudal productive relations in the Soviet Union, which reflected the superiority of the new productive relations and the superstructure over that period and promoted the development of productivity. However, with the further development of productive forces, that economic theory that negated the role of market came to hinder the further development of productivity, thus causing the transformation of social systems, which embodies the universality of the theory "productive relations must adapt to the development of productive forces".

5.1.3 *Mezzoeconomics and current production relations*

Since the 1970s, stagflation, in the coexistent form of massive unemployment and drastic inflation, raged over the capitalist world, which signified the malfunction of Keynesianism. Consequently, numerous economic thoughts and competing theories came into formation in current Western economic circles. In a sense, the malfunction of Keynesianism showed that this kind of economic theory could no more adapt to the current productive relations and that microeconomics and macroeconomics could not fully explain the complicated economic reality. A new superstructure must be called into forth to adapt to new productive relations, as the current world economic situation has changed tremendously, compared with the Keynesian times.

First, the increasingly expanding economic aggregate has made it difficult to rely simply on macro- and micro-level management to regulate the enormous economies in a timely and effective manner. In 2013, the gross GDP in America reached 16.6 trillion dollars, an almost 17 times' increase over that of 1928.

Second, urbanization accelerated to reach a high level, and the role of cities in the national economy has been strengthened to a considerable extent. The entire European population between 1920 and 1970 (except for the Soviet Union) increased by 42% (from 325 million to 462 million), and its urban population increased by 182% (from 104 million to 293 million). The rate of urbanization in China was less than 10% before 1949 and had risen to 53.73% by 2013.

Third, the economic structure has undergone transformation, and the industrial structure has undergone profound adjustment. Over the past one hundred years, there have occurred several major adjustments in industrial structure of the world economy, which are mainly characterized by: (1) the appearance of high and new technology industries that have been driven by the impetus of scientific and techno-logical advances and led by the information industry with industries of biological engineering, new materials, and new energy following its wake, which has grown substantially in the output value, driven the employment rate up and accounted for a greater proportion in the whole national economy; (2) the traditional cap-ital-intensive and technology-intensive manufacturing industries that have been applying information technology to promote industrial upgrading, with the pro-duction value growing continuously at lower speed, employment on the decline, and its proportion in the national economy gradually decreasing; (3) the shrinking of some labor-intensive manufacturing industries and the thorough remolding of some other such industries through applying high and new technology, with a sub-stantial increase in technical level and competitiveness and yet the ongoing pro-duction transfer from developed countries to developing countries on the whole, in the wave of globalization; (4) the flourishing of traditional and service industries in both output value and employment, with an increasingly greater proportion in the national economy and currently a new round of industrial restructuring.

Currently, developing countries, such as China, are still in the late period of industrialization or the beginning of post-industrialization, with their industrial structure gradually transiting to new and service industries. However, unlike developing countries, developed countries, such as the United States, through introspection about their domestic industrial structure after the international finan-cial crisis, have come to realize that the crisis has much to do with the serious imbalance of proportion between real economy and virtual economy. To improve the imbalance of industrial structure, the U.S. government has definitely proposed to reduce the proportion of the financial sector in the national economy, revitalize its manufacturing industry, strive strenuously to develop diversified industries, including traditional low-end manufacturing industries, and stand the American economy upon the "rock" rather than the "beach". To stabilize and promote eco-nomic growth, the world's major economies have preempted the commanding heights of economy and science and technology, entering into an unprecedented era of innovation and development of newly emerging industries, with the break-through of key technology and the promotion of strategic emerging industries as new economic growth points, and ascertaining the prioritizing domains.

Fourth, it is the effect of economic globalization. Since the 1990s, the rapid development of the high-tech industry with the information technology revolution as the center has not only broken through the national boundaries but also shrunk the distances across countries and regions to make the world economy integrated. However, the economic globalization is "a rapier with double blades", which has promoted the development of global productivity, accelerated world economic growth, and provided rare opportunities for a few developing countries to chase after developed countries on the one hand, and has intensified international competition, increased international speculation, and magnified international risks on the other hand. At present, economic globalization has shown strong vitality and exercised tremendous impacts upon the economic, political, military, social, cultural, and all other aspects of international life, even the ways of thinking. In addition, economic characteristics may vary from country to country in different stages of economic development, such as China's dual economic structure and differences of economic development between the east, central and west regions, etc.

In the face of economic relations characterized by increasingly larger volumes, more complicated structures and faster changes, the traditional binary theories of macroeconomic and microeconomic systems have proved to be powerless to answer why government and market failures coexist in Western countries or why China has been able to achieve economic miracles in the past 30 years of reform and opening up. Our long-term study of China's economic growth reveals that regional governments have played crucial roles in regional economic development, hence mezzoeconomics.

From the perspective of historical materialism, when micro- and macroeconomics can no longer adapt to the development of new productive forces and productive relations, a new theoretical system must come into forth to replace or ameliorate the old system so that it will adapt to and promote the development of new productivity. The proposition of mezzoeconomics, based on the GFL theory, embodies both chance and historical certainty. Mezzoeconomics helps to considerably improve and perfect the contemporary economic theories, to constitute the new superstructure of economics together with micro and macroeconomics, and facilitate and serve productive relations so as to promote the development of productivity.

First, mezzoeconomics can function as the experimental field for macroeconomy by means of its innovation and breakthroughs. In the mid-1980s, mezzoeconomic development models were explored and tested in certain regions of China in the light of their own situations, such as the South Jiangsu model, the Wenzhou model and the Pearl River Delta model, etc. Those models are the result of regional development on their own initiatives on the basis of their own situations and have played important roles in propelling macroeconomic development. Direct economic benefits can be generated by the messo-level to provide easy, direct and convenient service for new growth, which in turn can help to resolve certain urgent problems in mezzoeconomic development. These problems are also hot and difficult on the macroeconomic level and will gain national affirmation and central support once they are solved and generate favorable demonstrative and driving effects. The implementation of most of the reform measures and policies in China has followed the path of first "feeling stones" on the mezzo-level and then "crossing the stream" on the macro-level.

Second, mezzoeconomics can better perform the functions of stabilization and coordination and can effectively reduce excessive fluctuation in macroeconomy. Mezzoeconomy can act as the "stabilizer" and "compression release valve" for macroeconomy, which includes top-to-bottom and bottom-to-top flow of effects. In top-to-bottom flow, when there is large vibration of macroeconomy or when it is disadvantageous to mezzoeconomic development, full play should be given to the subjective initiatives of mezzoeconomy to "absorb" harmful "radiation" through each level of mezzoeconomy and reduce their harmful effects to the minimum. In the early 1980s, when national economic adjustments were conducted in China to reduce investment in infrastructural construction, some provinces gave full play to the regulatory function of mezzoeconomy so as to maintain the strong momentum of comprehensive growth in the main economic indicators under the great pressure of drastic decline in infrastructural construction investment. In the mid-1990s, after introducing the policy measures for national hypothermia of the real estate industry and squeezing "economic bubbles", the economy of Hainan was seriously affected, and yet through vigorously promoting tourism, high-efficiency agriculture and creating favorable external environment for microeconomy, the shock waves were reduced to the greatest extent possible, which revitalized and energized mezzoeconomy soon after short-term twists and turns. In bottom-to-top flow, when there occur bad signs on the microeconomic level, the mezzo-level can intervene in a timely manner and offset the inefficiency of macroscopic monitoring.

Finally, mezzoeconomics can help to complete the control system of national economy and diversify risks of centralized control. From the perspective of reform, the mezzoeconomic regulating and control system plays irreplaceable roles in the entire national economic system. According to the cybernetic theory, the optimization of multiple targets in the national economic system is, in the final analysis, seeking for the extremum of function. Under the condition of centralized control, the number of function arguments increases rapidly to drastically expand the optimization system of space, thus bringing about enormous difficulties in refined calculation. Meanwhile, the structure of the centralized control possesses high rigidity, and the adaptation of random and environmental variations for the system can only stem from its center. Although the centralized control can stabilize the system in the long run, the invariable structure of the system and the transitional and evolutionary contradictions of its various parts will eventually evolve to extremely sharpened conditions. Moreover, the centralized control can reduce the operative reliability of the system. Once failures occur in the control, it is difficult to prevent and rectify them in each subsystem, which will deteriorate the whole system. If different levels of decision making were proposed by diverse subjects and each subsystem has strong independence, it is termed hierarchical (or dispersion) control. The vertical division of authority of hierarchical control can overcome the weaknesses of the centralized control to a great extent and adapt to the variations of environment and systems, enabling the function of autonomous strain for each level. Simultaneously, the control efficiency will be improved with the increase of information accepted and processed by lower levels. The economic operational mechanism of hierarchical controls means that the central government takes charge of regions, departments and large groups, which in turn supervise and manage enterprises or microeconomic levels.

5.2 A research framework for mezzoeconomics

Economics studies productive relations that are determined by productivity and are in proportion to the developmental levels of productivity, namely the economic structure. Since focus is laid on the production mode in which productive relations must adapt to the development of productivity, it is essential to look into a few basic elements of productivity and productive relations on micro-, macro- and mezzoeconomic levels: the subject, the object and the tool. This section will follow the above logic for discussions.

5.2.1 Microeconomics

According to the microeconomic theory and the basic principle of productivity and productive relations, it is not difficult to find that in microeconomics, the subject is the single economic unit (mainly consumers and businesses), the object is the commodity, and the tools are costs and prices. Microeconomics takes into consideration the subject, the object and the tools as well as their mutual relations, which means it studies how consumers influence the production and consumption of goods via prices and how enterprises influence the production and consumption of goods through costs and prices.

Thus, microeconomics focuses exclusively on the economic behaviors of individual economic units, taking costs and prices of the commodity as its starting point and hereby extending to the enterprise's production and operation, the income and expenditure of the family, the number of certain types of products and their prices in the market, etc., thus forming the entire theoretical system of microeconomics, which includes: the equilibrium price theory, also termed as price theory, which studies the price decision of the commodity and how the price adjusts the operation of the economy as a whole; the consumer behavior theory, which studies how consumers distribute limited income to the consumption of various items to realize the utility maximization, which is the further explanation of demand as one of the price decision factors; the production theory, namely the theory of producer behavior, which studies how producers use limited resources to produce all kinds of goods and maximize profits, including the production theory that focuses on the relation between production factors and output, the theory of costs and profits, and the theory of the manufacturers' behavior, which studies manufacturer behavior under different market conditions, which altogether offers further explanation of another price decision factor – supply and discusses how manufacturers produce; the theory of distribution, which studies how products are allocated to different social subjects and the principles for allocation, namely how to decide the wages, interest, rent and profits, which explains the question of for whom to produce; the general equilibrium theory and welfare economics, which studies the realization of optimizing social resource allocation and the realization of social and economic benefits.

Modern microeconomics covers a wider range of issues, including property rights economics, human capital theory, etc. which have all developed on the basis of the principal theory of microeconomics.

5.2.2 Macroeconomics

In macroeconomics, the subject is the state, the object is national income, the tools include monetary policies and fiscal policies. Macroeconomics studies the interrelations between them, in other words, how the state employs monetary policies and fiscal policies to increase national income. Thus, macroeconomics takes the activities of the whole process of national economy as the research object and the national income as the starting point, extending through investigations of GDP and its growth and fluctuation, the total output level, the total price changes and the overall employment status, etc. to monetary policies and fiscal policies, which forms a complete theoretical system of macroeconomics. Its core theory is national income decision theory, including the theory of unemployment and inflation, the theory of economic cycles and economic growth, and the theory of open economy.

Macroeconomics covers issues like economic growth, fluctuation of economic cycles, unemployment, inflation, national finance, international trade, etc., which involve national income and the consumption of the whole society, savings, the ratio of investment and national income, the amount of currency in circulation, the velocity of circulation, price levels, interest rates, population size and growth rate, the rates of employment and unemployment, the national budget and deficit, import and export trade and balance of international payments, etc.

Macroeconomics pays the foremost attention to a country's economic growth, i.e. a country's growth of potential productivity. Macroeconomics holds that the government should and is capable of employing fiscal policies, monetary policies and other means to adjust aggregate demand, stabilize periodical economic fluctuation, overcome economic recession and avoid inflation in order to achieve "full employment equilibrium" or "full employment without inflation". The fiscal policies and monetary policies are interactive and mutually supportive, but different countermeasures, either expansionary or contractionary, are to be adopted in different periods and under different conditions, such as economic recession and inflation.

During the depression, expansionary fiscal policies and monetary policies are to be adopted. In terms of fiscal policies, tax reduction and expansion of government spending will be taken as the major measures. Tax reduction increases the income of enterprises and individuals after taxes to stimulate enterprises to expand investment and individuals to increase personal consumption. The expansion of investment demand and consumption demand will lead to the growth of aggregate demand and eventually overcome recession. In times of inflation, contractionary fiscal policies and monetary policies are to be adopted using the same tools as above but to make economy move in the opposite direction, namely the tightening mode rather than the expansionary mode.

Microeconomics and macroeconomics mainly differ in the following aspects:

(a) Objects. The research object of microeconomics is a single economic unit, such as family, manufacturer, etc. As concluded by the American economist J. Henderson, the optimized behavior of such individual units as households and manufacturers lays the foundation for microeconomics. Macroeconomics, however, focuses on the entire economic behavior and studies the operation mode and laws of the economy as a whole and analyzes economic issues from the angle of the gross volume. Samuelson once stated that macroeconomics analyzes the whole behavior of the economy on the basis of output, income, price level and unemployment. E. Shapiro, the American economist, emphasized the function of macroeconomics in investigating the national economy as a whole.

(b) Issues. Microeconomics aims to resolve problems concerning resources allocation, namely what to produce, how to produce and for whom to produce, in order to realize the maximized individual benefits. Macroeconomics takes the allocation of resources as the vested premise to study resources utilization within the scope of the society in order to maximize social welfare.

(c) Approaches. Microeconomics employs micro-analysis and studies how to decide the individual value of economic variables, while macroeconomics employs aggregate analysis and analyzes the decision of economic variables, their variations and correlations, reflecting the running situation of economic operation. The aggregate analysis covers two categories: the sum total of individual quantity and the average quantity.

(d) Assumptions. Microeconomics takes market clearing, entire rationalization and sufficient information as its fundamental assumption and considers that the "invisible hand" can adjust freely to optimize resources allocation. Macroeconomics assumes that the market mechanism is imperfect and that the government is capable of regulating economy and rectifying the defects of market mechanism through the "visible hand".

(e) Core theory and basic substance. The core theory of microeconomics is the price theory, including the consumer behavior theory, the production theory, the distribution theory, the general equilibrium theory, the market theory, the equity theory, welfare economics and management theories, etc. The core theory of macroeconomics is the national income decision theory, including the unemployment and inflation theory, the economic cycle and economic growth theory, and the theory of open economy, etc.

5.2.3 Mezzoeconomics

Just like the research frameworks of microeconomics and macroeconomics discussed previously, mezzoeconomics also has the subject (regional government), the object (resources allocation) and the tools (policies and measures) in its framework and studies the interrelations between them.

5.2.3.1 The subject – the regional government

In the mid-1970s, Hans Rudolf Peters, the German professor of national economics in The University of Attenborough, first proposed the concept of "mesoeconomy" (mezzoeconomy). In the mid-1980s, Wang Shenzhi, a Chinese scholar, attempted to elaborate upon Peters' mezzoeconomic theory in his book *Mezzoeconomics* (1988).

According to Peters, mezzoeconomics mainly covers three areas: sectoral economics, regional economics and group economics. Sectoral economics generally refers to the aggregation of one or more regions' economy of a similar kind, which is formed according to the product group, technological characteristics of material production or the nature and functions of economic activities, also known sometimes as industry. The interrelation and interaction between various departments jointly constitute the sectoral structure of economy of a country or a region (i.e. the industrial structure). Certainly, departmental division is based on different situations, different angles and even different needs. They may be divided by referring to various sectors of economic entities, such as the economic management organizations established by the government, like coal department, metallurgical department, forestry department and fishery department, etc. Another type is the intangible division, such as the primary industry, the secondary industry and the tertiary industry, or labor-intensive sector, capital-intensive sector and technology-intensive sector, etc.

Regional economy is the aggregation of a number of departments and different categories of affiliations in the same region characterized by comprehensiveness and relative independence, in which each region has its own features according to its regional advantages, and interrelations and interaction of different regions form the spatial structure of the national economy (productivity distribution). It must be mentioned that regional economy is not the general regional economy but the administrative regional economy, with the administrative region generally referring to administrative districts, like province, city and county, etc., and regions of other kinds fall into the scope of regional economics.

Group economy is generally thought of as the economy of enterprise groups and is the aggregation of sectoral economy and regional economy in the same economic organization, characterized by overlapping, comprehensiveness and independence. For professionalized groups, it is an aggregation of a single department in the same region or in different regions, and for comprehensive and integrated groups, it is an aggregation of a number of departments in the same region or in different regions.

Obviously, Peters and Wang Shenzi have proposed some ideas concerning mezzoeconomics, which reflects their thoughts on the deficiency in Western economic systems. However, without their direct involvement in the economic practices of China's reform and opening up, it was unlikely for them to realize underneath economic phenomena that regional governments with dual functions are the major subjects of economic activities, though they analyzed economic activities based on the concepts of mezzoeconomy relative to micro and macro economy through differentiation of economic scales. For various reasons, they failed to recognize the actual subject of mezzoeconomy, i.e. the regional governments with dual functions, which are the principal entity of productivity and productive relations at the mezzoeconomic level. Mezzoeconomic research should focus on regional governments, which jointly promote regional development through macro-regulation and control and regional competition, as regional governments share the characteristics of quasi-microeconomic entities similar to those of enterprises and of quasi-economic entities similar to those of the nation.

In addition, sectors or industries in Peters' and Wang Shenzhi's research are divided merely according to the same or similar product groups, technological characteristics of material production and the nature and functions of economic activities. They do not constitute the subjects in the real sense. For example, the telecommunications industry or the tertiary industry is merely an abstract conceptual synthesis, and there does not exist such a subject that stands for them and take economic action in the real economy. Moreover, the groups mentioned by Peters and Wang Shenzhi are essentially the principal enterprises in microeconomics, except that they may produce different products or conduct inter-regional production, such as multinational corporations in Western economics. Therefore, the analytical tools of microeconomics can be largely employed to analyze and explain the behavior of groups as the market economic subject.

It has been clarified in the previous analysis that the GFL theory mainly concentrates on regional economy and regional government and analyzes regional economy from the mezzoeconomic perspective. Regional government has the main characteristics of market economic subject, and the effects of its dominant role are of significant influence to regional economic development. In China, apart from competition between sole proprietors and companies, there is another type of competition with typical Chinese characteristics – competition between regional governments at the provincial, municipal, county, and even township level. This type of competition is the key factor behind China's economic miracle, which embodies the effects of GFL and forms the core background for mezzoeconomics studies.

Economic theories are derived from economic practices and are intended to explain economic phenomena and provide guidance for economic activities. Without taking into consideration regional government competition and the role of GFL, the mezzoeconomic system will be devoid of its theoretical significance and practical guidance either from the historical perspective of theoretical development of economics or from the angle of three-level logic induction of philosophy.

To sum up, mezzoeconomics lays its focus on the role of regional government with dual functions as the economic principal in productivity and productive relations.

5.2.3.2 The object – resources allocation

After the identification of the subject of productivity and productive relations in mezzoeconomics – regional governments with dual functions, what now needs to be clarified is its corresponding object – the object of mezzoeconomics.

Before answering this question, let us comb through the research framework of microeconomics and macroeconomics once again. In microeconomics, the subject is the consumer and the enterprise, the object is commodity, and the tools are costs and prices. Microeconomics studies the subject, the object and the tools as well as their interrelations, that is how consumers influence the production and consumption of goods through prices and how enterprises influence the production and consumption of goods through costs and prices. Thus, microeconomics aims at the economic behaviors of individual units, adopts costs and prices of the commodity as the research starting point and extends to the enterprise's production and operation, the income and spending of the family, the number and price of certain types of products, etc., thereby forming the theoretical system of microeconomics.

In macroeconomics, the subject is the state, the object is national income, and the tools are monetary and fiscal policies. Macroeconomics investigates the subject, the object and the tools as well as their interrelations, that is how the state employs monetary and fiscal policies to increase national income. Consequently, macroeconomics considers the activities of the whole process of national economy as its research object and national income as the starting point and extends through the investigation of the GDP of national economy, the GDP growth and volatility, the total level of output, the total price changes, and the overall employment situation to the monetary and fiscal policies, thus forming the entire theoretical system of macroeconomics. The core theory of macroeconomics is the national income decision theory, including the unemployment and inflation theory, the economic cycle and growth theory, the theory of open economy, etc.

The object of mezzoeconomics is mainly the allocation of resources. Resources refers to a kind of objective mode of existence which can create both material and spiritual wealth with a certain amount of accumulation, including natural resources (like land resources, mineral resources, forest resources, marine resources and oil resources, etc.), manpower resources, financial resources, industrial resources, and infrastructure resources, etc.

(a)   Natural resources

Natural resources are the material base of human survival and development and the source of social material wealth and one of the important bases for sustainable development, characterized by limitedness, regionality and entirety. The regional government should adopt market-oriented approaches and prohibitive, restrictive, guiding or supportive measures to adjust the price, usage modes and conditions for all kinds of natural resources in the light of their characteristics and to optimize the allocation of all kinds of natural resources, which not only ensures the favorable development of regional economy but also maintains the harmonious balance with natural resources and the realization of sustainable development. The marketization of natural resources can make the resources-based industrial sectors deepen the exploitation of natural resources, the processing industrial sectors reduce their demand for natural resources, and other industrial sectors (such as the construction industry, the transportation industry, etc.) strengthen their awareness of cherishing natural resources. The marketization of natural resources plays quite positive roles in inhibiting industrial demand for natural resources, improving productivity, reducing wastes and establishing the resource-conserving industrial structure.

(b)   Human resources

Human resources is a general term for people who can contribute to national economy and social development with capabilities for intellectual work and manual labor, with biological, epochal, initiative, duplicity, timeliness, continuity, regeneration characteristics in terms of quantity and quality. With the rapid development of modern science and technology, economic development chiefly depends on the improvement of population quality. Human resources will play more and more important roles in economic development with the extensive application of modern science and technology in production. Human resources, as a special and crucial type of resource, constitute the most dynamic and elastic part among all kinds of productive factors.

(c)   Financial resources

Financial resources refers to the sum of a series of objects or their aggregation in terms of structure, quantity, scale, distribution, effects and interactive relations of financial services' subjects and objects in the financial sector. It comprises three intimately related levels of resources: the general monetary assets, financial organizational systems and financial assets (tools) systems, the overall function of financial systems. Financial resources play the strategic role in the development of regional economy and express its effects through the macroscopic function of the integrity often as a sort of strategic resources. The capability and efficiency of resource allocation provided by financial resources for regional economic entities determine the comprehensive developmental level of the regional economy and potential growth capability. As a kind of special resources, financial resources are not only the object of resources allocation but also the instrument of resources allocation. The regional government makes sufficient use of financial leverage of modern market economy to drive the coordinated and healthy development of regional economy by means of rational financial resources allocation.

(a) Industrial resources

Industrial resources refer to the industries and their structure possessed by a country and region. In the broad sense, industry refers to all walks of life of the national economy, which ranges from production to circulation, to service, to culture, education, etc. and can be as large as sectors and as small as a single line of industry. Industries can be divided, according to the relative intensity of the three production factors of labor force, capital and technology in each industry, into labor-intensive industries, capital-intensive industries and technology-intensive industries. According to the system factors, regulatory mechanisms of industrial structure can be divided into government regulatory mechanisms, market regulatory mechanisms, and so on.

Industrial structure cannot be purely optimized conscientiously or spontaneously, and its optimization can only be a dual process of spontaneous and conscientious regulation. The efficiency of the allocation of resources via market regulating mechanism outclasses that of the planned regulatory mechanism. While bearing in mind that market is the chief means of resources allocation and structural adjustment, it is necessary for regional governments to formulate rational and foreseeable policies of industrial structure in case of the blindness of investment behaviors, to plan for preferential sectors for development and the development sequence of leading industries, fundamental industries and strategic industries, to enhance the function of government leading and improve regional economic benefits and the overall quality of economic structure.

The phenomenon of industrial agglomeration in industrial development can also facilitate innovation. The innovation of enterprises often stems from the interaction between enterprises and between enterprises and customers. Enterprises can more easily discover the gap of products or services and get enlightened so as to find market opportunities and research and develop new products. Industrial agglomeration increases opportunities of communication for employees from different enterprises to sparkle their thoughts and generate innovative thinking. The regular meetings and exchanges will bring innovative inspiration to enterprise managers and technicians of each enterprise in the same park, which is the embodiment of the spillovers of knowledge and technology. It also helps to foster the competitive advantage of enterprises. The four determinants in Michael Porter's diamond model of enterprise competitive advantages are the production factors, demand conditions, related and supporting industries, corporate strategic structure and competition within the trade, which are the requirements of enterprises possessing competitive advantages. Enterprises are the subject of regional economic development. If the clustered enterprises in industrial parks meet these conditions, it is possible for them to improve the competitiveness of their enterprises, their industries and their regions. Industrial agglomeration intensifies competition, which is in turn one of the important sources for corporations to acquire competitive advantages. Competition is not just manifested in the competition for market but also in other ways. For example, the same industries in the same region that have the scale plate of performance evaluation may conduct comparison between themselves, which brings the innovative pressure and power for corporations, compels them to continuously reduce costs, improve products and services, as well as catching up with the tides of technological changes. Enterprises in the agglomeration zone have stronger competitive advantages than those scattering outside of the zone, thus more likely to access the leading edge of the industry.

(b)   Infrastructure resources

Infrastructure resources refer to the material engineering facilities providing public services for social production and residential livelihood and the public service systems ensuring the nation's or region's socio-economic activities on the right track. They are the general material conditions for social survival and development. Infrastructure includes transportation, post and telecommunications, water and power supply, business services, scientific research and technical services, landscaping, environmental protection, culture, education, public health and other utilities. They are the foundation for national economic development. In the modern society, the more developed the economy, the higher the demand for infrastructure. Impeccable infrastructure accelerates socio-economic activities and promotes the morphological evolution of their space distribution patterns.

Infrastructure construction possesses the so-called multiplier effect, which can generate total social demand and national income that are several times of the amount invested. The complete infrastructure of a nation or a region is the important foundation for the long-term sustainability and stability of its economy. In the 1930s, President Roosevelt pursued the famous "Roosevelt's New Deal" to cope with the unprecedented great depression, part of which was the key policy of government-led large-scale infrastructure construction, which boosted employment, increased public income, and laid a solid foundation for the later development of the U.S. economy.

Infrastructure has the feature of antecedence and fundamentality. Thus, public services supplied by infrastructure are essential to production of all types of goods and services, without which other goods and services (mainly direct production and operational activities) would be difficult to produce or supply. Infrastructure, such as highways, airports, ports, telecommunications, water factories and other industries, also possesses the feature of wholeness and indivisibility and can render services or effectively provide such services under normal conditions only if it attains a certain scale. Small-scale investment will not produce the desired effects.

5.2.3.3 The tools – policy means

It has already been defined before that the subject of mezzoeconomics is regional government and the object of research is the allocation of resources. Then what are the research tools? It is our view that the research tools of mezzoeconomics, which originates from the GFL theory, should be various policies and measures adopted by regional governments, including the means of investment, prices, taxation, laws as well as the modes of innovation in organization, institution, technology, management and so on, which aim to achieve the efficient allocation of various resources and promote the sustainable development of regional economy. They can be roughly classified into economic means, legal means and administrative means according to the different properties of the policies and measures adopted by regional governments.

(a) Economic means

Economic means indicates that regional governments adjust the demand and supply of goods and affect the formation of prices to conscientiously regulate and guide regional economy on the basis of the law of value and with the aid of the regulating effect of economic leverage. Under market economy, economic means mainly include prices, taxation, and investment, etc. Under market economy, regional governments tend to adopt indirect economic measures to regulate and guide prices. With regard to local governments, reserve systems and the price adjustment fund systems of staple commodities are crucial marketized measures of price adjustment and control to ensure the relative stability of general price level in the region and to promote the harmonious development of regional economy, which enable the government to effectively adjust price operation of staple commodities in accordance with the law of value and the changing situation of market supply and demand and keep the price-rising range of staple commodities within bearable limits.

Something more must be said about price regulation fund, staple commodity reserve system and active regulation and control of prices of resources, such as land. Local governments utilize price regulation funds to stabilize market prices and lessen the burdens of urban and rural residents, especially low-income groups, so as to protect their interest and maintain social harmony and stability. The price regulation funds have three functions to perform: first, support prices of agricultural products through subsidizing producers, which is mainly applied when market prices of agricultural products are low. If production cost is higher than market price, farmers will suffer losses, as the saying goes, "low grain price hurts farmers". In this case, the government will subsidize producers to strike the balance between market price and target price by setting target prices so as to maintain stable supply.

Second, stabilize fluctuations in prices, especially when agricultural product prices rise at unusual speed. For example, the supply of agricultural products will decrease in the case of natural disasters, and their prices will go up sharply. Under such circumstances, a low-order price will be set and subsidies will be provided to strike a balance between market price and the set low-price limit to arrest inflation. If demand drives prices up, prices are to be stabilized through differential subsidies. If price rises continue, which is disadvantageous to residents, especially low-income groups, the government will provide consumption subsidies to consumers, in particular low-income groups, so as to stabilize demand and reduce prices.

Third, lower the equilibrium price by supporting construction of production bases and increase the level of supply so as to shift the supply curve to the right, which is a relatively long-term tactic, and its effects will not come out until after a given period of time. This measure is characterized by greater stability, relative to short-term price policies. Agricultural production possesses the mechanism of acting on agricultural product markets by means of both supply and price, so price regulation funds are applied extensively and are remarkable for their rapid price adjustment function in response to emergencies or important festive seasons. Besides, regardless of inflation or deflation, price regulation funds can effectively stabilize market supply and price fluctuations and protect the interests of the producers and consumers.

Viewed globally, agricultural policies are more subject to government intervention, which is determined by the supply and demand character of the agricultural sector. Owing to the actual reality, intervention organizations and policies vary from country to country in terms of agricultural policy implementation. The United States establishes such organizations as the federal government credit company, and the European Union the intervention center. Countries vary in terms of agricultural policies owing to specific situations but most of them regard pricing policies as the core, while the traditional pricing policies mainly employ price subsidies to maintain agricultural development and balance the interests of consumers and producers. Price regulation funding is an important part of China's supportive policies in the agricultural sector.

In addition to price regulation funding, the staple commodity reserve system is also an important means of regional governments regulating market prices. On August 31, 2011, for example, Guangdong provincial government issued "The Work Program about Promoting Pork Production and Stabilizing Prices" to maintain the stability of pork prices. It requires that the regulatory mechanism for preventing excessive pork price decrease and the mechanism for guaranteeing market supply, both of which are to be based on the reserve system, should be established to protect the legitimate interests of producers, consumers and operators, that the earlywarning index should be established to optimize the regulative means of taking in and sending out the reserves and prevent excessive increase and decrease of pork prices, that full play should be given to the guiding role of fair-price shops in stabilizing prices by maintaining pork supply at prices lower than the average market price and lower than over 10% of the average prices in the local markets when prices continue to rise, and that the initiatives of "stabilizing pork prices" should be actively mobilized to propose that all fair-price shops in the province reduce pork circulation cost by butt welding production and marketing or production, supply and marketing.

Guangdong provincial government also requires that the gross amount of pork reserves, as well as frozen pork reserve, be increased at the provincial level, the reserves of frozen pork and pigs be established and replenished according to local reality, pork reserves suffice to meet the demand of no less than 10 days in localities and in large and medium-sized coastal cities and no less than 7 days for other regions, and pork reserves be ready for timely market supply that follows the order of local cities and then provincial capitals.

Land is one of the three factors of productivity and is so important to government and enterprises that it acquires the title of "the mother of fortune". The prices of land and other resources determine, to a great extent, the production cost and market competitiveness of enterprises. Land resources are mainly under the control of government, especially regional governments. Even in Western countries, government possesses the right to manipulate land planning. Therefore, the pricing policies of regional governments for land resources are bound to exercise tremendous influence upon enterprise production and the formation of industrial structure.

Since China's adoption of the tax distribution system in 1994, the proportion of tax revenues local governments retain has somewhat increased, thereby tremendously arousing local government's enthusiasm of attracting investment, which has led to the escalating of competition for investment, the result of both game playing and interest seeking on the part of local governments. Starting from the 1990s, competition for attracting capital between local governments has become increasingly intensified, and new contending methods have been created, ranging from providing various kinds of preferential policies for foreign investors to contending with peer governments for foreign capital, to taking the initiatives of sending delegations abroad to invite investment, etc. Local governments mainly have two cards to play in investment competition: preferential institutional arrangement and cheap land resources.

In 1992, China conducted the institutional reform of land utilization to turn land into resources that were without price and are now priced, which endowed local governments with the role of "actual land manipulator". As a rule, capital chases profits, and in order to acquire maximum capital, local governments rationally chose to decrease the cost of capital flow into their administrative region, whereupon land resources became an important inductive tool, hence the "land price war". Local governments in many regions attracted investment at low land prices, which tempted a large number of productive enterprises to settle in their region. Situation started to change upon entry into the twenty-first century. Local governments, especially those in coastal developed areas, shifted their low-price land transfer lands to urban management. They put more emphasis upon land development, consolidation and rehabilitation and promoting urbanization through which to gain land revenues.

Why did significant changes take place in land prices adopted by regional government? Could it be that regional governments made irrational policies? The answer is certainly in the negative. The changes of land policies are the very price measures applied by regional governments for initiative adjustment of land prices in the light of differences in stages of economic development and industrial policies. In the initial stage of development zone establishment, land was supplied for short term and relatively infinitely, which could be considered the elasticity of land supply being inclined toward infinity with regard to demand, i.e. land supply curve presents itself in a horizontal line. Rational local governments would supply land on the basis of the principle of cost pricing (even below cost pricing) in return for long-term tax revenues and employment from enterprises. It also happened that local governments might take no account of actual contributions of the introduced enterprises to the improvement of industrial structure and regional economy and dispose land to foreign investors at prices below cost and even at symbolic prices merely for political achievements, which resulted in the inefficient allocation of land resources and land abuse. Under such circumstances, the earnings of fund introduction were inadequate to offset the reduction of resident welfare and the net loss of social welfare.

With the increasing maturity of development zones, land supply became more and more limited, and the cost of land supply increasingly heavy. Meanwhile, with the progression of industrialization and urbanization, residential real estate and commercial real estate driven by service industries ushered in vigorous growth. The opportunity cost would greatly increase if regional governments continued to supply land to industrial enterprises at low prices. If regional governments sensed that the benefits of attracted investments were less than their opportunity costs, they would no longer invite investment by land but utilize land for urban operation. That is precisely the basic logic of regional governments conducting industrial selection through land prices and market competition. More detailed analysis will follow in the third section of this chapter.

As mentioned previously, local governments mainly depended upon preferential institutional arrangement and cheap land resources as instruments for investment competition. After implementing the tax distribution system in 1994, local governments acquired independent authority in finance. Regionally, the institutional arrangement of various kinds of laws, regulations, policies and other soft environment, as public goods, is usually supplied by local governments. One means of competition between local governments is providing the institutional arrangement superior to that of other regions so as to attract external capital. That is why some scholars deem local government competition as institutional competition (Feng Xingyuan 2001). External capital investors choose those regions where the expected marginal efficiency of capital can be optimized according to their preferences for the institutional arrangement of specific regions. Among all the institutional arrangements, the taxation system is of the greatest interest to external investors. Local governments tended to provide such preferential policies tax exemption to attract investment and even more attractive preferential policies of taxation for certain key projects.

Regional governments have formulated different preferential taxation policies according to the magnitude of their financial solvency and the direction of their industrial development. Investors can take full advantages of the differences of taxation systems in different regions and regional tax dips to choose investment destinations and reduce the cost of investment to gain greater investment returns. There are generally 16 classes of regional privileges in China: (1) special economic zones; (2) coastal economic development zones; (3) economic and technological development zones; (4) high and new technology development zones; (5) coastal open cities; (6) Yangtze River and Pearl River open cities; (7) inland open cities; (8) border open cities; (9) national tourist resorts; (10) Suzhou industrial park;

(11) Fujian Taiwan Investment Zone; (12) Shanghai Pudong New District; (13) Hainan Yangpu Development Zone; (14) export processing zones; (15) tariff-free zones; (16) the Midwest and poverty regions.

Apart from regional differences, the focal points of preferential taxation policies vary from time to time. With varying degrees of continuous economic development, taxation preferences have been converted from direct privileges to indirect privileges and from regional privileges to industrial privileges so that taxation policies conform to a greater degree to the orientation and requirements of industrial policies.

Now let's come to investment means. Public investment plays a pivotal role in a country's economic development strategy, especially in long-term development. China's implementing the strategy of sustainable development once met with the problems of inadequate infrastructures and public investment. Moreover, the severe imbalance of regional economic development became the shackle for steady, rapid and sustainable socio-economic development. Thus, the promotion of regional economic development must resort to local governments' public investment.

Local government possesses duality. One the one hand, it must ensure the sustainable and stable development of regional economy as it plays the role of administering certain territorial areas and a certain population size, and on the other hand it must comply with the jurisdiction and guidance of the central government politically and economically and fulfill the duties and carry out the plans prescribed by the state and the central government. Therefore, macroscopic policies and goals for local regulatory investment should be decided through unified central decision making and reflect the unity of centralization and the interests of the whole. However, the level-to-level administration should be adopted for implementation to reflect the flexibility of the power of local government and the differences of group interests. All this points to the fact that local government is not only the principal to be regulated but also the administrator to regulate in investment. As an entity to be regulated, local government should fulfill the function of conducting national macroeconomic regulation and support regional construction of key national projects in investment and financing. As a regulator, local government should manage regional public welfare projects, create favorable investment environment and provide good services for investors.

The implementation of the tax distribution system enables regional government to possess relative financial autonomy and to adopt more investment means to optimize regional resources allocation and promote regional sustainable economic growth, including infrastructure investment (particularly land investment), subsidizing investment in infrastructure, the guidance funds of government industries, etc. Due to the fierce competition between regional governments, regional government frequently stimulate local economic growth through investment in such areas as infrastructure, as well as creating favorable institutional arrangement and investment atmosphere. The recent round of regulation has made local governments the main driving force for investment growth.

Apart from issues like regional government's status as agent and short-term investment objectives, which are to be elaborated upon in the third section of this chapter, regional government investment is often confronted with low efficiency, mainly embodied in its investment inclination toward economic construction and the short-term tendency of investment objectives. In regions where the market forces are weak, competitive project investment is most likely to be local government's rational choice, though it is hard for such offside government investment to gain ideal results. Local government tends to be tempted by economic construction projects, rather than those social projects with long-term effects, which leads to obvious deficiency of public expenditure for people's livelihood.

Due to its limited term of office, local government investment also manifests short-term defects. Assuming that local government investment earnings are measured by the index of net present value, which are the difference between the present worth of income and cost present value, the greater the index of net present value, the higher the efficiency of public investment. It could be discovered by analyzing the investment behavior of local governments with the indexes that when local governments choose investment projects, they would select projects with higher discount rates, as local government officials have strict terms of office. In the case of projects like environment protection programs that demand great costs to disburse at sight, it is likely for local government to delay investment, which causes undercapitalization; in the case of those projects that can bring about large sum of earnings at sight, it is likely for local government to show up strong investment impulsion, which then generates overinvestment. Furthermore, at times of election and change of terms, local government will be more likely to adopt expansionary economic policies, like increasing public expenditure, to stimulate and speed up economic growth, a typical reflection of political cycles. Periodical growth points can be detected from the statistics released by The National Bureau of Statistics in fixed investment in 1983, 1988, 1993, 1988 and 2003, when government changed its term of office.

Like the principle of preferential taxation mentioned previously, subsidizing infrastructure investment refers to regional government's direct investment in infrastructure chiefly used by enterprises to reduce investment costs and attract investment according to the needs of enterprises in addition to the traditional subsidies of land prices and tax preferences in the course of investment promotion. For instance, a provincial government in the Western region of China provided huge sums of fiscal subsidies and project operating subsidies to attract Samsung to settle down there by implementing the preferential policy of income tax, shortened as "ten exemptions and ten reductions to half" and providing free land and factory buildings, expressways, metros and other means of transportation and other supporting facilities, which was reported to have amounted to at least 200 billion yuan.

Government industrial guidance funding has been touched upon in the discussion of guaranteed credit funds for small and medium-sized enterprise in Shunde and will not be repeated here.

(b) Legal means

Regional government should employ legal forces, economic laws and judicature to regulate economic relations and activities. Economic legislation mainly includes the formulation of economic laws and regulations by legislative bodies to protect the rights and interests of main market players; economic judicature covers the procuratorial and trial proceedings of economic cases by judicial offices to maintain market order and punish and sanction economic crimes according to the laws and regulations.

Legal means cover economic legislation, judicature, and law enforcement. Regional government can apply legal means to realize the "rule of law": first to refrain government from random intervention in economic activities, and second to constrain the behaviors of economic beings and maintain market order, including the demarcation and protection of property rights, the enforcement of contracts and law, fair judges. To put it in a nutshell, macroeconomic regulation should be incorporated into legislation so as to enable the "visible hand" and the "invisible hand" to scientifically supplement each other.

The legal means of economic regulation has general characteristics of law, such as coerciveness and normalization. Compared with laws of other domains, it also possesses the distinct economic nature, which is mainly embodied in: (1) The subjects of regulation should at least include authorized functional departments of macroeconomic management or comprehensive economic sectors. Regulation and control are mainly intended to offset blindness arising out of spontaneous market adjustment and let market mechanism play a fundamental role in the allocation of resources. Consequently, regulation and control are indirectly conducted in accordance with law and with market as the intermediary agent within authorized limits and on the basis of the diversification of subject interests in market economy, instead of previous direct administrative orders under planned economy; (2) The objects of regulation and control are market economic relationships, ranging from economic relations between industries, markets, countries, enterprises and individuals to any segment of social reproduction, distribution, exchange and consumption, with a view to maintain national economic aggregate and the balance of economic structure; (3) The interaction between subjects and objects should not violate economic rules. The legislation and application of legal means must abide by market economic laws.

Characteristics of legal means determine their special function in economic regulation and control: (1) Orientation function, which is embodied in the pioneering function of legislation. Legislation must be based on social reality and is both the verification of existing facts and the guidance of future behaviors. It standardizes people's behaviors by stipulating their rights and obligations as well as the responsibilities required to assume while violating legal provisions, for instance, the selective guidance for subject behavior via stipulating norms of "what can be done" with a view to encouraging subject initiatives within the limits of law and the positive guidance for subject behavior via stipulating norms of "what should be done" with a view to preventing behaviors of disturbing market economic order; (2) predictive function, which means that due to the normalization and relative stability of law, market subjects can clearly predict the force of law brought about by their and other behaviors according to law and make reasonable arrangement for prospective economic activities so as to protect their own benefits; (3) supportive function, in which the establishment of "fair and free competition order" is the foundation for economic regulation and control, and the improvement of legal systems contributes to solving civil and economic disputes and provides system safeguard for the formation of good order, on the one hand and, on the other hand, market economy seeks both efficiency and justice, and its drawbacks need to be compensated for via legalized social security systems; and (4) incentive function, which exerts favorable influence upon the initiatives and creativity of subjects, as legislation grants guarantee to rights and interests of each subject in normative forms.

(c)   Administrative means

Administrative organizations adopt compulsory orders, instructions and stipulations, etc. to regulate economic activities so as to achieve the goal of regulation, control and guidance. Administrative means are characterized by authority, lengthways, gratis and quick reaction, such as the closure of heavily polluted small coal mines and oil fields upon government directives. Under market economy, regional government should not employ administrative means as its major instrument. Instead they should be used as the auxiliary tools of economic and legal means. Administrative means should be adopted to promote the implementation of economic and legal means.

5.3 Reflections upon mezzoeconomics

Based on the analysis of the role of regional government in economic activities, especially in China's economic practices of reform and opening up, the GFL theory is proposed with elaborate exposition of its background, justification, practices and prerequisites. Extensions are made from this theory to further propose that economics be divided into macroeconomics, mezzoeconomics and microeconomics and that a theoretical framework be established for mezzoeconomics, with the dual-role regional government as its subject, the allocation of resources as its object and various policies ad measures as tools.

5.3.1 *The revenues of regional governments*

5.3.1.1   *The components of government fiscal revenues in Western countries*

Local government here refers to government below the level of federal departments or ministries, and in the United States it covers all levels of government units below the level of state government, like counties, cities, townships, education districts, special districts, and so on. Local government is the major part of a state, regardless of a unitary state or a federal state. Public finance is essential to maintaining its operation and performing its administrative functions. There should be a clear definition of inter-governmental authorities of office and property. Local government takes responsibility for the supply of public products and services in its region and therefore should possess relatively stabilized sources of income. Government needs financial revenues and levies taxes from the public by virtue of public power so that it can provide public goods and maintain its operation. Local government obtains income according to relevant laws to perform its functions. Viewed globally, the fiscal incomes of local government are mainly constituted by tax revenues, transfer payments and other incomes. The proportion of fiscal revenues for local governments varies from country to country and reflects the value orientation of inter-governmental relations influenced by a country's history, politics, economy, culture and other factors.

(a)   Tax revenues

In terms of the composition of tax revenues, property tax is the main part of the tax system for local governments in the United States and Canada, and the administrative authorities of inter-governmental taxation are relatively independent, while revenues of local government in Germany mainly come from revenue sharing between the federal and the state government and their tax administrative authority is strictly controlled by superior governments. Real estates (property) tax has a long history in North America and is levied annually at the rates that are determined by the evaluation of land and buildings. It is the primary source of tax revenues for local governments in the United States and Canada and even the sole source in some regions, accounting for about 40% of the revenues going to the local authorities. The tax revenues of local governments in Germany account for about 35% of their local fiscal revenues, mainly including land taxes and industrial and commercial taxes levied since the nineteenth century, 15% of federal income taxes shared since 1969 and part of the value-added taxes shared since 1998. Over recent years, the proportion of industrial and commercial taxes has gradually decreased, and tax revenues of local governments in Germany have come increasingly from inter-governmental tax sharing.

(b)   Transfer payment

The transfer payments of local governments come from the subvention of the federal and state governments, which are the important source of local government revenues and account for about 30% and 40% in the United States and Canada respectively in their local government revenues. In the United States and Canada, subsidies from the federal government are limited and are used for special projects, such as education, urban development, transportation, etc. The main transfer payments come from the state (provincial) government. Subsidies are divided into the general type with unlimited conditions and the special type with restricted conditions for particular purposes. In Canada, owing to the constant growth of local public spending in the early twentieth century and the increasing deficiency of real estate taxes, the provincial government started to provide various kinds of appropriation to local governments, and most appropriations were conditional. The transfer payments of local governments in Germany include the budget allocation of the federation and states for different regions and fiscal appropriation as direct subsidies, which account for about 27% of revenues for local authorities.

(c)   Other revenues

Other revenues mainly include royalty revenues, territorial bonds, etc., which have become important means of generating revenues for local governments under fiscal difficulties. Royalty revenues are mainly the voluntary payment of the general public using public goods, such as the charges of electricity, water, sewage, roads and bridges, park tickets, and athletic facilities, etc. In the United States, Canada, and Germany, fiscal revenues paid by the users of public facilities have been on the increase over recent years. In Canada, for example, royalty revenues accounted for 6.5% of the income of municipal governments in 1965, 12.2% in 1980 and 21.3% by 2000 (Tindal and Tindal, 2008).

In the United States, local governments can raise funds for economic construction by issuing bonds according to the federal constitution to offset inadequacy of its financial funds, balance financial revenues and expenditures in the short term and raise funds for the construction of toll roads and bridges, which can be paid back by users in the long term. However, the provincial (state) governments in Canada and Germany impose strict restrictions upon local governments in issuing bonds that can only be used for infrastructure construction investment. Over the past decade, local governments of Germany have begun to sell local assets and enterprises of public utilities owned and operated by local governments to remit financial crises, with the proportion in local revenues rising from 3% in the 1980s up to 5% in the late 1990s.

5.3.1.2 The composition of fiscal revenues of local government in China

Since 1950, China's fiscal systems have experienced three stages: the unified system of collection and allocation of funds by the state from 1950 to 1979, the system of dividing revenues and expenditures and fiscal responsibilities from 1980 to 1993, and the system of tax sharing since 1994 up to now. Seven fiscal administrative modes were employed in the 30 years under the first system, and three modes under the second system (as shown in Table 5.1). The composition of fiscal revenues of local governments varied greatly with different modes of fiscal administration. After 1994, the fiscal relationship between the central and local governments tended to be stabilized, with only occasional adjustments of some tax types.

Table 5.1 China's national fiscal policies and administration

Implementation Time		Fiscal Administration Mode
First	1950	Highly centralized, unified collection and allocation
Stage	1951–1957	Dividing revenues and expenditures, hierarchical administration
	1958	Revenues determining expenditure, no change for five years
	1959–1970	Localized revenues and expenditure, planned responsibilities, regional coordination, total sharing, one year term
	1971–1973	Fixed expenditure and revenues, fiscal responsibilities, guaranteed turnovers to higher authorities (or difference subsidies), balance surplus retained, one year term
	1974–1975	Revenues reserved according to fixed proportion, different proportions for increased revenues, expenditures determined according to targets
	1976–1979	Fixed and coordinated income and expenditure, total divided according to proportions, one year term, experimenting "income and expenditure coordinated and sharing increased revenues"
Second Stage	1980–1985	Dividing revenues and expenditure and hierarchical responsibilities
	1985–1988	Classifying tax types, checking revenues and expenditure, and hierarchical responsibilities
	1988–1993	Fiscal responsibility system
Third Stage	1994 to present	Continuation of expenditure identification of central government from local government, classification of taxes into central tax, local tax, and shared tax by central and local government, determining tax base for central government, gradual standardization of transfer payments

The tax-sharing reform launched in 1994 determined the composition of existing types of revenues for the local governments, mainly including the shared revenues by the central and local governments and local fixed revenues (as shown in Table 5.2). However, these are not the whole, and sometimes even not the main component of local fiscal revenues. Local fiscal revenues in China can be classified by their sources into tax revenues, transfers from the central government, non-tax revenues, local debt income and other income (Category A). They can also be categorized by different managing modes into budget income, extra-budget income, debts and outside-system income.

It can be clearly seen from the fiscal balance sheet that the non-tax income is an important part of local fiscal revenues. The non-tax revenues refer to the fiscal income collected according to the law and administrative regulations by the state departments, social organizations and other groups at all levels when they perform management functions, exercise the ownership of state-owned assets or

Table 5.2 China's local budget revenues since the 1994 tax distribution system

Revenue Sources		Proportion (%)		Remarks
Revenues Shared by Central and Local Government	Value-added Tax	Central Local	75 25	The value-added tax reform that started in 2009 allows enterprises to deduct the value-added tax in equipment purchasing.
	Income Tax — Enterprise Income Tax	Central Local	60 40	Exemptions for railway transportation, postal services, four national banks, Sinopec, COSL, etc. 50% for both central and local government before 2003 and 60% for central government and 40% for local government after 2003.
	Individual Income Tax	Central Local	60 40	
	Resources Tax — Petroleum Resource Tax	Central Local	100 0	No tax collection for central government, but in the form of mineral royalty tax, which turns resources tax into a sole type of tax for local government.
	Other Resource Tax	Central Local	0 100	
Income Shared By Central and Local Government	Securities Exchange Stamp Tax	Central Local	97 3	Proportion was 50% for both central and local government before 1997 and changed to 80% for central and 20% for local government in 1997 and to 97% for central and 3% for local government. Only Shanghai and Shenzhen share the proportion.
Local Fixed Income	Transaction Tax	Local	100	Excluding transaction taxes of railway services, head offices of banks, headquarters of insurance companies.
	Urban Maintenance and Construction Tax	Local	100	Excluding the part jointly collected from railway services, head offices of banks, headquarters of insurance companies.
	Contract tax, real estate tax, vehicle and vessel tax, stamp tax, farming land occupation tax, tobacco tax, land value-added tax, rural and urban land employment tax, etc.			

Table 5.3 Fiscal revenues of China's local government

Category A	Components	Category B	
Tax income	Value-added tax (25%), enterprise income tax(40%), individual income tax (40%), transaction tax, urban maintenance and construction tax, contract tax, etc. and other tax types listed in Table 5.2	Budget income	
Transfer Payment From Central government	Tax revenue returns		
	General transfer payments (financial transfer payment)		
	Special transfer payments	Budget income	Extra-budget income
Non-tax income	Administrative and institutional charges collectable (Among the 236 items in the 2008 National & Central and Individual Administrative and Institutional Charges Catalogue, 141 items are related and collected by local financial authorities.) In addition, similar charges are collected by local government		
	Special income (pollution discharges, water resources, education, education additional charges, etc.)		
	Penalty charges		
	Government funds	Budget income	Extra-budget income
	State-owned capital operation income (profit turnovers from local state-owned enterprises)		
	Royalty income from state-owned assets and resources)		
	Other non-tax income, like lottery, donations for government, interest income from government financial capital, administrative permit income.		
Debt income	Direct debt income	Debt income	
	Indirect debt income, mainly liabilities from urban construction investment corporations		
Others	Funds, charges, fundraising, penalty and institutional deposits from outside system	Income outside system	

resources and provide particular services, etc. According to the National Treasury's final accounts data, the non-tax revenues collected by the local governments remained below 20% of the general budget revenues between 2005 and 2008 (as shown in Table 5.4).

However, Table 5.4 fails to give a complete picture of non-tax revenues of China's local government, not even the great part of them. The proportion of land transfer fees, which have recently taken a lion's share of local fiscal revenues, is considerably underestimated. According to the statistics of the Ministry of National Land Resources, the total land conveyance fees amounted up to

Table 5.4 Non-tax revenues of China's local government 2007–2012

Indexes	2007	2008	2009	2010	2011	2012
Budget revenues(hundred million)	23,572.62	28,649.79	32,602.59	40,613.04	52,547.11	61,078.29
Non-tax revenues(hundred million)	4,320.5	5,394.68	6,445.15	7,911.56	11,440.37	13,759.21
Non-tax revenues(percentage)	18.33%	18.83%	19.77%	19.48%	21.77%	22.53%

Source: www.mof.gov.cn

Table 5.5 Proportion of land lease to local fiscal revenues

	2009	2010	2011	2012
Local fiscal revenues (hundred million)	3,260.259	4,061.304	5,254.711	6,107.829
Total land lease price(hundred million)	1,425.38	2,939.798	3,347.7	2,888.631
Percentage of land lease income to local fiscal revenues	43.72	72.39	63.71	47.29

Source: WIND

760 billion yuan in 2006 and then rose to 1,300 billion in 2007. It remained high to be 960 billion in spite of the financial crisis in 2008. That figure from 2009 to 2012 was 1,430 billion, 3,000 billion, 3,350 billion and 2,890 billion, respectively.

For years, local public finance has depended too much upon land convey-ance fees, and the proportion of land conveyance fees in local public finance has remained to be over 40% over the same period, even reaching a height of 73% in 2010, as shown in Table 5.5. In some cities and counties, the land conveyance fees has taken over 50% of extra-budget fiscal income, and even over 80% in others.

There are two distinct features in the structure of China's local fiscal revenues in comparison with that of the United States. One of them is that the non-tax rev-enues take up a greater proportion so that China's local fiscal revenues are of less stability. The other is that the land transfer income and governmental debts are high, bringing about potential financial risks. In China, the local government can raise revenues by two means. It can boost local economic growth to collect more taxes from the expanded tax base, and it can also gain non-tax revenues from land selling and transfers, etc. At the time of a flourishing real estate market, such a structure of fiscal revenues in which land-related income accounts for a great proportion enables the government to obtain more revenues for the investment in urban construction and economic growth. However, if the golden time of real estate market fades away, the land-oriented revenue structure will possibly cause great fiscal risks.

Due to the central government's regulation policy on the real estate market in 2011, the land transfers in China's 130 cities totaled 1,863.44 billion yuan, decreasing by 13%. Many cities witnessed a sharp decline in land conveyance fees, and they were faced with the increasing pressure upon their fiscal security. The reason is that the municipal governments have borrowed a lot of land-related loans through various local financial platforms to support the large-scale industrial and infrastructural projects at the peak of the prosperity of the real estate market. These projects were more driven by the fierce inter-jurisdictional economic and political competition, so they usually have long period of investment return.

5.3.2 Explaining development zones and industrial parks from the perspective of mezzoeconomics

In the years of 1993 and 1994, China witnessed an upsurge of development zones that were mushroomed in many regions. Although many of them were soon called off by the central government, more and more industrial parks emerged in the following waves of investment promotion. As a promising innovative energy-saving industry, for instance, the LED industry soon became the new favorite of the local governments and their industrial parks. The enterprises entering the industrial parks enjoyed such preferential policies as low-cost land and capital subsidies, causing a massive influx of capital into this this new industry and resulting in repeated construction and serious overcapacity. The investment on the production of LED sapphire substrate might be the most overheating, causing an unexpected sharp and fast decrease in the price. Only from January to July of the year 2011, the price of two-inch sapphire substrate dropped by averagely 50%, from US$35 to US$13 to $15 a piece. The price of LED chip also went down by 25% on the average. This phenomenon motivates us to think about why the local governments were so keen on the construction of development zones or industrial parks since 1993 and 1994.

5.3.2.1 Reform in taxation and state-owned enterprises and strategy of regional operation

A glimpse at the history may help understand the motivations that drove the local governments to operate their regions like enterprises. Around the year of 1994, China launched two influential reforms. One of them was the tax-sharing reform that brought about a changeover in the revenue-sharing structure, in which the local governments had taken the lion's share since the 1980s. That year, the fiscal revenue of the central government climbed up to 290.65 billion yuan, more than the local fiscal revenue of 231.16 billion yuan. However, the fiscal responsibilities imposed on the local governments were not accordingly reduced, so the local fiscal deficits soon emerged. The other reform of the enterprise system was conducted in 1995 with emphasis on the privatization of state-owned enterprises. The local governments could no longer set up and run local enterprises, which used to be an important source of revenues. As a result, these two reforms forced the local governments to pave a new way of "regional operation" that focused on local land developing, including establishing development zones or industrial parks.

The mode of regional operation means that the local government operates its jurisdiction as it runs an enterprise. Like a land owner, the government composes the plan of development and create favorable environments to attract investments. It adjusts the industrial structure and cultivates the leading industries and key enterprises to increase the economic output. The local government sets up the goals of local economic growth and formulates accordingly the plans of land use, infrastructural construction, investment solicitation and industrial structure adjustment. The administrative power and financial resources are employed to put these plans into operation. The local governments exercise direct control upon public operative projects and regional factors of production to ensure the implementation of plans, including land development and management, construction and operation of industrial parks and their supporting infrastructure, investment services, preferential policies for leading industries and key investors. In terms of land utilization, local governments grant the rights of project investment and operation to investors by means of "investment solicitation and introduction",

This practice shares similar characteristics with "shopping mall" in that the owner plans, invests and manages the mall, but he does not directly operate individual counters. The owner provides good shopping environments and operational conditions, advertises for the whole mall, and attracts commercial tenants by renting the counters. The owner has income from renting the counters and sharing sale revenues. There is thus a dual-leveled operating structure in such shopping centers that combines the management of the whole mall and the dispersed operation of individual counters, which form together the mode of operation and competitive strength of the shopping mall.

Steven Cheung (2009) believes that the county economy of China has the similar dual-leveled operating structure as the shopping center. In his words, "A county can be seen as a huge shopping mall run by an enterprise (i.e. the county government), and the investors as the commercial tenants. They pay a fixed amount of rent plus a part of sales revenue, as the land price and taxes paid by the investors. As the owner of the shopping center tends to make a careful choice of his tenants and provide various services to them, the county government offers favorable policies to the investors."

According to Hu Wei (2007), the local government no longer treats the investment programs of a specific enterprise as their own projects by offering financial and fiscal supports. Instead, it takes the whole county as an enterprise, in particular in developing industrial parks. On the one hand, the government changes its way from supporting certain enterprises to guiding the overall direction of industrial development, cultivating the leading industries and investing in industrial parks. On the other hand, the government centralizes fiscal resources previously devoted to individual enterprises and focuses on the construction of public infrastructure and supportive facilities.

Consequently, the relationship between the local governments and the enterprises has changed. Hu Wei (2007) believes that the local government plays a role similar to that of an "enterprise service corporation" in its jurisdiction, providing investment services to all enterprises as well as some special services to certain enterprises. In this respect, the biggest innovation of local governments is the establishment of development zones and industrial parks. "The relationship between the development zones and their enterprises is in fact the relationship between the government and enterprises. The job for development zones is to do what lies outside the walls of the enterprises well, like maintaining good investment and production environments. To put it metaphorically, development zones are like large enterprise service companies, which offer everything the enterprises acquire outside their walls." (Hu Wei 2007) In addition, having under control the factors of land, communications, power supply, etc., the local government assumes the role of facilitator in local economic development.

The local governments turned to new approaches mainly because they were faced with different external environments as a result of the market-oriented reform and the tax-sharing reform promoted by the central government. The local governments found that their fiscal revenues could hardly support their fiscal responsibilities imposed by their superior government. They had difficulty in reducing the rigid demand of financial expenditures, and they could no longer return to rely on the income from state-owned enterprises. Under the new system, the local governments' disposable income had mainly two sources. One of them was the value-added income associated with land transfers, and the other was the locally preserved taxes like the income tax, construction and real estate tax, etc., boosted by investment solicitation and urban expansion (Jiang Shensan, Liu Shouying 2007). With the goals of increasing local fiscal revenues and promoting the officials' personal career development, the local government had to keep such productive factors as land under its close control. The government thus governed its jurisdiction like running an enterprise so as to avoid losing in the inter-regional competition.

5.3.2.2 Industrial agglomeration theory

From a different perspective, the development zones and industrial parks are driven by the local government which follows the theory of industry cluster in promoting local economic growth. This theory is among the most important economic laws for messo-economic analysis.

Industry cluster often refers to the phenomenon that a group of related enterprises gather together in certain geographic locations in industrial development. Closely linked and mutually supportive to one another, these clustered enterprises in general belong to the same industrial chain and occupy different specialized positions in an industrial network that is horizontally and vertically organized. The enterprises benefit from the economies of scale and the competitiveness of the entire industry is thus strengthened with the help of the spillover effects associated with the sharing of technology, information, talents, policies, etc.

The theory of industrial cluster has drawn high attention from the scholars across the world. They explored the causes and formation of industrial clusters from the perspectives of economic externalities, industrial location, competition and cooperation, technology innovation and competitive advantage, transaction costs, progressively increasing returns, etc.

(a)   The theory of economic externalities

In the time of classical political economics, Adam Smith (1776) touched upon the industrial agglomeration in his famous work *The Wealth of Nations*. Based on the theory of absolute advantage and from the perspective of industrial division, he argued that the industrial cluster is a group of enterprises united together to complete a product.

For the first time in the book *The Principles of Economics*, Alfred Marshall (1890) put forward the concepts of the industrial cluster, internal agglomeration, and the externalities. He investigated the economic motivations for industrial clusters under the conditions of the economies of externality and scale. He pointed out that the so-called internal economy refers to the economy that is contingent upon resources, organization and operating efficiency of individual enterprises that undertake industrial production, while the external economy refers to the general developed economy that depends on the production of such industries. He proposed three causes of industrial agglomeration. First, the agglomeration promotes the development of professional industrial services. Second, it creates a labor market and attracts the workers with specific skills to a certain location where there would be neither the shortage of labor nor the high rates of unemployment. Third, the agglomeration can generate spillover effects of technology and information that increase the output of production of the clustered enterprises.

Furthermore, Marshall pointed out that the agglomeration of more enterprises of the same industry in one space would induce the agglomeration of the productive factors needed by these enterprises, including labor, capital, energy, transportation, and other resources. In turn, the agglomeration of these productive factors helps to reduce the average production cost of the whole industry and thus to increase the efficiency and competitiveness of enterprises located in this space. In the light of such reasoning, Marshall formulated the concept and theory of industrial zones (industrial districts). According to Marshall, the economy of agglomeration is rooted in that the connections between the enterprises, institutions and infrastructure in a space can bring about the economies of scale and scope in production as well as the breeding of a general labor market and the concentration of professional skills. All these promote eventually the interaction between the producers and consumers in sharing the local infrastructure and other productive facilities. In short, by pointing out the existence of labor "pool", Marshall (1920) proposed that the availability of non-traded inputs and the externalities of knowledge spillovers would cause industrial concentration. However, his analysis applies more reasonably to one industry and fails to explain the agglomeration of different industries.

(b)   The theory of industrial location

Johann Heinrich von Thünen (1783–1850) put forward the creative location theory with focus on spatial transportation differences. In the first part of his book *"The isolated state in relation to agriculture and national economics: studies on the influence of grain prices, the richness of soil and the yields from crop farming"* (1826), he attempted to develop a framework to explore the patterns of agricultural activities on the outskirts of a representative city before Germany's industrialization. He might be the first to explain economic agglomeration by examining a variety of elements. The hypothesis of endogenous market in the Thünen Kreise model typically combines the assumption of constant returns to scale and perfect competition, and he is thus named the founder of marginalism economics.

Alfred Weber (1868–1958) proposed the creative concept of agglomeration in *Über den Standort der Industrie* (*Theory of the Location of Industries*, 1909). His theory of industrial location was derived from the location choice of enterprises. By assuming an enterprise minimizing its production cost, he concludes that the optimal choice of location minimizes the cost. The industrial agglomeration can bring down the cost, and whether the enterprises gather together depends on the comparison between the benefits and costs of agglomeration. By defining agglomeration as cost saving, his theory pays little attention to the causes of agglomeration and just assumes it as the outcome of internal economies of scale. He aims to explain the causes for such agglomeration rather than agglomeration economics itself. The factors shaping the choice of location are classified into regional factors and agglomeration factors, and the agglomeration factors evolve in two stages. In the first stage (also the primary stage), the advantages of agglomeration are mainly generated through the expansion of enterprises themselves. But in the second stage, the individual enterprises are connected and organized in the industrial network, which is the most important to boost local industrialization.

August Lösch (1906–1945) (1940) studied the interactions between industrial agglomeration and urban formation and urbanization. He pointed out that the location of a large enterprise may sometimes bring forth a city, and in this case, it is the location of massive enterprises that are engaged in a kind of integrated production of goods and services. Viewed from the perspective of location theory, the so-called integrated production can also result in several industrial locations that are related to the integrated production. He argues that urbanization is essential for industrial cluster, which results from the spot-by-spot gathering of non-agricultural activities. Furthermore, he identifies the agglomeration into free agglomeration and location-constrained agglomeration. The former can occur in any location, such as the gathering of enterprises surrounding a large enterprise, the gathering of enterprises of the same or different industries, and the gathering of consumers, etc. However, the latter is under the constraints of locations and under the influence of such inherited factors as population density, terrain, wealth and spatial differences.

(c)   The theory of transactional cost

The neoinstitutional economists explain industrial agglomeration with the help of the concept of transactional cost. The core idea is that the enterprises emerge as a substitute of the market, which manage resources by forming organizations to save the cost of market transactions. In the opinion of Coase (1937), the production can be effectively coordinated by means of price mechanisms in the market, but the managers should play the role of organizing production inside the enterprises with the absence of transaction. Although these two means are different, they assume the same function of coordinating production. By putting forward the transactional cost theory, Coase analyzed the boundary problems of organizations. As he illustrated, the role of the enterprises or other organizations is to organize the owners of different factors to form a unit to participate in market exchanges. By this means, the number of the traders in the market is reduced and so are the degree of information asymmetry and the transactional costs. Derived from this theory is that the industrial agglomeration generates economic benefits, say, lower transaction costs.

According to Coase and Williamson, industrial agglomeration helps to reduce the uncertainty of environment, change small amount conditions, overcome the opportunism in transactions and improve the symmetry of information, thus reducing the transactional costs. Therefore, from the economic perspective, the rationale behind the constructions of development zones and industrial parks by the local governments is consistent with the theory of industrial cluster. As industrial cluster often takes place within a limited range of space, the theory of industrial agglomeration is an important part of mezzoeconomics.

Industrial agglomeration occurs under certain conditions. A type of industry may run well in one place but does not at all in another, as a Chinese old saying tells, the orange changes with the environments, hence the concepts of resource endowment and industrial structure, as will be discussed below. If the local government does not follow the basic economic laws in boosting local industries, they will be punished by unexpected consequences, as happens to the LED industry.

5.3.2.3 Resource endowment and industrial structure

Resource endowment, also known as endowment of factors, refers to the extent of abundance of productive factors in a country or a region, including labor, capital, land, technology, management, etc. The concept of industrial structure is generally defined as the proportions of different branches of industries in the whole range of industry and the connections between them. The upgrading of factor endowment mainly depends on capital accumulation, which in turn determines the optimal industrial structure in a region.

The Swedish economists Heckscher and Ohlin propose that a country should make its industrial policies in accordance with its domestic factor endowments in which the comparative advantage of this county is rooted. The country should make full use of its relatively abundant factors in production to improve welfare.

Later on, their theory was furthered by the Polish economist Tadeusz Rybczynski. He argues that the increase of one factor will reduce the output of products intensive in another factor. It can be derived that the labor-intensive industries will experience a decline and thus should no longer be protected in the countries where the stock of capital grows. In contrast, the development of capital-intensive or technology-intensive industries may be untimely in the developing countries where the supply of labor is still to increase. Otherwise, it is likely to result in the loss of comparative advantages and the phenomenon of "more haste and less speed" in economic growth.

When an industry develops according to the structure of factor endowments, it will acquire comparative advantages and produce products with comparative advantage. It thus receives higher returns of profit as well as faster accumulation of capital. The enterprises in pursuit of maximized profits are reasonably to organize their production in accordance with their factor endowment structure. Figure 5.1 shows how the choice of production is determined by the structure of factor endowments. There are three representative counties numbered 1, 2 and 3 with different factor endowment structures. Country 1 is capital-intensive, Country 3 is labor-intensive, and Country 2 is in between them. The three countries have different iso-cost curves, which intersect with the iso-quant curves and result in different optimal choice of production. Country 1 chooses capital-intensive technological R & D in new products, Country 2 prefers the chip production, and Country 3 the labor-intensive assembly. With such choices, the three countries can achieve the same level of output and maximize their profits. In conclusion, the

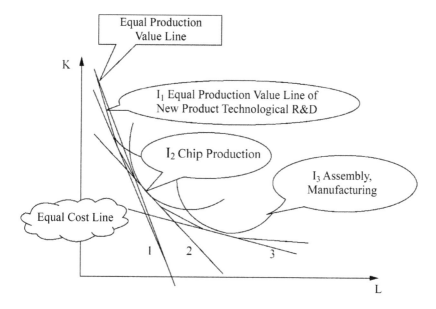

Figure 5.1 Factor endowment structure

structure of factor endowments shapes the comparative advantages of a country or region, which in turn determines the optimal industrial structure and even the optimal product chosen in the same production line.

The analysis of factor endowment and industrial structure above may offer some tips for the local industrial development. If one region has no factor endowments necessary for the development of a certain industry, it would be better not to insist in introducing such an industry. Otherwise, for lack of comparative advantages, the cost of such development will go too high and the effect of industrial cluster will be greatly discounted.

5.3.3 Explaining land finance from the perspective of mezzoeconomics

5.3.3.1 The definition and characteristics of land finance

Land finance in China refers specifically to the income local governments earn through transferring land utility rights to maintain local fiscal expenditure. It falls into the category of off-budget revenues, also known as the secondary fiscal revenues. China's "land finance" mainly relies on incremental land to create revenues, which means selling land to meet financial needs.

In many regions, the secondary fiscal income has surpassed the first budgetary revenues. According to the report released by the State Council Development Research Center, in some places, direct land taxation and indirect taxes derived from urban expansion accounted for 40% of local budget revenues, and the net income from land sales and leases more than 60% of government budget revenues. In terms of "land finance", the major practice of some local governments is land consolidation and rehabilitation, which means that local governments use their administrative power to integrate collective land or land for other purposes for action and take land yields.

The most serious dependence upon land finance is found in underdeveloped cities in Central China and in coastal regions where development zones have not become the pillar of industrial development, and land finance is currently the main source of government revenues in less developed cities and newly emerging areas where related supporting industries are not well developed.

Over the past decade or so, there has been a rapid increase in land sales income and in the proportion of local fiscal revenues. Statistics shows that in 2001–2003, China's land sales income reached over 910 billion yuan, about 35% China's local fiscal revenues over the same period, and the 2009 land sales reached 1.5 trillion yuan, about 46% of China's local fiscal revenues over the same period. In some counties and cities, that took more than 50% of their non-budgetary income, and even more than 80% in some others.

Judging from an objective perspective, over the past decade or so, land finance proved to be of great significance to alleviating local financial insufficiency, easing difficulties in financing for public goods supply, creating employment opportunities and improving urbanization. The outcries for land finance have arisen from its somewhat irrational and unfair operation and a series of malpractices. The most seriously criticized is its benefit coupling mechanism. Years of land finance has, in fact, created a scrolling mode of "land acquisition, land sales, tax collections, mortgages, and then land re-expropriation". Huge profits from land acquisition and land sales even enticed occasional illegal use of land.

Driven by this benefit coupling mechanism, high land prices have become inevitable, followed in turn by high housing prices. The continuing rise of housing prices causes housing to be owned by wealthy families, and most other households will have poor financial capability, and their opportunities have been diminishing, which eventually leads to social inequality. Land finance also causes the excessive flow of capital into real estate industry, which is not conducive to optimizing economic structure. Over the recent years in China, the real estate industry has become such a "field of capital attraction" that some large enterprises in garments and home appliances industry have transformed themselves into housing developers.

Land mortgage revenue growth for local governments has also intensified financial risks. According to the National Auditing Administration, by the end of 2009, in the 18 provinces, 16 cities and 36 counties that were audited and investigated, the balance of government debt amounted to 2.79 trillion yuan. The ratio of the balance of government debt to the financial resources available in that year in 7 provinces, 10 cities and 14 counties was more than 100%, with the highest being up to 364.77%. From August to September 2013, an extensive auditing of government debts was conducted by a huge army of 54,400 auditors collected by the National Auditing Administration in 31 provinces, autonomous regions and state-level cities, covering 391 municipalities, 2,778 counties and 33,091 townships.

The results show that local governments in the whole of the country were liable for a total debt of 20.07 trillion yuan, 2.9 trillion guaranteed debt, and another 6.65 trillion that local governments were likely to shoulder the rescue responsibilities, totaling 30.3 trillion yuan. In addition, local government debts were to a great extent dependent upon land conveyance fees. By the end of 2012, 11 provinces, 316 municipalities and 1,396 counties pledged to repay their debt residues of 3.5 trillion yuan, accounting for 37.23% of the total 9.4 trillion yuan. A large proportion of local government loans depended on land sales for repayment. When market prospects are good and land sales are successful, local governments are able to repay the loans through well-paid land sales, and once housing prices go sharply downward and land prices will also fall, risks are inevitable for banks and local finance.

The collection and abuse of land finance has seriously overdrawn future earnings. As far as local governments are concerned, land sales are made for the accumulative total rent within fixed numbers of years that is charged once and for all and is used for current spending, which will increase fiscal revenues in the short term but overdraw decades of future earnings and is bound to harm future interests and cause deficit spending.

It can be concluded that land finance is unsustainable. A city's land resources are limited. Once sold out, its subsequent fiscal spending is not guaranteed, and what is worse is the serious waste of such resources. Revenues from land sales have long been collected and spent by local governments without standardized regulations and supervising mechanisms. Rent-seeking and corruption are not uncommon.

Land finance has played an important and positive role in China's industrialization and urbanization. However, with the deepening reform, the disadvantages of the previous practices have more and more obviously become the obstacle for China's sustainable development in future. Mainland China has mainly learned from Hong Kong in land leasing system. However, no such unfavorable circumstances have occurred in Hong Kong's land management and lease, which suggests that even under the land lease system policies may also come into being that are suitable for economic development.

5.3.3.2 Land finance in America

Let us have a look at how land finance works in the United States before we begin our analysis of it from the economic perspective. The fiscal revenues associated with land in the United States mainly fall into three categories. First, the government receives the income by selling the land as assets. Second, the government levies taxes on the land and the real estate built on it. Third, the government also collects some non-tax revenues that are related to land.

(a)   The evolution of land revenues in the United States

The evolution of land finance in the United States can be divided into several stages. In the first stage (1776–1861), the government gained land-related revenues predominantly by means of selling state-owned land. At the early time, the U.S. federal government was seriously entrapped in the deficit budget. In pursuit of a fast increase in the federal and state fiscal revenues, the U.S. government had to sell state – owned land. It passed a set of bills to nationalize the land in the vast west and then sell or grant it to private household or enterprises. The *Land Ordinance* of 1785 and the *Northwest Ordinance* were passed respectively in 1785 and 1787 to lay legal foundations for the privatization of state-owned land, which occupied almost 90% of the total American land at that time. Obviously, the land policies employed by the U.S. government in this stage were mostly motivated by the pressing political and economic difficulties. So with the economic development, the government relied less on the sales of land in raising the revenues, as the privatization of state-owned land was often regarded as unfair for the public.

The second stage covered the period from the Civil War to the year of 1900, which was marked by the collection of property tax in many states. The sale of land was drawn to an end and was replaced by property tax. Although the detailed tax system varied from state to state, most of them levied property tax, which was an indispensable source of revenue for the state and sub-state government, especially for county and township governments. In general, the property taxes were collected at the levels of state, county (city) and township, with immovable property (chiefly real estate) being taxed, sometimes business movable property and family property, etc. as well.

The third stage (1900–1942) was a transitional stage focusing on property tax. The state government gradually relegated the authority of collecting property tax to local governments, which led to a substantial reduction of the proportion of property taxes in the state budget and a corresponding increase in the budget of local governments. In the early twentieth century, new types of tax were set up and levied first upon automobiles and gasoline and then upon sales and income. The proportion of property taxes collected by the state government in its total fiscal revenues and total tax revenues went down from 52% in 1902 to less than 10% in its total revenues, which indicates that property taxes began to gradually transfer from the state government to lower-level governments, which made it possible to maintain the proportion of property taxes in the fiscal revenues of local governments at a high level, accounting for over 40%, and the proportion in the total tax revenues of local governments reached 80%.

The fourth stage began from the mid-1940 up to present, during which period local governments in America began to property taxes were fully developed as the main form of fiscal revenues of local finance. Land revenues mainly include property taxes, inheritance and gift taxes, housing and community development income, environmental resources income and immovable property proceeds. The proportion of property tax in the total revenues began to decline over this period but remained an important part. Relative to the total fiscal revenues of local governments, it has stayed at more than 20%, and the proportion in the total tax revenues once stayed at more than 70%.

(b) The evolutional path for America's land revenues

In the first stage, the land sales revenues went basically to the federal government, and property taxes mainly to the state government. After the Civil War, the authority of collecting property taxes was relegated to lower-level governments, and property taxes were shared by the state and local government. America's land revenues began to assume the following characteristics from the beginning of the twentieth century: (1) property taxes shared by the state and local government, though local governments' proportion is far greater than that of the state government; (2) the proportion of property taxes levied by the state government in its total fiscal revenues and total tax revenues fell steadily and sharply, but by 1936, the downward trend was slackening, and it has maintained at a low proportion since 2004; (3) the proportion of property taxes in local governments' fiscal revenues and tax revenues presented the downward trend in the initial phase of collections and continued until around 1980, but it was then arrested and has remained at about 25% and 70%; (4) the proportion of local property taxes in the total fiscal revenues of local governments has been far higher than that in the state's fiscal revenues, which suggests that relative to the state government, property taxes have increasingly become the main source of both fiscal and tax revenues of local governments; and (5) the state government has gradually turned to other types of taxes rather than property taxes as the main sources of their fiscal and tax revenues.

In the early stage, land revenues in America accounted for a greater proportion in its total revenues, reaching over 60%, and then began to decline but slowly. In the early twenty-first century, the proportion went down to less than 30%, with no great variations. It is evident that the proportion was following a pattern of initial declining and then steady progression, but land revenues have remained significant in the fiscal revenues of local government.

In the composition of land revenues, land sales income constituted a key part in the early stage. After the privatization of state-owned land, property taxes derived from land and immovable property ownership became a significant part and remained stable after a sharp rise in the proportion of land revenues. While local governments also levied inheritance and gift taxes, their proportion in the total land revenues was rather low. Though there was an increase in other charges associated with land, the total amount was still rather limited.

(c)   Lessons learned from American experience

It can be seen from land finance in the United States that land policies are intimately related to a country's political and economic environment. There is a natural and temporal logic rationale behind assets earnings from land as the main source of land finance over a certain period of time. The land privatization in the early days of the founding of the United States brought the U.S. government a large amount of non-tax revenues from land sales. In times of fiscal revenue shortage, land nationalization and then land sales can be the most convenient, the least costly, and the quickest means of acquiring revenues.

It follows that in the primary stage of China's economic construction, it is natural and inevitable to use land finance as accrual to government fiscal revenues. However, revision and amelioration of the original practices and land policies are necessary after a long-term sustained economic growth and financial strength enhancement. Even today in America, land finance still exists, but no longer focuses on assets earnings. Instead it focuses on land utilities tax, a more stable tax class.

A review of the evolution of America's land revenues shows that America's land revenues has gradually shifted from the federal government to the state and local governments. The classification of property tax, which has stable sources and is suitable for state and local government collections, as belonging to state and local governments and the transfer of land fiscal revenues into the budgetary income of local governments not only ensure stable fiscal revenues for the state and local government budget but also embody the spirit of taxes being collected from the people and being used for the people. Such arrangements lead the state and local governments to use property tax for local public environment, education, construction and maintenance of economic environment, and local socio-economic development.

5.3.3.3 The institutional logic of land finance

China's land finance started as of 1992, which has profound institutional moti-vations behind it. The tax distribution system reform in 1994 changed the pro-portional structure in which local fiscal revenues accounted for a larger share since the 1980s. In 1995, the enterprise system reform privatized state-owned enterprises, and it became impossible for local governments to directly set up and run enterprises. Under the new system, local governments had only two control-lable income sources: the land value-added income when land is liquidated and the accrual of local taxes, such as income tax, construction and real estate tax, etc. through investment promotion and capital introduction and urban expansion.

Even so, local governments' governance was not curtailed, and their rigid expenditure amplified fiscal deficit spending. Caught in such a predicament, local governments had to turn to the regional operation mode that focused on land development, including development zones and industrial districts, which also opened up the road of nearly 20 years' land finance.

Just like land finance focusing on asset returns in the initial stage of the found-ing of the United States, it is natural and unavoidable for China to the use land finance to increase government revenues and to facilitate economic development and local construction in the early stage of its economic construction.

As a result of the central government implementing market-oriented reform and the tax distribution reform, the external environment changed for local gov-ernments. Under this new situation, local financial authorities and responsibili-ties did not match, and it was difficult to reduce the rigid demand of local fiscal spending. The old practice of local governments setting up and running state-owned enterprises was abolished, and local governments could only seek help from land, which is the endogenous outcome of regional competition under the circumstances of the central government formulating unified tax rates, maintain-ing the unified national product market and capital market: local governments, in order to achieve the politically optimal economic growth target, need to attract sufficient private investment; in order to attract private investment, they need to invest in productive public goods and provide attractive preferential policies; in order to keep the cost of investment of productive public goods to their affordable range and to have the capability to provide investors with attractive preferential policies, they need to employ the rights of land supply and pricing and therefore the rights to control land development.

That is the institutional logic of land finance. At the time marking the 20th anni-versary of the tax distribution system launched in 1994, a new round of tax reform is well underway. On June 30, 2014, *The General Scheme for Deepening Reform in Public Finance and Taxation* was passed and promulgated and will provide solid foundations and support for that new round of reform in public finance and taxation. As the 1994 reform was aimed at constructing a system framework "con-gruent with socialist market economic system", so the 2014 scheme is to set up a solid base for public finance and taxation "congruent with the modernization of national governance and administrative capabilities" so as to provide foundations and support for the well-coordinated economic, political, cultural, social and eco-logical development.

5.3.3.4 Investment promotion and capital introduction or land selling – from the perspective of short- and long-term government income functions

For local governments, their income function can be defined as a combination of tax + non-tax revenues, among which land revenues constitute the major part of non-tax revenues.

Assuming that income function Y = T + NT, Y is fiscal revenues, T is tax, NT is non-tax revenues.

As is known to all, tax revenues and economic growth are related, namely T = a * GDP (assuming that "a" stands for the composite tax rate and that GDP represents economic growth).

In real economy, economic growth is a long-term process. It will not experience sudden rise or fall. As a result, GDP growth is limited.

NT falls into impact variables and is controlled by government under normal market conditions. Meantime, NT can indirectly drive the growth of GDP.

Assuming that one regional government has a plot of land (100 acres), a pro-ductive enterprise expects the government to conduct investment promotion and capital introduction and grants the preferential policy of land price reduction (real estate market price rises to 2 million yuan/acre, and the enterprise wants the gov-ernment to provide the land at the price of 1 million yuan/acre), the government has two options: either providing the land to the enterprise at the price of 1 million yuan/acre so that factory buildings can be constructed and the government can have an annual tax collection of 50 million yuan for eight successive years in two years' time, or putting the land on the real estate market for bidding at the price of 2 million yuan so that 100 million yuan of tax revenues can be generated in two years on a real estate development.

If the local government is assumed to be in office for a term of 10 years, they are likely to appraise the present value of future cash flows (PV) the above two options will bring. In this case, PV (option 1) = 333.41 million yuan, PV (option 2) = 264.46 million yuan. Rational government officials should choose scheme 1, i.e. investment introduction to the enterprise rather than land sales to real estate developers.

However, assuming that the government will be in office for a term of only 5 years, they appraise the present values of the two options on the basis of a 5-year cycle. In this case, PV (option 1) = 203.95 million yuan, and PV (option 2) = 264.46 million yuan. The government will choose to sell the plot of land for real estate development rather than soliciting long-term investment that will be of long-term benefits to local economy. The shorter term of office for the local gov-ernment, the more likely they will sell land for real estate development.

In China, government terms of office are usually short. The analysis of above functions explains why, under such administrative arrangements, the local gov-ernment is more likely to sell land for real estate development. And, of course, the above model is the most abstract analysis of short- and long-term functions of government income, which has filtered various factors that may cause changes, such as whether investment introduction enterprises will have definite tax contributions, whether real estate market prices continue to rise or fall, whether the higher-level government will look at only fiscal revenues or other factors as well in its assessment of the lower-level government performance, etc. If these factors change, the local government's decision will be likely to change accordingly.

China's real estate market came into the economic scene only after the implementation of the housing system reform in the 1990s. Before that, real estate prices underwent almost no change and growth, and land price maintained at a low level. In this context, local governments were more inclined to investment promotion strategies rather than land sales for real estate development.

With the rapid development of real estate market, opportunity costs for the local government to conduct investment promotion and capital introduction increased gradually, especially short-term opportunity costs. Under such circumstances, the short-term motivation for local governments to sell land became naturally intensified. If land development is basically saturated, or if there is small room for real estate price rise, the land finance of local governments will transit from short-term income of land sales to property tax revenues represented by real estate tax. At this point, similarities are found between the Chinese case and the American one.

Previously, the main indicators of government performance evaluation mainly included single indexes, such as GDP. However, composite indicators, such as green environmental protection indexes, sustainable growth indexes, and indexes of people's livelihood, will be introduced into the evaluation system so that the past practices of government decision making focusing on short-term results will be changed, which will bring forth positive economic Pareto optimization.

5.4 Some mezzoeconomic concepts relating to local government behavior

5.4.1 The externalities of local government's behavior

Over one hundred years since it was proposed by Marshall, the concept of externality has been widely applied to the analyses of society and economy. There are two kinds of externalities, i.e. the market externality and the government externality. The market externality is further classified into the capital externality and technological externality. The former refers to the externalities generated via market mechanism between the manufacturers with an emphasis on the interdependence of the price system, and the latter refers to the externalities generated purely by technology or other relations with an emphasis on the interdependence of production functions. The government externality is the by-product of political activities that the government changes the rule of social games or conducts administrative trading. According to Allan Schmid (1978), professor of the Michigan State University, the government externality does not directly change the costs and benefits of the stakeholders; instead, it does so indirectly by changing the rules of game or the control of property rights.

In regional economic activities, it is difficult to define the geographical limits of mobile resources such as rivers, air and human resources. As a result of this technological externality, the local government has no motivation for the protection of rivers, pollution abatement and talent cultivation. The local government may employ administrative measures to set up the entry barriers to enterprises outside the region so as to protect their own enterprises, thus changing the cost of other market stakeholders and causing capital externality.

The market-oriented reform in China since the 1990s was essentially a process of administrative power decentralization. The central government delegated the power of economic control to the local governments, thus making them independent economic units with their own interests and goals. Under the tax-sharing system and the classified budget management, the local governments have strong incentives in the pursuit of local economic performance. Whether in policy making or the construction of public facilities, the local governments intend to benefit the enterprises in their jurisdiction so as to maximize their own utility.

The current evaluation system of the local officials' performance focuses on the indicators of economic growth and fiscal revenues, etc., which are closely related to the income of microeconomic units. As there are strong positive correlations between the local economic development and the growth of local enterprises, the governments and their enterprises are of highly common interests. Economic activities are often both regional and trans-regional, and the influence of local governments often extends beyond their administrative boundaries. Therefore, the behavior of local governments will inevitably intervene in the free flow and combination of economic factors, which in turn will affect the optimal solutions of regional economic activities and give rise to the externality.

5.4.2 The principal-agent relation and adverse selection

In the world of neoclassical economics with complete information and without transactional cost or externalities, both the central and local government would seek maximizing social welfare and conduct no opportunist behavior. However, that is far from the real world with asymmetric information, transactional costs, externalities and incomplete contracts. The local government plays its game in the very complicated principal-agent relationships with the central government, the creditors (including financial institutions and individuals) and the citizens. Such multi-fold principal-agent relationships often generate serious agency principal-agent problems and incur high agency costs for the local government that acts as a representative of both the central government and local residents.

According to Jensen and Meckling (1996), the agency cost is composed of three parts. The first of them is the supervision cost that the principal has to pay for monitoring and inspiring the agent to do the best job. The second is the warranty cost that the agent swears to do no damage to the principal's interests and pays for the loss in case of any damage. The third is the cost of residual loss that is an evaluated loss resulting from the difference between the decisions made by the principal and agent, even in case that they both possess the same information and capability in decision making. Evidently, the first two costs are produced by formulating, implementing and managing the contracts, and the third is the opportunity cost that is generated by the incomplete compliance and execution of even an optimal contract.

The local government is prone to problems of adverse selection and moral hazard in the course of institutional transformation mainly because it performs the function of bidirectional agency. It seeks relatively independent economic interests, and it also has information advantages in the games with the central government.

The first agency problem is the hidden action that causes moral hazards. The local government usually expects the help from the central government in case of local fiscal difficulties. That is not far from the truth. Particularly in a unitary country, the local government is nothing but the sent-out agency of the central government. Even for the sake of its own reputation, the central government would give a hand to bail out instead of sitting by and watching the local defaults. Consequently, the local government tends to be excessively in debt or fail deliberately to pay the debt.

The second agency problem is the hidden information that causes adverse selection. The local government is often unwilling to disclose honestly the true and complete information about their financial status. It follows that the local government with worse financial status is likely to borrow more.

The third agency problem involves the creditors. They will not carefully evaluate the solvency of the local government in the lending decision when they surely know that the central government would stand to bail out local financial difficulties. This kind of agency problem will be even worse if the borrowers are the state-owned or government-controlled enterprises, as they themselves are simultaneously the agency of the government and thus care less about the quality of loans without strict constraints from private shareholders.

The principal-agent problem of the local government varies greatly from country to country due to the huge difference in their political system, legal system, history and culture. However, in the course of economic transition, the local government not only stands for local economic interests but also for its own interests, resulting in the increasingly expanding difference of interests between the central and the local government. In the case of asymmetric information, the serious problem of adverse selection and moral hazard will arise in the bargaining of interests between the local government and the central government.

Bibliography and references

An, Tongliang. 2003. The Technology Choice of Chinese Enterprises. *Economic Research Journal*. Issue No. 7, 76–84

Block, Fred. 2008. Swimming Against the Current: The Rise of a Hidden Developmental State in the United States. *Politics & Society*. Volume 36 Issue No. 2

Block, Fred and Matthew R. Keller. 2009. Where Do Innovations Come from? Transformations in the US Economy, 1970–2006. *Review of Social Economy*. Volume 7 Issue No. 3

Boadway, Robin W. 1984. *Public Sector Economics* (second edition). Little Brown

Brenner, Robert. 2003. *The Boom and the Bubble*. London: Verso

Brown, C.V. and Jackson, P.M. 1991. *Public Sector Economics* (fourth edition). New York: Wiley-Blackwell

Buchanan, James M. 1989. *Liberty, Market and State*. New York: New York University Press

Cao Zhenghan. 2008. *System Transformation of Xiaoshan Public Enterprises and Strategic Transformation of Local Government*. Hangzhou: Zhejiang University Press

Chen Jian. 2002. *Study on the 21st Century Development Strategy of Japanese Economy*. Beijing: China City Press

Chen Kang. 1994. The Decentralization and Central-Local Relation in Transition Economies. *Reform*. Issue No. 3, 136–142

Chen Qingyun. 1996. *Public Policy Analysis*. Beijing: China Economic Press

Chen Shiqing. 2009. *China's Economic Explanation and Reconstruction*. Beijing: China Modern Economic Publishing House

Cheung, Steven. 2009. *The Economic System of China*. Beijing: China CITIC Press

China Statistical Yearbook (1985–2002). China Statistics Press

Chomsky, Noam. 1998. *Profit Over People: Neoliberalism and the Global Order*. New York: Seven Stories Press

Coase, Ronald, et al. 1994. *Property Rights and Institutional Changes: The Proceedings of Property-Right Economics and New Institutional Economics*. Translated by Liu Shouyinget al. Shanghai: Shanghai People's Publishing House

Cong Shuhai. 1999. *Analysis of Public Expenditure*. Shanghai: Shanghai Finance and Economics Press

Cong Shuhai. 2002. *Study of Fiscal Expenditure*. Beijing: China Renmin University Press

Dai Wenbiao. 2002. *Introduction to Public Economics*. Shanghai: Shanghai People's Publishing House

Day, Richard H. 1996. *Chaos Economics*. Shanghai: Shanghai Yiwen Publishing House

Deng Xiu-e. 2012. *Selections of K. Marx and F. Engels* (volume 2–4). Beijing: People Publishing House

Deng Ziji. 2001. *Public Finance*. Beijing: China Renmin University Press

Ethridge, Don E. 2014. *Research Methodology in Applied Economics* (second edition). New York: Wiley-Blackwell

Fan Gang. 2003. Deflation, Efficiency Price-Falling and Economic Cycles in China, *Economic Research Journal*. Issue No. 7, 3–9

Fan Gang, Wang Xiaolu and Zhu Hengpeng. 2007. *Neri Index of Marketization of China's Provinces 2006 Report*. Beijing: Economic Science Press

Fang Fuqian. 2000. *Public Choice Theory: Political Economy*. Beijing: China Renmin University Press

Feng Xingyuan. 2001. On Inter-Governmental Competition over Systems. *Journal of National School of Administration*. Issue No. 6, 27–32

Feng Zhaokui. 1998. *Japanese Economics*. Beijing: Higher Education Press

Frederickson, George. 1996. *The Spirit of Public Administration*. Wiley: Jossey-Bass

Freeman, Christopher and Louca, Francisco. 2002. *As Time Goes By: From the Industrial Revolutions to the Information Revolution*. Oxford: Oxford University Press

Freeman, Christopher. 1987. *Technology Policy and Economic Performance: Lessons from Japan*. New York: Pinter Pub Ltd

Furubotn, Eirik G. and Richter, Rudolf. 2005. *Institutions and Economic Theory: The Contribution of the New Institutional Economics* (second edition). Ann Arbor: University of Michigan Press

Fu Yong and Zhang Yan. 2007. Chinese Decentralization and Fiscal Expenditure Structure: The Cost of Competition for Growth. *Management World*. Issue No. 3, 4–12

Gao Binghua. 2001. The Government Failure and Its Precautions. *Journal of Central China Normal University* (Humanities and Social Sciences Edition). Issue No. 1, 43–48

Gao He. 2006. Fiscal Decentralization, Economic Structures and Local Government Behavior: A Theoretical Framework of China's Economic Transformation. *The Journal of World Economy*. Issue No. 10, 59–68

Gao He. 2006. The Reasons for Non-Performing Loans of China State-Owned Banks: An Analysis Framework Based Economic Transition. *Finance & Economics*. Issue No. 12, 1–9

Gao Hongye. 1996. *Western Economics* (volume 1). Beijing: China Renmin University Press

Gao Peiyong. 2000. *Public Finance, Said the Economists*. Beijing: Economic Science Press

Gao Peiyong. 2003. Seeking Breakthrough on Active Fiscal Policy from Perspectives of Theory and Implementation. *Finance & Trade Economics*. Issue No. 7, 9–15

Gao Yanni. 2009. Principal-Agent Relation between the Central and Local Governments. *Reformation & Strategy*. Issue No. 1, 29–30

Gao Yumei and Ou Yangqiao. 2010. An Important Initiative of the European Union Supports Innovation: A Summary of the European Institute of Innovation and Technology (EIT). *Yunnan Technological Management*. Issue No. 4, 51–52

Gregory, Paul R. and Stuart, Robert C. 2003. *Comparing Economic Systems in the Twenty-First Century* (seventh edition). Boston, MA: Cengage Learning

Guo Qingwang. 2002. *Finance*. Beijing: China Renmin University Press

Guo Qingwang and Jia Junxue. 2004. Explanation of China's Economic Fluctuations: The Shocks of Investment and Total Factor Productivity. *Management World*. Issue No. 7, 22–28

Guo Yuanxi. 1997. *Capital Operation*. Chengdou: SouthWestern University of Finance and Economics Press

Guo Zhibin. 2002. *On the Incentive Regulation of Government*. Beijing: Law Press

Han Tingchun. 2002. *Financial Development and Economic Growth*. Beijing: Tsinghua University Press

Hicks, John. R. 1975. *Value and Capital* (second edition). Oxford: Oxford University Press

Hua Min. 1994. *An Overview of the State-Owned Enterprises in the World's Major Countries*. Shanghai: Shanghai Yiwen Publishing House

Huang Shichu and Li Bin. 2001. Research Review of the Relationships between the Central and Local Governments in Recent Years. *Journal of Hubei University* (Philosophy and Social Sciences Edition). Issue No. 2, 22–24

Hu Daiguang and Li Yining, et al. 2004. *Development and Evolution of Keynesianism.* Beijing: Tsinghua University Press

Hu Wei. 2007. *Government Behavior in Township During the Process of Institutional Change.* Beijing: China Social Sciences Press

Jiang Manyuan. 2007. *Competitive Problem Study of Local Government in Regional Sustainable Development.* Beijing: China Agriculture Press

Jiang Xiaojuan. 1999. Utilizing Foreign Capitals and the Transform of Economic Growth Form. *Management World.* Issue No. 2

Jones, Charles I. 1997. *Introduction to Economic Growth.* New York: W. W. Norton & Company

Kenichi Imai and Ryutaro Komiya. 1995. *The Business Enterprise in Japan.* Cambridge, MA: MIT Press

Krugman, P.R. 1979. A Model of Innovation, Technology Transfer and the World Distribution. *Journal of Political Economy.* Issue No. 3, 253–266

Lei Qinli. 2003. *Institutional Change, Technical Innovation and Economic Growth.* Beijing: China Statistics Press

Lewis, Arthur. 1955. *The Theory of Economic Growth.* London: Unwin Hyman

Li Baoyuan. 2000. *Human Capital and Economic Development.* Beijing: Beijing Normal University Press

Li Huiming. 2001. A Theory of Non-Market Failure and China's Process of Market Economy. *Reform.* Issue No. 6, 22–28

Li Hair and Chen Zhiguo. 2003. *Path Selection of China's Economic Take-Off.* Beijing: China City Press

Li Jingwen and Wang Tongsan. 1998. *Theory and Policy of China's Economic Growth.* Beijing: Social Sciences Academic Press

Lin Guoxian. 2001. The Stages of Market Institution and the Consociations of the Means of Institution Evolution. *Journal of Fujian Agriculture University* (Social Science Edition). Issue No. 4, 20–25

Lin Jiabin. 2005. *Perspectives and Reflections on the Upsurge of City Management.* Beijing: Central Party Literature Press

Lin Shangli. 1998. *Intergovernmental Relations in China.* Hangzhou: Zhejiang People's Publishing House

Li Shantong and Liu Yong. 2002. Central-Local Administrative Rights Division and the Regional Management Mode in China. *Review of Economic Research.* Issue No. 14, 2–9

Liu Changli. 2002. *Introduction to Modern Japanese Economics.* Dalian: Dongbei University of Finance and Economics Press

Liu Hanping and Liu Xitian. 2003. Local Government Competition: Decentralization, Public Goods and Institutional Innovation. *Reform.* Issue No. 6, 23–28

Liu Lingling and Feng Jianshen. 1999. *Public Finance China.* Beijing: Economic Science Press

Liu Rongcang. 2000. *Control and Development: Theory and Policy Research.* Beijing: Social Sciences Academic Press (China)

Liu Shangxi. 2002. The Scope of Public Expenditure: Analysis and definition. *Economic Research Journal*. Issue No. 6, 77–85

Liu Shucheng and Li Shi. 2000. An Investigation and a Study of US "New Economy". *Economic Research Journal*. Issue No. 8, 3–11

Liu Wei. 2006. Historical Change of the Reform and Fundamental Transition of the Economic Growth Mode of China. *Economic Research Journal*. Issue No. 1, 4–10

Li Yihua. 2002. *Local Government Investment in China* (unpublished doctoral dissertation). Xiamen: Xiamen University

Lou Hong. 2004. Public Investment Policy in Long-Run Economic Growth – General Congestion Public Infrastructure in Long-Run Growth Model. *Economic Research Journal*. Issue No. 3, 10–19

Lou Jiwei. 2002. *Chinese Government Budget: Institution, Management and Case*. Beijing: China Financial and Economic Publishing House

Luo Haocai. 1999. *The Science of Administrative Law* (new edition). Beijing: Peking University Press

Lu Wenpeng. 2003. Learning, Path Dependence and Late-Development Disadvantage: Adjustment of China's Economic Development Strategy. *Economic Review*. Issue No. 1, 55–58

Lu Xiyue. 2002. *Science and Technology as a Great Source of Value Creation*. Beijing: Economic Science Press

Lv Yuanli. 1999. *Political Culture: The Transformation and Integration*. Nanchang: Jiangxi People's Publishing House

Ma Dehuai and Yu Wenguang. 2000. The State Indemnity of the Injury by the Public Infrastructure. *Cass Journal of Law*. Issue No. 2, 14–19

Ma Guoxian. 2000. On the Framework of Public Expenditure System in China. *Collected Essays on Finance and Economics*. Issue No. 2, 20–25

Mansfield, E., Schwartz, M. and Wagner, S. 1981. Initiation Costs and Patents: An Empirical Study. *The Economic Journal*. Volume 91: 907–918

Mao Chuanxin. 2001. Local Government Actors in the Transition: An Analytical Framework. *Shanghai Economic Review*. Issue No. 12, 31–38

Mao Shoulong. 1998. *Administrative Reform in the Western Countries*. Beijing: China Renmin University Press

Marx, Karl. 1992. *Capital* (volume 1, reprint edition). London: Penguin Classics

Ma Shuanyou. 2003. *Fiscal Policy and Economic Growth in China*. Beijing: China Financial and Economic Publishing House

Miao Helin. 1997. *Capital Operation*. Beijing: Economic Science Press

Mueller, Dennis. 1979. *Public Choice*. Cambridge: Cambridge University Press

Mu Fang. 2001. On the Standard Drawing a Line of Demarcation of the Public Expenditure Range in China. *Journal of Central University of Finance and Economics*. Issue No. 8, 28–31

Newman, Peter. 1998. *The New Palgrave Dictionary of Economics and the Law*. London: Macmillan Reference Limited

Niu Ruohan. 1997. The Overall Strategy of Invigorating State-Owned Economy. *Reform and Theory*. Issue No. 7, 5–8

North, Douglass C. 1982. *Structure and Change in Economic History*. New York: W.W. Norton & Company

Nozick, Robert. 1977. *Anarchy State and Utopia*. New York: Basic Books

The OECD Report on Regulatory Reform, www.oecd.org

Olson, Mancur. 2000. *Power and Prosperity*. New York: Basic Books

Osborne, David and Gaebler, Ted. 1993. *Reinventing Government*. New York: Plume

Ostrom, Vincent. 2007. *The Intellectual Crisis in American Public Administration* (third edition). Alabama: The University of Alabama Press

Peng Hongfang. 2002. Experiences of Public Expenditure Management in Foreign Countries. *The Theory and Practice of Finance and Economics*. Issue No. 1, 108–110

Peng Zaimei. 1999. On the Reasons and Countermeasures of Government Failure. *The Theory and Practice of Finance and Economics*. Issue No. 6, 71–74

Porter, Michael E. 1998. *The Competitive Advantage of Nations*. New York: Free Press

Qi Shouyin. 2002. *The Public Economic System Reform and Outline of Public Economics in China*. Beijing: People Publishing House

Qian Yinyi. 2002. Understanding Modern Economics. *Comparative Economic and Social Systems*. Issue No. 2

Qiu Dong. 2001. *National Statistics*. Dalian: Dongbei University of Finance and Economics Press

Ricardo, David. 1951. *The Works and Correspondence of David Ricardo*. Cambridge: Cambridge University Press

Romer, David. 2005. *Advanced Macroeconomics* (third edition). New York: McGraw-Hill/Irwin

Romer, Paul Michael. 1990. Endogenous Technological Change. *Journal of Political Economy*. Volume 98 Issue No. 5

Rosen, Harvey S. 2004. *Public Finance* (seventh edition). New York: McGraw-Hill/Irwin

Rostow, Walt W. 1971. *The Stages of Economic Growth* (second edition). Cambridge: Cambridge University Press

Sachs, Jeffrey and Hu Yongtai. 2003. The Structure Factors of Economic Reform in China, Eastern Europe and the Soviet Union. *Economic Policy Journal* (Quarterly). Issue No. 2

Samuelson, Paul A. and Nordhaus, William D. 1998. *Economics* (sixteenth edition). New York: McGraw-Hill Companies

Schiavo-Campo, Salvatore and Tommasi, Daniel. 1999. *Managing Government Expenditure*. Manila: Asian Development Bank

Schumpeter, Joseph. 1982. *The Theory of Economic Development*. NJ: Transaction Publishers

Schumpeter, Joseph. 1962. *Capitalism, Socialism and Democracy* (third edition). New York: Harper Perennial

Sheng Hong. 1991. On Seeking Stability Form of Reform. *Economic Research Journal*. Issue No. 1, 36–43

Shen Kunrong and Fu Wenlin. 2006. Tax Competition, Region Game and Their Efficiency of Growth. *Economic Research Journal*. Issue No. 6, 16–26

Shen Kunrong and Ma Jun. 2002. The Characteristics of "Club Convergence" of China's Economic Growth and Its Cause. *Economic Research Journal*. Issue No. 1, 33–39

Shen Kunrong and Zhang Jing. 2007. *Regional Financial Development and Growth Performance in the Context of Fiscal Decentralization: An Empirical Study on Perspective of Local Government Intervention*.

Shi Xuehua. 1998. *Theory of Government Power*. Hangzhou: Zhejiang People's Publishing House

Shu Huai. 1997. Industrial Structure of Singapore: Historical Development and Revelations Therefrom. *Journal of Shantou University*. Issue No. 3, 22–29

Shu Yuan and Xie Shimao. 1998. *Models of Economic Growth*. Shanghai: Fudan University Press

Smith, Adam. 2013. *The Wealth of Nations*. New York: Create Space Independent Publishing Platform

Smith, Adam. 2013. *The Theory of Moral Sentiments*. New York: Economic Classics

Stiglitz, Joseph. 1998. *Why Is the Government Intervention in the Economy* (Chinese edition). Beijing: China Material Press

Stiglitz, Joseph E. and Walsh, Carl E. 2006. *Economics* (fourth edition). New York: W. W. Norton & Company

Sun Liping, Shen Yuan and Liu Shiding. 1997. Workaround for Institutional Operation and Way of Institutional Change. *Social Sciences in China* (Quarterly). Winter Issue

Sun Yongrao. 1998. Analysis of Investment Value of Companies from the Aspect of Capital Structure. *China Securities Journal*. Issue No. 1

Tan Chongtai. 1999. *New Development of Development Economics*. Wuhan: Wuhan University Press

Tanzi, Vito, et al. 2000. *Public Spending in the 20th Century*. Cambridge: Cambridge University Press

Tu Yonghong. 2009. *Goldman Sachs: Rebirth from Fire*. Beijing: China Financial Publishing House

Wang Bangzuo, et al. 1998. *Introduction of New Politics*. Shanghai: Fudan University Press

Wang Baoshu. 2000. The Legal Concepts to Perfect State-Owned Enterprise Reform Measures. *China Legal Science*. Issue No. 2, 24–35

Wang Chunfa. 2001. New Economy: A New Techno-Economic Paradigm. *World Economics and Politics*. Issue No. 3, 36–43

Wang Jinying. 2001. *Human Capital and Economic Growth*. Beijing: China Financial and Economic Publishing House

Wang Lei. 1998. The Research of Constitutional Law of Administrative Legislation Power. *Deiking University Law Journal*. Issue No. 5, 58–63

Wang Qin. 1996. On Singapore's Industrial Structure and Economic Growth. *Southeast Asian Affairs*. Issue No. 3, 31–37

Wang Shaoguang. 2008. The Great Transformation: Bi-Directional Movement in China since the 1980s. *Social Sciences in China*. Issue No. 1, 129–148

Wang Shuxian and Zhang Gaixiang. 1999. The Effect of Local Government Economic Behavior on Economic Aggregate Equilibrium Model. *Productivity Research*. Issue No. 5, 46–48

Wang Wenbo, Chen Changbing and Xu Haiyan. 2002. The Model of Economic Growth of China Including Institutional Factors and Its Experimental Analysis. *Modern Economic Science*. Issue No. 5, 33–37

Wang Xuebiao and Wang Zhiqiang. 2001. *Fiscal Policy, Financial Policy and the Co-integration Analysis*. Dalian: Dongbei University of Finance and Economics Press

Wang Yongjun. 2000. *An Empirical Analysis of China's Public Expenditure*. Beijing: Economic Science Press

Wang Yuanlong. 1995. On Marx's Theory of Resource Allocation. *Contemporary Economic Research*. Issue No. 2, 1–7

Wang Zeke. 2000. Silicon Valley's Not the Product of Economic Planning. *Southern Weekend*. Issue No. 8, 38–48

Wen Guanzhong. 2002. Market Mechanism and Government Positioning and Rule of Law. *Comparative Economic and Social Systems*. Issue No. 1, 1–11

Wolf, Charles. 1993. *Markets or Governments* (second edition). Cambridge, MA: MIT Press

World Bank Group. 1997. *World Development Report 1997: The State in a Changing World*. Oxford: Oxford University Press

Wu Bin. 2000. On the Legal Regulation of Government Investment. *Xiangtan University Journal* (Philosophy and Social Sciences Edition). Issue No. 1, 44–46

Wu Jinglian. 2004. Economist, Economics and China Reform. *Economic Research Journal*. Issue No. 2, 120–127

Wu Jinglian, et al. 1996. *Progressive or Radical: Choice of Chinese Reform*. Beijing: Economic Science Press

Wu Shuqing and Hu Naiwu. 1987. *Mode, Operation, Regulation and Control*. Beijing: China Renmin University Press

Wu Yifeng. 2003. Study on the Issue of Insufficient Demand in China from the Perspective of Western Market Economy Theory and Policy. *Macroeconomics*. Issue No. 2, 14–19

Wu Yujin and Qi Shirong, et al. 1994. *World History: Modern History* (volume 1). Beijing: Higher Education Press

Xiao Yun and Gong Liutang. 2003. Money, Taxes, and Federal Transfer in an Endogenous Growth Model with Multiple Levels of Government. *Economic Research Journal*. Issue No. 1, 45–53

Xiao Zesheng. 1999. On Character of Governmental Purchase. *Nanjing University Law Review*. Autumn Issue, 146–159

Yang Jie. 1999. *Business Innovation*. Beijing: Economy and Management Publishing House

Yang Ji and Yang Wei. 2003. A Summary of the Theory of Public Expenditure from Endogenous Growth Theory. *Economics Information*. Issue No. 5, 68–71

Yang Junchang. 1985. *Keynesian Revolution*. Chengdu: Sichuan Remin Press

Yang Long. 2007. *Government Economics*. Tianjin: Tianjin University Press

Yang Ruilong. 1994. On the Way of Institutional Change and Conflict and Coordination of the System Target Selection in China. *Economic Research Journal*. Issue No. 5, 40–49

Yang Ruilong. 1998. The "Three Stages Theory" of the Way of Institutional Change Conversion in China. *Economic Research Journal*. Issue No. 1, 3–10

Yang Shanhua and Su Hong. 2002. From Agent-oriented Managers of Political Power to Profit-seeking Managers of Political Power. *Sociological Research*. Issue No. 1, 17–24

Yang Xuedong. 2004. Technology Innovation and Local Governance Reform. *China Public Administration Review*. Issue No. 1

Yin Qiang. 2008. *Study on the Efficiency of Public Investment in China*. Beijing: Economic Science Press

Yu Jingliang. 2000. On the Pulling Function of the Government Investment for the Economic Growth. *Modern Finance and Economics*. Issue No. 10, 42–45

Yu Keping. 2005. *Theory and Practice of Government Innovation*. Hangzhou: Zhejiang People's Publishing House

Yu Keping. 2000. *Governance and Good Governance*. Beijing: Social Sciences Academic Press

Yu Minsheng. 1995. On Legislative System of China. *Legal & Economy*. Issue No. 3, 28–31

Zhang Haixing. 2003. The Empirical Research on the Financial Expenditure Structure and the Economic Growth. *Review of Investment Studies*. Issue No. 6, 15–17

Zhang Jianhua. 1998. On Carrying out the Research of Government Economics. *Inquiry into Economic Issues*. Issue No. 1, 6–9

Zhang Jie. 1995. *Analysis of Financial Growth in China*. Beijing: China Economic Press

Zhang Jun. 2002. Capital Formation, Industrialization and Economic Growth: Understanding China's Economic Reform. *Economic Research Journal*. Issue No. 6, 3–13

Zhang Jun, Gao Yuan, Fu Yong and Zhang Hong. 2007. Why Does China Enjoy So Much Better Physical Infrastructure? *Economic Research Journal*. Issue No. 3, 4–19

Zhang Junzhou. 1995. *Analysis of China Regional Finance*. Beijing: China Economic Press

Zhang Jun and Zhou Lian. 2008. *Growth from Below: The Political Economy of China's Economic Growth*. Shanghai: Truth and Wisdom Press & Shanghai People's Publishing House

Zhang Weiying and Li Shuhe. 1998. Inter-Regional Competition and Privatization of State-Owned Enterprises in China. *Economic Research Journal*. Issue No. 12, 13–22

Zhang Yu. 1997. *The Road to Transition: Political Economy Analysis of China's Gradual Reform*. Beijing: China Social Sciences Press

Zhang Yuyan. 1993. *Economic Development and the System Choice*. Beijing: China Renmin University Press

Zheng Bingwen. 2003. "Welfare State" in the Economic Theory. *Social Sciences in China*. Issue No. 1, 41–63

Zhou Keyu. 2000. On the Role of China's Local Governments and the Optimization of Their Economic Operations in the Transitional Period. *Journal of East China Normal University* (Philosophy and Social Sciences). Issue No. 2, 93–99

Zhou Li'an. 2007. Governing China's Local Officials: An Analysis of Promotion Tournament Model. *Economic Research Journal*. Issue No. 7, 36–50

Zhou Qiren. 1995. Rural Reform in China: Changes in Relations of State and Land Ownership. *Social Sciences in China* (Quarterly). Issue No. 6, 147–155

Zhou Ri. 2003. *Regional Financial Development and Economic Growth in China* (1978–2000). Beijing: Tsinghua University Press

Zhou Xiaochuan, et al. 1992. *Problems and Way out for China's Tax System*. Tianjin: Tianjin People's Publishing House

Zhou Ye'an. 2003. Local Government Competition and Economic Growth. *Journal of Renmin University of China*. Issue No. 1, 97–103

Zhou Zhenhua. 1999. Behavior of Local Government and Independent Development of Local Economy. *Study & Exploration*. Issue No. 3, 32–40

Zhou Zhiren. 1999. *The Comparative Study of Contemporary Foreign Administrative Reform*. Beijing: National School of Administration Press

Zhuang Ziyin and Zou Wei. 2003. Does Public Expenditure Boost Economic Growth: An Analysis of China's Experience. *Management World*. Issue No. 7, 4–12

Zhu Peibiao. 2001. The Analysis on the Inertia of Fiscal Expenditure's Stimulating the Economic Growth. *Journal of Central University of Finance & Economics*. Issue No. 9

Zhu Qianwei. 2002. *Public Administration*. Shanghai: Fudan University Press

Zhu Zejun. 2006. *Metropolitan and Satellite Cities: An Empirical Study on Development Model of Zengcheng County, Guangdong Province* (unpublished doctoral dissertation). Guangzhou: South China Agricultural University

Zou Hengfu. 2000. *Public Finance, Growth, and Dynamic Economic Analysis*. Beijing: Peking University Press

Index

Note: Page numbers in *italics* indicate figures and tables.

For Product Safety Concerns and Information please contact our EU
representative GPSR@taylorandfrancis.com
Taylor & Francis Verlag GmbH, Kaufingerstraße 24, 80331 München, Germany